Journeys 2017

An Anthology of International Haibun

Edited by
Angelee Deodhar

Journeys 2017
An Anthology of International Haibun
Copyright © 2017 by Angelee Deodhar

All Rights Reserved. No part of this publication may be reproduced or utilized in any form or by any means, electronic or mechanical, including photocopying, recording, or by any information storage and retrieval system, without prior written permission of the publisher, except by a reviewer, who may quote brief passages in a review.

First Edition:	March 2017
ISBN:	978-1541387034
Printed By:	CreateSpace, An Amazon.com Company
Cover Photograph:	Ray Rasmussen
	Stone Lantern from the Japanese Garden
	in Esquimalt Gorge Park, Victoria, B.C. Canada
Book Design:	Angelee Deodhar
Mailing Address:	House No. 1224, Sector-42 B,
	Chandigarh, U.T. 160036, India
Email:	angeleedeodhar@gmail.com
Frontispiece Quote:	Author Unkown
Back Cover Quote:	Matsuo Bashō from Haruo Shirane's
	Traces of Dreams: Landscape,
	Cultural Memory, and the Poetry of Bashō

This book is dedicated to my grandson Aryan, who helps me rediscover the joy of bugs, birds and flowers and who teaches me that following a snail's trail can be a journey in itself.

Angelee Deodhar

Sometimes we need to move away from the busyness of the world around us and search out the quiet places–places where we may seek understanding, take time to organize our thoughts, get in touch with our deepest selves–and then be ready to give all that is asked of us to our world again.

Author Unknown

Contents

Preface 13

Introduction 15

Form in Haibun: An Outline 19

Section I: Early Adaptors 41

John Ashbery 43
    Haibun 44
    Haibun 2 45
    Haibun 3 46
    Haibun 4 47
    Haibun 5 48
    Haibun 6 49

Jerry Kilbride 51
    Oslo, 1977: Notes From A Journal 52
    Fort Mason 54
    Another View Of Fuji 56
    The Muezzin's Call 57
    Steinbeck 59

Kenneth C. Leibman 61
    Oleno 62
    Hōryūji 63

Paul F. Schmidt 65
    Kyoto Temples 66

Edith Shiffert 75
    Yama-Biko: Mountain Echo 76

Rod Willmot 83
    Excerpts from The Ribs of Dragonfly 84
    Unanswered Questions 97

Section II: Contemporary Writers of Haibun..........101

Melissa Allen..........103
- Where We Live..........104
- Post Office..........106
- Wave and Particle..........107
- Misdirection..........108
- What Was His Is Mine..........110

Cherie Hunter Day..........111
- Fifth Floor..........112
- Inclement Weather..........113
- Boo..........114
- Aftermath..........115
- Soft Landings..........116

Lynn Edge..........117
- Midnight..........118
- Glory Days..........119
- Trucker..........120
- On My Mind..........121
- Frida and Me..........122

Judson Evans..........123
- Work, Labor, Play..........124
- Window Washer..........125
- Soundings..........126
- Windswept Style..........127
- Backpack..........128

Chris Faiers..........129
- The Day We (Sort Of) Met George Harrison..........130
- Meeting Eel Pie..........133
- The Buddhist Monastery..........136
- The Three Fishes..........142
- Hare Krishna..........144

Charles Hansmann..........147
- Low Tide..........148
- Birthday Hike..........149

    Camouflage.. 150
    Contact... 151
    Rash.. 153

Jeffrey Harpeng..**155**
    Horse Tale.. 156
    The Ghost in the Haibun... 157
    Birdlings Flat... 159
    Seven Teas–Sixth Tea –Hamasa Yukki Bancha..................... 162
    Liberation... 164

Ed Higgins..**165**
    So one day.. 166
    The Letter... 167
    Ida's Parmesan Cheese.. 168
    He drank... 169
    Forging a Fishmonger's Knife.. 171

Ruth Holzer...**173**
    Cefalù.. 174
    Dinner at Timmy's... 175
    Gros Morne.. 176
    Niklasstrasse 36... 177
    Smoking.. 178

Roger Jones...**179**
    Global Warming.. 180
    Yosemite Recollection.. 181
    Galveston, 2010... 182
    Publish or Perish... 183
    Calling Home... 184

Gary LeBel...**185**
    Bridge.. 186
    Circuit... 188
    Machinery... 189
    Noisy Things.. 190
    Watermelon.. 191

Tom Lynch **193**
    Thunder Season 194
    White Sands Dunes 195
    A Beginner's Mind 196

George Marsh **203**
    The Higgs Boson 204
    The Ruined Church 206
    Langstone Harbour 208
    Waiting at the Ferry café 210
    How little is left 211

Michael McClintock **213**
    Sea of Cortez 214
    Men of Property 215
    Raspados 216
    Koi in Winter 217
    Ordinary Seductions 218

Beverly Acuff Momoi **219**
    Lifting the towhee's song 220
    Yellow flag 221
    Holding fast 222
    Assisted living 223
    Broken 224

Lenard D. Moore **227**
    East 92nd Street 228
    Manhattan Chronicle 229
    A Blueberry-Picking Day 230
    This Autumn Night 232
    In The Owl's Claws 233

Peter Newton **235**
    Cold Comfort 236
    One Thing 237
    Simple Folds 238
    My America 239
    The Anatomy of Hope 240

Jim Norton **241**
    Out of the Blue 242
    When You Need It 243
    Knockree 245
    Sandscript 246
    A Tear of the Sun 247

Stanley Pelter **249**
    sonata 250
    City of Gifts 251
    Always Discordant 253
    Glen Catacol 254
    insideoutside 255

Dru Philippou **257**
    Between Peaks 258
    The Visitation 259
    Sýko 260
    Learning English 261
    The Spinning Top 262

Richard S. Straw **263**
    First Impressions 264
    Stone by Stone 265
    Perennials 266
    Desert Places 267
    Whether Together or Apart 268

Bill Wyatt **271**
    Homeless in the Universe 272
    The Early Days of Throssel Hole Priory 276
    Ancestral Voices on Kos 281
    Cicada Immortals part 2 283
    Dragon's Breath and Mountain Madness 285

Section III: Excerpts from Japanese Books **287**

Travel Diaries and the Development
of Modern Haibun **289**

Awesome Nightfall: The Life, Times,
and Poetry of Saigyō.. 305

The Journal of Sōchō.. 313

Traces Of Dreams: Landscape, Cultural Memory,
and the Poetry of Bashō.. 327

Dew On The Grass: The Life and Poetry
of Kobayashi Issa... 337

A Translation of Kurita Chodō's
Sketches of Moonlit Nights...341
    The Third and Fourth Day Moons............................... 342
    The Waxing Moon... 343
    The Tenth Day Moon.. 344
    The Midpoint of Autumn... 345
    The Sixteenth Night... 346
    The Last Quarter of the Moon....................................... 347
    The Moon That Rises in Early Morning...................... 348
    Daybreak..349

Masaoka Shiki: His Life and Works.. 351

Literary Creations on the Road–Women's
Travel Diaries in Early Modern Japan....................................353

Slocan Diary.. 363

Biographies of Other Contributors... 377

Publishing Credits... 383

Acknowledgements... 387

Preface

When Matsuo Bashō wrote *Journey into the Interior*, a classic of Japanese literature three hundred and fifty years ago, he could not have imagined the popularity haibun would come to enjoy as a serious poetry genre among English-language poets. Although *Oku no hosomichi* is accepted as being the first haibun ever written, other travel journals and diaries were being written by men and women, courtiers, princesses, entertainers, hermits, nuns and commoners several centuries before Bashō's lifetime. Many of them influenced his writing style.

The lack of critical literature aroused my interest in assembling the three Journeys anthologies. Today we have many online and print haiku journals and even some main stream poetry publications carry haibun, but it is still difficult to find the work of some of the early adaptors of prose with verse. This is because some journals that carried these early haibun forms ceased publication and many personal chapbooks were also only printed in short limited runs.

The first two Journeys (*Journeys* and *Journeys 2015*) highlighted the personal selections of the published work of our most prominent current international writers, as well as featuring the work of early adaptors of the genre. Encouraged by the reception of both anthologies and feeling that work of more contemporary and early adaptors is needed, I embarked upon putting together *Journeys 2017*. This features the work of twenty-two current writers and six early adaptors who employ a wide range of writing styles and subjects. In addition, this collection features not so familiar excerpts from eight Japanese poets, whose works are vital to the understanding of the roots of haibun.

It is my sincere hope that the *Journeys* trilogy will inspire poets and promote a deeper understanding to the serious study of this genre.

While putting together this series, I would pause from time to time to go over a particular piece, to savour an exquisite turn of phrase or the depth and poignancy of a particular experience from the poet's *milieu interior*, a fascinating journey in itself.

I am very grateful to all the poets who have generously shared their work with me for this third collection. It has been an honour to travel with them.

Angelee Deodhar
Chandigarh, India

Introduction to Journeys 2017: The Exploration Continues
By Rich Youmans

This third volume of the *Journeys* series continues one of today's most ambitious explorations of English-language haibun. Over the past several years, editor Angelee Deodhar has truly been on a journey of discovery. She has assembled work from some of the leading practitioners of the form–from all parts of the world, representing all manner of styles–and presented them side by side, so readers can see the range of what's being written today. But she wasn't content to just present a "best of" series; she also delved into the history and heritage of the haibun, presenting its earliest practitioners and, in this volume, its roots in the Japanese diary writing and kikobun that date back as far as the Heian era. Each volume has successively expanded the scope of the journey until, together, they compose an extended treatise on what exactly a haibun was, is, and, perhaps, will be.

There are a few implied questions in *Journeys 2017*–Where are we? Where have we been? Where are we going? These are important, since they are being asked not just by newcomers to the field, but also by those who have been writing haibun for years. For instance, the first volume of the *Journeys* series offered an "anthology" of haibun definitions by leading writers and editors, and a quick scan shows just how widespread the views of haibun are. Most of the definitions agree on certain core points–brevity, concrete language, the absence of abstractions, the leap that should occur between prose and haiku. But you don't have to go too far before things get murky. The late Ken Jones, a former editor of *Contemporary Haibun Online* and one of the genre's foremost practitioners/proponents, tries to be more prescriptive: He says that haibun prose should, among other characteristics, be "light handed, elusive and even ironic, 'in the style of haiku.'" Contrast that with the opinion of Michael McClintock (whose work can be found in this present volume): "There need be few or any constraints at all, except that it be written as an aesthetic whole, not a fragment."

Even the use of haiku isn't agreed upon. Several definitions (including the official one from the Haiku Society of America) proffer that a haiku is optional, while others highlight its use as *the* key element. Stanley Pelter puts it memorably, "No self-respecting haibun shows its face in public unless haiku is incorporated as an integral part of its structure." Perhaps the definition that best sums up the current state of affairs is that of Jeffrey Woodward, the founder of the *Haibun Today* online journal: "Haibun as a genre is fluid and ill-defined, volatile and subject daily to change, invisible to the public-at-large and widely misapprehended by haiku editors and commentators. Haibun is richly varied, by its foremost practitioners, in matter and technique but paradoxically Lilliputian in character when this achievement is measured against what appears to be its inexhaustible promise."

That fluidity, volatility, richness, and, yes, promise are all in evidence in this current volume. You'll find many family and childhood memories, several travel accounts, a few diary-like memoirs of time spent in a commune or a religious retreat (Paul F. Schmidt's "Kyoto Temples," Chris Faiers' remembrances of his days at the Eel Pie commune); such topics are the longtime staples of haibun. But we also encounter memorable portraits (like those in Lynn Edge's "Trucker" or Cherie Hunter Day's "Boo"). Some, such as Melissa Allen's "Misdirection" and "Wave and Particle," border on the surrealistic. And in the work of Judson Evans we find a rich, resounding language that can mesmerize.

And there will be some, yes, that will leave you scratching your head. Take the six haibun written by John Ashbery. Ashbery has been lauded as one of the greatest poets of the 20th century and also one of the more difficult, and the haibun presented here bear witness to the truth of both labels. How can one not do a double-take at a work ("Haibun 6") that compares every phase of theater production to the perfection of when "a large, fat, lazy frog hops off his lily pad like a spitball propelled by a rubber band," that manages to include an image of "floundering cattle" being deposited in trees and "so on to who know what horrible mischief," and ends with the following haiku: "Striped hair, inquisitive gloves, a face, some woman named Ernestine Throckmorton, white opera gloves and more." After several readings, I still can't wrap my head around this haibun totally, but I also can't help but appreciate and be somewhat floored by it.

Ashbery is among six "early adaptors" referenced in this volume. As in *Journeys 2015*, this section highlights some of the earliest writers of English-language haibun, showing how varied their efforts could be. But in *Journeys 2017* the editor is not content simply to go back several decades in pursuit of modern haibun's roots; instead, she goes back several centuries. In the final section, "Excerpts from Japanese Books," you'll find the works in which the haibun genre is rooted. The excerpts range from explorations into the "pantheon" of haikai writers–the haibun of Bashō and Issa, the diary writing of Shiki–as well as examples of Japanese travel diaries that date as far back as the sixteenth century. In its disparity, the section seems to be a bit of a "grab bag"– but one that holds many treasures, and in which the modern haibun writer can find influences that still inspire and inform. Even something as seemingly out of place as the "Slocan Diary," written by a Japanese woman sent to a Canadian internment camp during World War II, has its place: Read through Kaoru Ikeda's descriptions of life in her new environment–the red maples vivid against deep green mountains, the hikes in search of matsutake mushrooms, the sightings of paw prints and bear droppings–and her attention to detail will soon call to mind that of the best haikai travel writers. "[W]hatever place one lives in offers unique pleasures," she writes, and those words should be remembered by any writer of haibun.

As you read the haibun in this and the earlier *Journeys* volumes, you will undoubtedly come across many instances in which you'll wonder how such disparate works can occupy the same genre, seemingly connected only by the inclusion of a haiku (which, by practice, seems to have become a defining trait of haibun). Some may view this as a negative– shouldn't anthologies present a unified vision, a "best practices," a communal understanding? Personally, I see it as the true genius of this series: To present the genre in all its chaotic volatility and inchoate promise, so that we can come to a better understanding of not just where the haibun is, but where it can go.

Form in Haibun: An Outline
By Jeffrey Woodward

I. Introduction by Way of Simple Definition

The modest purpose of the present study is to offer the reader a concise outline of those forms commonly used in the composition of haibun. This objective can be achieved most readily by first drawing a distinction between standard haibun and haibun that depart from the norm. The standard is so dominant in haibun today as to justify the use of the adjective "anomalous" to describe those rare exceptions to its rule.

Standard haibun combine the two modes of writing–prose and verse. Haibun's predilection for employing haiku as its verse component distinguishes haibun from other types of prosimetra (i.e., mixed prose and verse writings). One can extrapolate from this circumstance a basic unit–one paragraph, one haiku–that defines the norm for haibun composition.

Because haibun is a hybrid genre that joins two modes of writing, and because its basic unit or building block is one paragraph and one haiku, it is reasonable to anticipate that variation in the number and placement of haiku in relation to the prose will have a bearing upon the final character of the haibun and upon its reception by the reader. Differences in the quantity and position of haiku, in fact, best define the various forms of standard haibun.

The role of the title, parenthetically, lies outside of the present investigation of haibun form, but well within any examination of an individual haibun's meaning. An article by Ray Rasmussen recognizes the corresponding relationships of the title to its haibun, the haiku's fragment to its phrase, and the haibun's prose to its haiku. The latter relation has largely occupied the attention of the genre's critical commentators.

Anomalous haibun lack one of the two components of standard haibun, the prose or the haiku. An examination of these exceptional haibun, however, will reveal that there is compensation for the missing element. If prose is absent, a verse form other than haiku is juxtaposed to the haiku. If haiku is absent, a structural device of verse composition, such as lineation, or an organizational principle of haikai, such as internal comparison, is applied and one segment of prose finds itself juxtaposed to its neighboring segment.

In the outline of standard and anomalous forms below, the format for each entry will be (a) the name and description of the form, (b) an illustrative example of the form from the current literature, (c) a commentary on the example, and (d) a list of other references or examples pertinent to or illustrative of the form.

The selection criteria for each haibun under discussion were that the sample fulfill the form's promise by being well-written and that it be representative of the current practice of the form that it was chosen to illustrate. Examples are generally limited to one haibun per form in order to focus on formal properties and to restrict this paper to an acceptable length. The commentaries that follow each haibun, therefore, should be read in the spirit in which they were written, as provisional observations intended to spur further study and discussion, observations that are willing to confess the limits of our knowledge of haibun without surrendering the hope that continued curiosity may tomorrow enlarge our comprehension.

II. Standard Forms in Haibun

A. Preface, Headnote or Header—The paragraph precedes the haiku.

Rose Madder

A few months ago the neighbors across the street lost their second child in late term. Their house stands empty this morning, the curtains drawn open, a few lights on, lifeless, sold. I hardly knew them. Upstairs our two teens are sleeping like royalty in their rooms: what do I know about sorrow?

morning twilight
I crack the ice
for thirsty dogs
    –Gary LeBel

Commentary: No form of haibun composition will be encountered more frequently than this, the basic unit of one paragraph and one haiku. The reader may verify this observation by a casual survey of any venue, in print or online, that promotes haibun. Various historical and aesthetic reasons for the omnipresence of this form might be posited; that one paragraph plus one haiku is haibun's fundamental building block is certainly answerable, in some degree, for the form's dominance.

Gary LeBel's "Rose Madder" is representative of the basic unit at its best, offering, in the prefatory prose, a vignette that focuses upon detail carefully chosen for its significance to the motif and a closing haiku's sensory perceptions compared with or contrasted to the imagery of the preceding paragraph. This form, while well-adapted for the abbreviated anecdote or descriptive sketch, may find its efficacy called into question with the introduction of greater expository or narrative complications. One concluding haiku will rarely balance well with a story that employs multiple characters and requires hundreds of words for the telling.

B. Afterword, Footnote or Footer–The haiku precedes the paragraph.

On the Path

on a bramble
puffed up
a sparrow

Morning without birdsong, boots shifting over the wetland's sheet of snow–the right, alongside coyote tracks; the left, beside the rabbit's.

    –Tish Davis

Commentary: Inversion of the basic unit–placement of the haiku first–changes the tenor of a haibun by altering the relationship of haiku to paragraph. The prose and verse components are still juxtaposed, their respective imagery still compared or contrasted, but the emphasis of the two elements is not the same. In the preface or headnote, the closing haiku caps the prose and is often the culminating point of the composition; perhaps haikai readers, too, are trained to anticipate this crest, to view the introduction of the haiku as a sign of the haibun's fulfillment.

In the inverted form of afterword or footnote, placement of the haiku first and the prose last disrupts our common expectation. In the inversion, the haiku adopts some of the narrative or expository qualities that we ordinarily associate with the prose, whereas the paragraph that now concludes the composition acquires, to some degree, the climactic characteristics that we customarily ascribe to the haiku. Tish Davis' "On the Path" demonstrates this well, with her opening haiku's sketch of a sparrow whose fragility and vulnerability in this winter scene foreshadow the mute violence of the paragraph's parallel coyote and rabbit tracks.

Compare this with Bashō's "Concerning the Beautiful Scenery at the Home of Master Shūa." Bashō's haiku, by hyperbole, relates that the mountains have joined host and guest in the large parlor with its scenic window. The paragraph then follows and identifies Master Shūa, his occupation and the location of his mansion, the prosaic but necessary background to the poetic reverie on the landscape and the Creative (*zōka*) that dominates the latter half of the prose.

C. Prose Envelope–Paragraph, then haiku, then paragraph.

As the Dew

How many tunnels by train from Tauramanui? Tahora is a country store and in the valley behind half a dozen houses, a school, and the church is the hall. Tarmac ends with gravel to the cattle grid, then dirt past the dog boxes up to the shearer's quarters and shearing shed full of folk song. And one Aussie accent to "rattle ya dags." Swell of hills all around, his hill the highest between here and there. And tomorrow,

dew above the fog
from the valley the tears
of a mournful song

At the hilltop a sense of the earth's curve, snowcapped volcanoes far to the east and west, and one sweet voice below.

—Jeffrey Harpeng

Commentary: The prose envelope begs comparison with both the preface or basic unit and with the afterword or inversion of the basic unit. Why? Its first paragraph prepares the way for the haiku's appearance and the reader's expectation of fulfillment, in the manner of the preface, but the paragraph that follows the haiku, because of its position, inherits some of the climactic properties, as does the afterword, that are normally reserved for the haiku in the basic unit.

In "As the Dew," the closing paragraph constitutes a lyrical envoy with its "one sweet voice below" providing an echo or amplification of the haiku's "mournful song." A poetic tone at closure, whether haiku or paragraph claims the exit line, may be customary for haibun. To infuse the writing with divine fire throughout, however, is less common. In "As the Dew," not even exposition escapes Harpeng's lyrical prowess as this alliterative passage, craftily balanced upon /t/ and /h/, clearly shows:

> How many *t*unnels by *t*rain from *T*auramanui? Ta*h*ora is a country store and in the valley be*h*ind *h*alf a dozen *h*ouses, a school, and the church is the *h*all.

Jim Kacian's "No Place," another haibun written as a prose envelope, devotes the opening paragraph to mood, to showing the reader how, in happy anticipation of a journey's end, everything becomes "greener as we move closer to home." The haiku then relates, with quiet irony, that

returning home
the chessmen have maintained
my lost position

The closing paragraph depicts an airport, a last stopover, and this description reinforces the haiku's "lost position," the ultimate sentence telling us with sober precision: "The airport is brightly lit, generic, not any place specific but a place between places; really, no place." The thematic climax, again, resides not in Kacian's fine haiku but has been inherited, along with the closing position, by the last paragraph.

D. Verse Envelope–Haiku, then paragraph, then haiku.

Maria Distasio, 10, Killed in the Great Molasses Flood of 1919

winter sun
glistening drops
from an icicle

I read your name on the list of fatalities and wonder how you died. Did rivets popping off the tank like bullets from a machine gun mow you down? Or were you crossing the street when two million gallons of molasses came barreling down on you at 35 miles an hour? There are so many ways to die. Who would have expected this to be one? I will never again say "slower than molasses in the winter time" without thinking of you.

daydream
the last of the light
caught in the blinds

—*Bob Lucky*

Commentary: Haibun commonly invite the reader to study the relation of the haiku to the prose. Many haibun employ one haiku only, as in the preface, afterword or prose envelope forms, and this fact further encourages the reader to focus upon the juxtaposition of the standard haibun's two components, prose and verse. In the verse envelope, where one paragraph of prose is sandwiched between two haiku, a careful reading must account for the further complication of how the opening and closing haiku relate not only to the prose, but also to one another.

The two haiku in Bob Lucky's "Maria Distasio . . ." share one motif–light–but afford a meaningful contrast that underscores the subject, the molasses flood. Light, in the initial haiku, is embodied by an icicle that drips slowly; in the final haiku, however, the diminished light, now "caught in the blinds," has neither movement nor life.

The verse envelope, as is evident from the above, lends itself to the treatment of the haibun as a journey between two points, between the textual landmarks of the introductory and of the concluding haiku. The paragraph is, at once, the vehicle that transports the reader from start to finish and the explanation of much that transpires in that passage.

E. Interlaced or Alternating Prose and Verse Elements–This follows the universal form of call and response, with the two elements, prose and verse, playing the role of chorus and anti-chorus. Either element may lead but in the example that follows the haiku comes first.

Dog Star

tea kettle whistling–
steam clouds
the windows

Thursday night. Another wife-daughter fight with raised voices, crying, doors slamming, I grab my jacket, call the border collie and bolt into the frigid night. The ravine trail is barely visible, the stream frozen . . .

beneath
the skin of ice–
dark waters

An owl calls. I pause, wait for the next call, let the silence sink in. Branches sweep toward a star-filled sky. The dog presses close, warm fur, her tail wagging . . .

> Sirius
> on the horizon—
> a nudge toward home
>
> —Ray Rasmussen

Commentary: The steady alternation of prose and haiku poses a special difficulty, particularly where the distribution of the two elements is symmetrical, that is, where one paragraph is repeatedly answered by one haiku. Careful consideration must be given, by the author of such a work, to varying sentence structure and prose tempo from paragraph to paragraph. If this task is neglected, a rhythm is soon established like that of the metronome, and the arrival of each subsequent haiku is not only easily predicted by the reader, but also increasingly met with resentment as an unwanted disruption in the narrative or exposition.

Ray Rasmussen avoids such monotony in "Dog Star" by his reliance upon brief telegraphic sentence fragments and simple but expressive details whose very abbreviation, paradoxically, increases the gravity of the two short paragraphs. Notable, also, is the functional aspect of the first two haiku. The whistling tea kettle, in the opening haiku, signals a delineation of the domestic setting that is then elaborated upon by the prose. The second haiku, with its dark water and thin ice, is concerned largely with mood and renders for the reader the emotional state of the haibun's narrator. Both haiku and paragraph are subordinate here to the purpose of the total composition. The closing haiku, on the other hand, connects the protagonist's border collie to Sirius in a startling wedding of near and far, of familiar and alien—an apt resolution of the haibun's theme.

F. Verse Sequence—The presentation of two or more haiku, in any position in the haibun composition, without interruption by the prose element.

> *Gauze in the Wind**
>
> pulling in the dusk
> fluttering pages of the
> *Knapsack Notebook*

That calls to mind Matsuo Bashō, traveling from Edo to one god-enshrined temple and another, searching for the scent of blossoms, passing a monk in high clogs, watching the fishermen catch kisugo in Suma, and resting under a bright moon, dreaming about art and poetry as he opens his satchel:

evening dew
dampens his inkstone . . .
the haiku's *joie de vivre*

the stroke of his brush
wordless word after word
in black ink

each pink sasanqua
blossom . . .
the only blossom

infused with
the sea's fragrance
his wind-dried haiga

—Dru Philippou

* "Gauze in the wind" was Bashō's pen name

Commentary: One trait of the verse sequence—the presentation of two or more consecutive haiku without prose intermission—lies in its tendency to possess some of the properties typically reserved for the haibun's prose: exposition or narration.

Another trait of the verse sequence in haibun arises from the fact that the presence of multiple haiku requires the reader to study not only the relation of haiku to prose but to study also the relation of each haiku in a series to its immediate predecessor and heir. These associations can become quite complex with the sequence simultaneously contributing to the narrative and to the metaphorical or analogical threads of the complete work.

The four haiku that close Dru Philippou's "Gauze in the Wind" illustrate clearly the propensity of the haiku sequence to encroach upon the paragraph's domain. The Bashō that Philippou summons from her reading of the *Knapsack Notebook* has only reached into his satchel when the prose gives way to the depiction, in the four haiku, of the master respectively preparing his inkstone, drawing with his brush, admiring the "only blossom" and, at last, letting his haiga dry in the sea breeze. The haiku sequence thus completes the delineation of the action that the prose initiates. In addition, the individual haiku also have the poetic value we frequently associate with haiku; they establish a mood, convey an atmosphere, hint at matters left unwritten. Bashō's "wind-dried haiga" of the last haiku neatly recalls the "fluttering pages" of the first haiku; this repetition of a motif stamps the last line with a satisfying sense of finality.

The haiku sequence, when not a participant in exposition or narration, serves other functions. Bashō's "An Account of the Moon at Mount Obasute in Sarashina," for example, comes to a close with two haiku on the moon that is the subject of the preceding paragraph. The first haiku amplifies the local legend of abandoning elderly women just recounted in the prose, while the second emphasizes Bashō's "lingering" at Sarashina. These haiku have no expository or narrative value but repeat, in a modulated voice, motifs first broached in the prose preface.

III. Anomalies or Variations from the Norm

A. Haibun Minus Haiku

1. Lineation

Postcard

We sit in the back, each with an arm crooked out a window, miles on end, not passing a word. Pressed to our doors, undeclared, we compete: whose left

will tan darker than whose right? Ladybug

on the odometer, numbers flipping, travel trailer in tow, I

tell you now, on this final stretch home, I'm as close to
my sister as I seem to know how, leaning

as far from her arm as this Ford will allow.

—Charles Hansmann

Commentary: Haibun without haiku often compensate and substitute, for the missing verse component, another structural feature that invites comparison and contrast between the haibun's parts. Charles Hansmann's "Postcard," in harmony with ideas he first enunciated in his article, "Haibun Poem: A Definition," introduces to the haikuless prose a fundamental feature of versification: lineation or the line-break. In "Postcard," this technique colors the whole haibun with an air of hesitancy, of slight ambiguity at the point of the line-breaks, of the lively but nervous tension, in fact, of the rival siblings. His lineation acts as camouflage for the presence of the treble rhyme of "now," "how" and "allow" while, in seeming contradiction, calling upon measure to draw the haibun to a proper close. For what is Hansmann's last line

as **far** from her **arm** as this **Ford** will **allow**

if not a strict anapestic tetrameter in which the alliteration of "far" and "Ford" reinforces our confidence in our scansion as well as in our comprehension of Hansmann's intent?

2. Internal Comparison or Juxtaposition

Finding My Way

another address to locate in an unfamiliar city i can now find my way to the Autistic Centre but accommodation has been offered in an unused nursing home a young woman social worker offers to pilot me across town 'city drivers' i almost lose her at the first set of lights and how will i find my way back it isn't as simple as retracing my steps because many of the streets are one way exhausted but one more effort is needed to get up the steep driveway to the home i unload the car as Tony runs from room to room exploring the place which is to be our home for the next week at the school the others laugh telling ghost stories of how those who have passed away in the home still wander the hallways at night the kitchen is bleak with windows which look out to a block retaining wall holding a cut-away bank in the hillside most of the nursing home is closed off from use by the fire doors half-way down the long hallway Tony and i the only occupants feeling enclosed i walk towards the glass doors and the main entrance beyond as i walk a ghostly figure in a long night gown approaches from the opposite direction for a moment i feel the panic then i realise as i stand in front of the wide glass doors that my reflection is looking anxiously back at me

–Janice M. Bostok

Commentary: Another method of haibun sans haiku is the application of a well-known structural feature of haiku, that of the principle of internal comparison, to the prose itself. Harold G. Henderson, in *An Introduction to Haiku* (1958), defined the operation of this principle as one in which the haiku's two parts "are compared to each other, not in simile or metaphor, but as two phenomena, each of which exists in its own right" and one in which "the differences are just as important as the likenesses." Internal comparison can also be understood as a juxtaposition of two images wherein both correspondence and contrast have their say.

This technique can be discerned in a close reading of Janice M. Bostok's "Finding My Way." Here, the protagonist's anxiety about being suddenly immersed in a strange environment is exacerbated by the fear that she will be unable to retrace her steps and find her way back to that familiar place from whence she came. The narrator's immediate surroundings are described in concrete terms–"a block retaining wall" and "fire doors." These physical barriers, firm in their bleak reality, are compared to the alienated protagonist who is reduced to an apparition, "a ghostly figure in a long night gown," an insubstantial "reflection" that mimics the disembodied countenance of its author.

The reader will discover this method, also, in Bashō's "Words in Praise of the Pine in Narahide's Garden," where enjoying a pine "preserved for a thousand years" is juxtaposed with the variable but fleeting pride and pleasure of nurturing exotic flowers or prized fruit, with the poet coming down firmly in favor of the former pursuit.

B. Haibun Minus Prose

> *Looking out on Research Triangle Park*
> *and remembering the white clouds at*
> *Great Lakes Naval Training Station*
>
> I gaze out a cafeteria window
> at loblollies and clipped lawns
> a songbird dips in the haze
> gray clouds hang distended
> four decades ago I joined the Navy
> landlocked now and off course
> I wait to enter a wider sea.
>
> a crow
> between rainfalls
> high in a pine
>
>   *—Richard Straw*

Commentary: Haibun that eschew the prose element commonly substitute a verse form other than haiku for the paragraph. The selection of verse type and quality of the versification have a direct bearing upon the final character of the haibun. Because of the availability of many poetic forms and the countless variations that meters permit, coming to any firm conclusions about haibun without prose as a formal option is problematical. A comparative study of known examples would be useful in increasing our understanding of the form's promises and limitations.

In Richard Straw's "Looking out on Research Triangle Park," the clear sketch of the poet's immediate environment, a rather mundane scene, evokes memories of his stint in the Navy "four decades ago." The voice is one of middle-aged detachment and resignation, of reflection upon vanished youth and youth's broad horizon. These qualities, along with the extended descriptive title, remind one of Tang poetry, of the *shih* or couplets of the poet and painter Wang Wei. The crow and pine of Straw's haiku are not unlike Bashō's famous crow and bare branch, while both haiku share an affinity with the ink and wash paintings of Sesshū and of the Song Dynasty landscape painters that preceded him.

No syllabic or accentual norm can be discerned in this writing; Straw's versification, therefore, is free. The lines do show grammatical order or design, however, and might be described, with one exception, as organized in unrhymed couplets with each distich completing one image or thought:

> I gaze out a cafeteria window / at loblollies and clipped lawns
> a songbird dips in the haze / gray clouds hang distended
> four decades ago I joined the Navy
> landlocked now and off course / I wait to enter a wider sea.

The exception lies in "four decades ago I joined the Navy," a single verse in lieu of the third couplet, although it does complete the unit of thought and thus has sufficient weight to balance well with the other distichs. That we find four couplets here reminds us, also, that the literary *shih* of the Tang Dynasty are similarly structured and are often rendered, in English translation, as eight lines. Straw's "Looking out on Research Triangle Park" could hold its own if placed among them.

IV. Conclusion by Way of Digression: Other Issues

A. Symmetry and Asymmetry in Form

The haibun chosen for discussion employ simple, symmetrical forms where the prose and verse elements are present in the ratio of one to one or where asymmetry is slight and due only to interruption of the alternating round of paragraph and haiku. The prose envelope, for example, falls one concluding haiku short of a doubling of the basic unit of paragraph plus haiku.

Many variations can be derived from the standard haibun forms by compounding one or both elements and introducing greater asymmetry. The interlaced haibun, as we discussed above, must avoid the metronomic beat of a steady alternation of paragraph and haiku; one of the simplest ways it may do so is to introduce asymmetry, often in the form of an added paragraph before the next haiku–paragraph, haiku, two paragraphs, haiku. Consider the prose envelope, again, and add a second haiku–prose, two haiku, prose. The result is symmetrical in quantity–two paragraphs, two haiku–but perhaps not so in quality, insofar as the interaction of adjacent haiku may enlarge their scale or gravity, a sequence being more than the sum of its parts.

B. Verse Other Than Haiku

Haibun is one type of prosimetrum. Some types of mixed prose-plus-verse writings show a predilection for a specific verse form, while others do not. The saga literature of Iceland and Scandinavia strongly favored Old Norse court-measures such as the dróttkvaett or "lordly verse." The poetic forms in Dante's *La Vita Nuova*, as in that of Boethius' *Consolatio* before him, are diverse but derived from a common Mediterranean and classical heritage; this meant the sonnet, canzone, and ballata in Dante's case.

The two types of prosimetrum issuing from Japan, haibun and tanka prose, can be distinguished by their respective preferences for haiku and tanka. Every verse form has conventions–metrical and cultural. Haiku, for example, was historically composed of 5-7-5 syllables with a cutting word (*kireji*) to divide the verse into two parts, a metrical requirement and convention. Haiku also required a season word (*kigo*), a cultural tradition and convention. Such properties, which differ from the conventions of other verse forms, are not without influence on their prose accompaniment.

In the commentary on haibun sans prose, I placed some emphasis on the fact that such works "commonly substitute a verse form other than haiku for the paragraph." To substitute haiku for the paragraph would be simply to join haiku to haiku, to write a haiku sequence, and not to write haibun. If I did stress "other than haiku," what of tanka, haiku's venerable ancestor? Can tanka replace the paragraph in haibun? The past few years have witnessed the publication of many sequences that mix tanka and haiku. See, for examples, those tanka anthologies referenced below. These compositions are what their authors claim them to be—verse sequences—and have little in common with haibun or, in my opinion, with the greater unity and cohesion of a tanka-only sequence.

If we rule out haiku and tanka as substitutes for the paragraph, the first because of common identity and the second because of its familial relationship with the verse side of haibun's basic unit, can every other known verse form, then, claim a place in haibun's toolbox? The question is open to the proof of future practice, of course, but among the examples of haibun sans prose already published, the diversity of verse forms used in lieu of prose includes iambic and accentual meters as well as free verse.

What common characteristics, if any, might be ascribed to these various stand-ins for the prose? Two features are noteworthy. First, the verses employed are Western forms, even where, as in the Straw haibun, the inspiration may have been China. Second, those forms heavily favored are stichic and not stanzaic; they are based upon a normative line and not upon a fixed arrangement of lines. This is significant and should be examined in any future study of the subject. Stanzaic forms are sharply defined, while stichic forms are relatively less so and thus closer to the unmetered language of prose. Strict stanzas, in theory, need not necessarily be proscribed from haibun and might juxtapose well with haiku. Common sense would seem to dictate, however, that such meetings, if they are to succeed, must be brief. Stanzas exhibit a high degree of organization where the number, length and order of the lines as well as the rhyme scheme are each prescribed. This architecture serves to place the stanza at a greater remove from prose and common discourse. One can imagine the haiku holding its own against a solitary epigrammatic couplet or quatrain . . . but more?

C. Descriptive Schematic

A simple notation system will allow us to provide a shorthand description of an individual haibun's form and to classify, for comparison, the form of many haibun.

P	paragraph
H	haiku
V	verse other than haiku
2, 3 . . .	the number of P, H or V in sequence
>	transition from element to element
(P > H)2	the series in parentheses is multiplied
[-P], [-H]	the element in the brackets is absent

If we employ these symbols, we can describe each of the standard haibun forms discussed above.

Preface	P > H
Afterword	H > P
Prose Envelope	P > H > P
Verse Envelope	H > P > H
Interlaced	P > H > P > H or (P > H)2
Verse Sequence	H > P > H4

The last notation on verse sequence describes our example, Dru Philippou's "Gauze in the Wind."

In speaking of symmetry and asymmetry above, we mentioned how, to avoid the regular alternation of paragraph and haiku in the interlaced haibun, the poet might choose to "introduce asymmetry, often in the form of an added paragraph before the next haiku–paragraph, haiku, two paragraphs, haiku" or P > H > P2 > H.

The anomalous forms may be notated as well, though interesting questions arise when doing so. Bostok's "Finding My Way," cited as an example of haibun sans haiku, can be diagrammed quite simply as P [-H]: one paragraph minus haiku. Hansmann's "Postcard," where lineation has invaded the prose and where, as we demonstrated, one line can be scanned as normative meter, cannot be so easily described. If one sets the lineation aside momentarily, it is clear that read as simple prose, "Postcard" consists of one paragraph. That is not the author's intent, however, as we know from the lineation on the page and from his article on the subject. If we respect Hansmann's lineation, then, we might diagram "Postcard" as P > V > P > V [-H] or, more succinctly, as (P > V)2 [-H]: paragraph, verse other than haiku, paragraph, verse other than haiku, minus the haiku. This notation, while not entirely satisfactory, can claim one small virtue; it affords a partial explanation of Hansmann's experiment whereas an interpretation of his work as a structure of one paragraph discloses little and evades much.

Straw's haibun without prose, "Looking out on Research Triangle Park," can be recorded shorthand as V > H [-P] or verse other than haiku plus haiku, minus prose. This is neither wholly accurate nor efficient, I admit, and if a study of the various haibun composed without prose were conducted, the author of such a study would want to define and compare the precise verse forms employed–the "verse other than haiku," I mean–in order to better understand their influence upon and relation to the haiku. What is the meter of the verse or line? What stanza, if any, is employed? How many verses are present? Are there other metrical considerations? Perhaps a close reading of this nature would render the notation system of little profit.

Introduction Bibliography:

- Ray Rasmussen, "A Title Is A Title Is A Title, or Is It?–The Unexplored Role in Haibun," *Frogpond 33: 3*(Fall 2010), pp. 74-82

- Jeffrey Woodward, "The Elements of Tanka Prose," *Modern English Tanka V2, N4* (Summer 2008), pp. 194-206

- Jeffrey Woodward, "Prose and Verse in Tandem: Haibun and Tanka Prose," *Modern Haibun & Tanka Prose 2* (Winter 2009), pp. 154-163

- Jeffrey Woodward, "Thinking It Through or A Few Innocent Questions: One Relation of Haiku to Prose in Haibun," *Frogpond 32: 3* (Fall 2009), pp. 85-87

Selected Preface, Headnote or Header Examples:

- Ruth Holzer, "Heimerzheim," *Modern Haibun & Tanka Prose 1* (Summer 2009), p. 43

- Gary LeBel, "Rose Madder," *Haibun Today* (December 19, 2007)

- Richard Straw, "Dolor," *Haibun Today* (March 28, 2008)

- Jeffrey Winke, "Gathers the Volume Up," *Haibun Today* (December 4, 2008)

Selected Afterword, Footnote or Footer Examples:

- Matsuo Bashō, "Concerning the Beautiful Scenery at the Home of Master Shūa," in David Landis Barnhill (translator), *Bashō's Journey: The Literary Prose of Matsuo Bashō*, SUNY Press, 2005, pp. 113-114

- Tish Davis, "On the Path," *Modern Haibun & Tanka Prose 1* (Summer 2009), p. 114

- Cherie Hunter Day, "Inclement Weather," *The Unseen Wind: BHS Haiku Anthology 2009*, p. 18

- Jeffrey Harpeng, "Marked," in Jeffrey Harpeng, et. al., *Quartet: a string of haibun in four voices*, PostPressed, 2008, p. 19

- Ralph Murre, "In Apartment 3-B," *Haibun Today* (July 24, 2009)

Selected Prose Envelope Examples:

- Jeannine Hall Gailey, "Love Story (with Fire Demon and Tengu)," *Haibun Today* (April 7, 2008)

- Jeffrey Harpeng, "As the Dew," in Jeffrey Harpeng, et. al., *Quartet:*

a string of haibun in four voices, PostPressed, 2008, p. 14

• Jim Kacian, "No Place," *Border Lands*, Red Moon Press, 2007, unpaginated

• Beth Vieira, "She Says," *Contemporary Haibun Online V2, N2* (June 2006)

Selected Verse Envelope Examples:

• Bob Lucky, "Maria Distasio, 10, Killed in the Great Molasses Flood of 1919," *Contemporary Haibun 11*, 2010, p. 49

• Stanley Pelter, "liquorice allsorts," *past imperfect*, George Mann Publications, 2004, p. 56

• Patricia Prime, "Barber Shop," *Contemporary Haibun Online V3, N1* (March 2007)

• Jeffrey Woodward, "Nebraska," *Frogpond 31:2* (Spring/Summer 2008), p. 51

Selected Interlaced Examples:

• Graham High, "Lost City," *Haibun Today* (November 30, 2008)

• Ruth Holzer, "Venetian Glass," *Modern Haibun & Tanka Prose 1* (Summer 2009), p. 44

• Ray Rasmussen, "Dog Star," *Lynx XXII:3* (October 2007)

• Lynne Rees, "Living Things," *Contemporary Haibun 10*, 2009, p. 74

Selected Haibun Minus Haiku Examples:

• Matsuo Bashō, "Words in Praise of the Pine of Narahide's Garden," in David Landis Barnhill (translator), *Bashō's Journey: The Literary Prose of Matsuo Bashō*, SUNY Press, 2005, pp. 131-132

• Janice M. Bostok, "Finding My Way," *Stepping Stones*, Post Pressed, 2007, p. 36

• Charles Hansmann, "Haibun Poem: A Definition," *Haibun Today* (November 17, 2007)

- Charles Hansmann, "Postcard," *Haibun Today* (November 26, 2007)

- Harold G. Henderson, *An Introduction to Haiku*, Doubleday Anchor Books, 1958, pp. 18-19

- Tracy Koretsky, "On a Hill Over Haifa: Haibun Sans Haiku, Experiment and Commentary," *Haibun Today* (January 12, 2008)

- Jeffrey Woodward, "Dead Letter Office," in Jeffrey Harpeng, et. al., *Quartet: a string of haibun in four voices*, PostPressed, 2008, p. 20

- Jeffrey Woodward, "Haibun Minus Haiku," *Haibun Today* (November 30, 2007)

Selected Verse Sequence Examples:

- Matsuo Bashō, "An Account of the Moon at Mount Obasute in Sarashina," in David Landis Barnhill (translator), *Bashō's Journey: The Literary Prose of Matsuo Bashō*, SUNY Press, 2005, pp. 110-111

- Ruth Franke, "Summit Ice," *Haibun Today* (July 26, 2008)

- Ken Jones, "Such Stuff as Dreams are Made Of," *The Parsley Bed*, Pilgrim Press, 2006, pp. 87-89

- Dru Philippou, "Gauze in the Wind," *Modern Haibun & Tanka Prose 1* (Summer 2009), p. 132

- Diana Webb, "The Gate," *Modern Haibun & Tanka Prose 1* (Summer 2009), p. 139

Selected Haibun Minus Prose Examples:

- Owen Bullock, "Karangahake Gorge," *Modern Haibun & Tanka Prose 2* (Winter 2009), p. 119

- Bob Lucky, "This and That," *Haibun Today* (April 5, 2008)

- Michael McClintock, "Courage in November," *Contemporary Haibun Online 5:1* (March 2009)

- Stanley Pelter, "'Thunderguy'–Isle of Arran," *insideoutside*, George

Mann Publications, 2008, p. 116

- Richard Straw, "Looking out on Research Triangle Park," *Modern Haibun & Tanka Prose 2* (Winter 2009), p. 142

Selected Verse Other Than Haiku Examples:

- Michael McClintock and Denis M. Garrison (editors), *The Five-Hole Flute: Modern English Tanka in Sequences and Sets.* Baltimore, MD: Modern English Tanka Press, 2006.

- Michael McClintock and Denis M. Garrison (editors), *The Dreaming Room: Modern English Tanka in Collage and Montage Sets.* Baltimore, MD: Modern English Tanka Press, 2007.

Acknowledgment

I'm indebted to Richard Straw and Ray Rasmussen for their patient reading and practical criticism of the various drafts of this essay. Their queries and observations were invaluable resources for my revisions. Any errors or shortcomings in this paper, of course, must be credited to the author alone.

Section I:
Early Adaptors

John Ashbery

Jerry Kilbride

Kenneth C. Leibman

Paul F. Schmidt

Edith Shiffert

Rod Willmot

John Ashbery

John Ashbery was born in Rochester, New York, in 1927. He earned degrees from Harvard and Columbia, and went to France as a Fulbright Scholar in 1955, living there for much of the next decade.

His most recent book of poetry is *Commotion of the Birds*, forthcoming from Ecco/HarperCollins in 2017. Other collections include *Breezeway* (2015), *Quick Question* (2012), *Planisphere* (2009) and *Notes from the Air: Selected Later Poems* (2007), which was awarded the 2008 International Griffin Poetry Prize. *Self-Portrait in a Convex Mirror* (1975) won the three major American prizes–the Pulitzer, the National Book Award, and the National Book Critics Circle Award–and an early book, *Some Trees* (1956) was selected by W. H. Auden for the Yale Younger Poets Series.

The Library of America published the first volume of his collected poems in 2008. A two-volume set of his collected translations from the French (poetry and prose) was published in 2014. Active in various areas of the arts throughout his career, he has served as executive editor of *Art News* and as art critic for *New York magazine* and *Newsweek*. He exhibits his collages at the Tibor de Nagy Gallery (New York). He received the Medal for Distinguished Contribution to American Letters from the National Book Foundation (2011) and a National Humanities Medal, presented by President Obama at the White House (2012). His work has been translated into more than twenty-five languages.

His book *A Wave* (1984), which featured six haibun, won both the Bollingen Prize in Poetry and the Lenore Marshall Poetry Prize.

http://www.flowchartfoundation.org/arc.

Haibun

Wanting to write something I could think only of my own ideas, though you surely have your separate, private being in some place I will never walk through. And then of the dismal space between us, filled though it may be with interesting objects, standing around like trees waiting to be discovered. It may be that this is the intellectual world. But if so, what poverty—even the discoveries yet to be made, and which shall surprise us, even us. It must be heightened somehow, but not to brutality. That is an invention and not a true instinct, and this must never be invented. Yet I am forced to invent, even if during the process I become a *songe-creux*, inaccurate dreamer, and these inventions are then to be claimed by the first person who happens on them. I'm hoping that homosexuals not yet born get to inquire about it, inspect the whole random collection as though it were a sphere. Isn't the point of pain the possibility it brings of being able to get along without pain, for awhile, of manipulating our marionette-like limbs in the straitjacket of air, and so to have written something? Unprofitable shifts of light and dark in the winter sky address this dilemma very directly. In time to come we shall perceive them as the rumpled linen or scenery through which we did walk once, for a short time, during some sort of vacation. It is a frostbitten, brittle world but once you are inside it you want to stay there always.

The year—not yet abandoned but a living husk, a lesson

Haibun 2

. . . and can see the many hidden ways merit drains out of the established and internationally acclaimed containers, like a dry patch of sky. It is an affair of some enormity. The sky is swathed in a rich, gloomy and finally silly grandeur, like drapery in a portrait by Lebrun. This is to indicate that our actions in this tiny, tragic platform are going to be more than usually infinitesimal, given the superhuman scale on which we have to operate, and also that we should not take any comfort from the inanity of our situation; we are still valid creatures with a job to perform, and the arena facing us, though titanic, hasn't rolled itself beyond the notion of dimension. It isn't suitable, and it's here. Shadows are thrown out at the base of things at right angles to the regular shadows that are already there, pointing in the correct direction. They are faint but not invisible, and it seems appropriate to start intoning the litany of dimensions there, at the base of a sapling spreading its lines in two directions. The temperature hardens, and things like the smell and the mood of water are suddenly more acute, and may help us. We will never know whether they did.

Water, a bossa nova, a cello is centred, the light behind the library

Haibun 3

I was swimming with the water at my back, funny thing is it was real this time. I mean this time it was working. We weren't too far from shore, the guides hadn't noticed yet. Always you work out of the possibility of being injured, but this time, all the new construction, the new humiliation, you have to see it. Guess it's OK to take a look. But a cup of tea—you wouldn't want to spill it. And a grapefruit (spelled "grap-fruit" on the small, painstakingly lettered card) after a while, and the new gray suit. Then more, and more, it was a kind of foliage or some built-in device to trip you. Make you fall. The encounter with the silence of permissiveness stretching away like a moonlit sea to the horizon, whatever that really is. *They* want you to like it. And you honor them in liking it. You cause pleasure before sleep insists, draws over to where you may yet be. And some believe this is merely a detail. And they may be right. And we may be the whole of which all that truly happens is only peelings and shreds of bark. Not that we are too much more than these. Remember they don't have to thank you for it either.

The subtracted sun, all I'm going by here, with the boy, this new maneuver is less than the letter in the wind

Haibun 4

Dark at four again. Sadly I negotiate the almost identical streets as little by little they are obliterated under a rain of drips and squiggles of light. Their message of universal brotherhood through suffering is taken from the top, the pedal held down so that the first note echoes throughout the piece without becoming exactly audible. It collects over different parts of the city and the drift in those designated parts is different from elsewhere. It is a man, it was one all along. No it isn't, It is a man with the conscience of a woman, always coming out of something, turning to look at you, wondering about a possible reward. How sweet to my sorrow is this man's knowledge in his way of coming, the brotherhood that will surely result under now darkened skies.

The pressing, pressing urgent whispers, pushing on, seeing directly

Haibun 5

Bring them all back to life, with white gloves on, out of the dream in which they are still alive. Loosen the adhesive bonds that tie them to the stereotypes of the dead, clichés like the sound of running water. Abruptly it was winter again. A slope several football fields wide sprang out of the invisible foreground, the one behind me, and unlaced its barren provocation upwards, with flair and menace, at a 20-degree angle—the ascending night and also the voice in it that means to be heard, a pagoda of which is visible at the left horizon, not meaning much: the flurry of a cold wind. We're in it too chortled the rowan berries. And how fast so much aggressiveness unfolded, like a swiftly flowing, silent stream. Along its banks world history presented itself as a series of translucent tableaux, fading imperceptibly into one another, so that the taking of Quebec by the British in 1629 melts into the lollipop tints of Marquette and Joliet crossing the mouth of the Missouri River. But at the center a rope of distress twists itself ever tighter around some of the possessions we brought from the old place and were going to arrange here. And what about the courteous but dispassionate gaze of an armed messenger on his way from someplace to someplace else that is the speech of all the old, resurrected loves, tinged with respect, caring to see that you are no longer alone now in this dream you chose. The dark yellowish flow of light drains out of the slanted dish of the sky and from the masses of the loved a tremendous chant arises: We are viable! And so back into the city with its glimmers of possibility like Broadway nights of notoriety and the warm syrup of embarrassed and insistent proclamations of all kinds of tidings that made you what you were in the world and made the world for you, only diminished once it had been seen and become the object of further speculation leading like railroad ties out of the present inconclusive sphere into the world of two dimensions.

A terminus, pole fringed with seaweed at its base, a cracked memory

Haibun 6

To be involved in every phase of directing, acting, producing and so on must be infinitely rewarding. Just as when a large, fat, lazy frog hops off his lily pad like a spitball propelled by a rubber band and disappears into the water of the pond with an enthusiastic plop. It cannot be either changed or improved on. So too with many of life's little less-than-pleasurable experiences, like the rain that falls and falls for so long that no one can remember when it began or what weather used to be, or cares much either; they are much too busy trying to plug holes in ceilings or emptying pails and other containers and then quickly pushing them back to catch the overflow. But nobody seems eager to accord ideal status to this situation and I, for one, would love to know why. Don't we realize that after all these centuries that are now starting to come apart like moldy encyclopedias in some abandoned, dusty archive that we have to take the bitter with the sweet or soon all distinctions will be submerged by the tide of tepid approval of everything that is beginning to gather force and direction as well? And when its mighty roar threatens in earnest the partially submerged bridges and cottages, picks up the floundering cattle to deposit them in trees and so on to who knows what truly horrible mischief, it will be time, then, to genuinely rethink this and come up with true standards of evaluation, only it will be too late of course, too late for anything but the satisfaction that lasts only just so long. A pity, though. Meanwhile I lift my glass to these black-and-silver striped nights. I believe that the rain never drowned sweeter, more prosaic things than those we have here, now, and I believe this is going to have to be enough.

Striped hair, inquisitive gloves, a face, some woman named Ernestine
  Throckmorton, white opera glasses and more

Jerry Kilbride

Jerry Kilbride Born February 25, 1930, in Denver, Colorado. Died November 3, 2005. Attended grammar and high schools affiliated with St. Mel Roman Catholic Parish in Chicago's west side, 1936-1948. United States Army, 1951-1953. Studied at the Kansas City Art Institute, Mexico City College, The School of the Art Institute of Chicago. Member of the Small Press Traffic Writers' Workshop, San Francisco, 1979-1986. Vice-President of the Haiku Society of America, 1989. A co-founder of the Haiku Poets of Northern California and the American Haiku Archives. Museum of Haiku Literature Award, 1987. Japan Air Lines Haiku Conference Awards, First Prize, 1987. Henderson Awards, First Prize, 1987. Henderson Awards, Third Prize, 1988. Mainichi Daily News Awards, First Prize, 1989. HPNC President's Gavel Award, 1991. Retired as senior bartender of the Olympic Club, San Francisco, March 1995. Participant in the 16th Annual Summer Writers' Workshop, Irish Writers' Centre, Dublin, Ireland, August 1995. Member of the Irish Literary and Historical Society, San Francisco. Widely traveled, Jerry Kilbride served as the Honorary Curator of the American Haiku Archives from 1998 to 1999.

Oslo, 1977: Notes From A Journal

>   midsummer night
> between the sun and the moon
>   a dusting of stars

We dock an hour before midnight. There is still some light in the sky—the sun is behind hills to the north and the moon is up. A peculiar light . . . like skimmed milk, clear and yet opaque. It can be understood in the physical sense, but the emotions want somehow to deny it. Leaving the docks, I walk deserted streets to the East Railroad Station and find the doors locked. Hmmm . . . the woman at Norwegian National Railways in London told me I could spend the night in the station. My train leaves for Stockholm at 8:15 AM and I don't want to take a hotel room for a few hours, careful of money as a long journey is ahead. Finding a door open at the back of the building, I enter cautiously. A bird flies frantically under the vaulted roof seeking a way out, its winging the only sound in the spectral quiet. I find a bench, remove my rucksack and settle down. Vending machine lights bite into the night, their colors in muted reflections on tracks leading to Sweden. A yellow light flickers on-and-off out beyond the end of the concrete platforms. The spookiness is huge! I take out Persig's *Zen and the Art of Motorcycle Maintenance* and try to read when a man approaches out of nowhere. His eyes are like eroded craters and the line of his mouth barely discernible. He informs me in railway-guard English that I must leave immediately as the station is locked until 6 in the morning. I can't believe he is kicking me out at this hour, but then see resolve in his thin bureaucratic smile. Orders from headquarters eclipse everything, including kindness. I tell him about the woman in London as he takes out keys and rattles them in my face.

Massive block buildings stand sentinel on the empty square in front of the station. Only an occasional passing automobile disturbs the quiet. In the half-light, I sit on the station's steps and think back to the rug seller of Istanbul . . . to the flaw in the rug. It is the summer of 1967 and I am in the Egyptian Bazaar. A very old Armenian merchant is selling me a small carpet. I put my finger on a flaw, a place where the wool has not been dyed. The old man tells me, as we both sip at glasses of tea, that Armenian weavers purposely leave imperfections in their rugs–they point to the fact that only God can weave the perfect carpet and that the carpets of God are not readily available. What he is really telling me is to take a closer look at life. Sucked-in by his eloquence and liking the little rug, I tell him I'll take it. And now, ten years later, with the wisdom of Armenians, I know that only God can take the perfect journey.

> midnight streets
> sounds at the edge
> of audibility

A solitary old man walks by . . . eyes me . . . goes down to the corner . . . pauses . . . turns . . . approaches.

He stares at my rucksack on the steps below me. I recognize the searching look he gives while asking if I am in difficulty. I tell him of being locked out. He seems wounded, then says in English with a thick Scandinavian accent, *But, my friend, this is scandalous!* His sad eyes look inwards as if weighing the wisdom of taking me home. His face relaxes and he walks away. Half-way across the square he turns and shouts loudly, *But, my friend, this is scandalous!* He fades into the stillness.

After lingering for another few minutes, something visceral tells me to cross the square to the Viking Hotel and ask permission to sit in the lobby. I enter and approach the desk clerk whose handsome Nordic face has waxed full in goodness. He is disturbed when I tell him of my predicament. The man tells me to take a couch in the shadows at the back of the lobby, he will wake me before the day shift comes on. I feel relieved and thank him. Pulling a flannel shirt from my rucksack, I roll it into a pillow and fall into a deep dream. I see moon changes and phases of the human condition: a cruel man, a lonely man, a compassionate man–in the night I see reflections of myself.

> far north
> dawn and dusk merge
> to claim the sky

Fort Mason

    san francisco fog
a troop transport moves
    through memory

Almost fifty years ago and still ghosts are encountered in the parking lot whenever I return. Spirits follow me up the stairs and into the white high-walled room in Building C where quarterly meetings are held. Tall windows open onto shipping piers and parking lot. The screech of gulls punctuate the rounds of haiku being intently read and listened to. Unable to give the poems full attention, I am prodded and sometimes chilled by the first circumstance that brought me to Fort Mason. Memory becomes as immediate as the haiku-moment and it is again a very foggy and very wet and very cold morning in November 1952. There are 4,300 of us lined up on that wide expanse of asphalt between Building C and the structure just to the east . . . long, orderly, slow-moving, switched-back files. Weighing heavily on our shoulders and carried through roiling air are 4,300 duffel bags with names and serial numbers stenciled in white on the coarse olive-drab fabric. During unshouldered pauses, several quietly smiling Red Cross women—with all of the kindness they can muster!—hand a cup of hot coffee to each soldier . . . a donut . . . a paperback book. I am given a copy of *The Autobiography of Benjamin Franklin*. Coffee, donuts, paperback books and military music from an Army band playing out-of-view at the end of the pier . . . the band also giving out with Kay Starr's poignant anthem to those of us caught up in what is to become a constantly muddy and forgotten little war. *Oh, wheel of fortune, keeper erpinning around . . . spinning, spinning, erpinning . . . winning, winning . . . fortune or . . . fame.* Shouts and whistles, of course. A troop transport's mighty horn and the good ship General Meigs cargoed with the soon-to-be-slain . . . and those lucky enough to dodge that fate and continue to pencil days off of the calendar. *Yeah*, we say to ourselves, *The Golden Gate in 58!* or *Ain't no use in goin' back, 'cause Jody's got your Cadillac.* Fog so thick and so dark and the Golden Gate Bridge barely visible as we pass below. And then the music is no longer there and the huge ship begins to rock gently in a westerly direction.

                        haiku reading
            the quiet space around each poet
                          each poem

Another View Of Fuji

On a clear afternoon in the late autumn of 1952, during the Korean War, I stood with my buddies on the roof of ASAPAC Headquarters, which was housed in the old Tokyo Arsenal at Oji. The perfect cone of Fujiyama was shining in the distance, snow-covered, quietly majestic; all of us were seeing the mountain for the first time and felt a deep sense of awe, something akin to a religious experience. A few weeks later, I found myself in a bucket-seat deep inside one of those cavernous C-124s on an early morning flight between Tachika-wa Air Base and Okinawa. I felt extremely lucky to be next to one of the few windows, as it seemed that just minutes after takeoff the sacred mountain was below us, rising up through the clouds as if draped in purple velvet, an atmospheric condition caused by the combination of snow, angle of dawn light, reflection of sky. That incredible sight was held in my vision for as long as possible as the huge Globemaster continued to fly south over the island of Honshu. Now, years later, after learning more about life, art and Japanese culture, I think of that day whenever I come across one of Hokusai's 36 Views of Mt. Fuji and wonder if the Edo Period printmaker had ever longed to see the mountain from high in the morning sky.

     hokusai woodblock
    stepping into the moment
      of his intent

The Muezzin's Call

> through the windshield
> of the mountain bus
> —nothing but sky

We came down from Marrakech in one exhausting day, and many Moroccans on the bus vomited into paper bags as we crossed the High Atlas mountains. A man took off a shoe and was sick into it; other passengers were nauseous to the side of the rising, falling, twisting road, as the driver, compassionately, made frequent stops. David and I did not get sick, although the air on the bus grew nauseating, even with the windows open; we fought vertigo by burying ourselves in books we were reading.

Arriving in Ouarzazate in the white heat of afternoon, we checked into a hotel with thick mud walls on the eastern edge of town, not far from the El Glaoui Casbah. A long corridor bore from the registration desk to our room like a tunnel through a coal mine—dim, cool, claustrophobic. We dropped our rucksacks on the floor, stripped naked, and fell onto bunk beds. Sleep lasted for a couple of hours.

The western sky held a hundred shades of red as we walked to the center of town to get a meal, and, at the edge of the Sahara that evening, I came to the full understanding of what T. E. Lawrence meant when writing that the finest scent was that of the empty desert.

> afterglow
> thoughts of travelers
> who passed this way

A Greek restaurant was along the thread of concrete that extends from the Atlantic Coast to Ksar es Souk, passing through Ouarzazate in the blink of a camel's eye. The only occupants of Demitri's were a blond and sunburned young couple seated just inside the door; they nodded as we entered. We took a table nearby and introduced ourselves.

Traveling together, Missa was beautiful and Birger was handsome; both were Swedish. Experienced wanderers: Missa had been in the United

States and wore a Navajo necklace; Birger's Australian sheep herder's hat rested on the tabletop. They were leaving in the morning for Tinehir, where they would visit a miniature version of the Grand Canyon. Missa had heard it was wonderful and urged us to see it.

David and I spent the early hours of the following day visiting the El Glaoui Casbah, and marveled at ramparts and towers of fretted clay. Much later, we strolled along a dusty road in the direction of a crumbling casbah, a mile to the southeast. Some of the passing men greeted us in French; heavily veiled women averted their eyes; children giggled at the sight of two strangers; dogs sniffed at our trousers.

Busses traveling across that country depart for destinations before dawn to avoid the heat of the day. As we walked to the bus station, the first call to prayer came from the town's minaret while the sky held bright stars. The air was still.

> the muezzin's call . . .
> the face
> on the full moon

We had decided that the canyon might be worth a visit. Our original intention was to travel directly to the military outpost of Ksar es Zouk, a yellow cluster of buildings facing the Algerian border; a taxi would be taken from there to where the sand dunes began. Birger met the bus in Tinehir, hoping against hope that we had taken Missa's suggestion. He was frantic, as the police had come to their hotel room the previous evening and demanded a marriage certificate; not married, they were breaking Moroccan law. She, being the woman, was jailed for thirty days; he was set free. Instinct demanded the young Swede not leave town; he pleaded with us to continue our journey and speak in Missa's behalf at a European consular office in Meknes. David and I reboarded the bus—we experienced, only in imagination, the wonderful canyon of which Missa spoke.

> empty desert . . .
> yet, the blue turquoise
> of her necklace

Steinbeck

Out early for coffee: sheets of rain in the murky dawn and moments of absolute calm. The air is clean as that coming off snow-melt during spring back in Illinois–I recall its coolness on the hands and face, how it seems to reach across the prairie from white vastnesses in Canada. A copy of Jay Parini's biography of John Steinbeck is under my jacket where it will stay dry. I have learned from the book that my neighborhood was a favorite of Steinbeck's during student days at Stanford, when he hung out weekends on Bush Street, on Van Ness. A gust of wind: for a moment my umbrella becomes testy and unmanageable. My trousers are soaked through from the knees down; no matter, it is one of those mornings in San Francisco when you can taste the rain, the fresh air. I enter Caffe Espresso, Sutter and Powell, and find only a few other customers. Louis smiles–pleasant fellow that he is–and serves me at the stand-up counter, takes my dollar bill, tells me how excited he is about his new voice teacher. I sit at a window table looking out on Powell Street. The wind-blown puddles outside are alive in reflections of neon and the lights of a few passing automobiles. A cable car angles up Nob Hill; bell silent, the conductor lets the diminishing rain do the talking. The soggy trousers glove my legs in a chill; my socks are wet, but what the hell . . . warm coffee, warm place. I open the book to 1930, and join Steinbeck and Ed Ricketts as they make the rounds of the waterfront joints in Monterey.

                gathering light
                 pools of rain
           leave the night behind

Kenneth C. Leibman

Kenneth C. Leibman (1923-2001), biochemical pharmacologist, university professor, and haiku poet.

Ken Leibman, well-known and respected throughout the American haiku community and long active in the Haiku Society of America, died in Gainesville, Florida, on September 2, 2001, after a long illness. He was 78.

A native of New York City, Ken moved to Gainesville, Florida, in 1956, when he was offered a faculty position in the Department of Pharmacology of the University of Florida. Ken was a Quaker and a member of the Religious Society of Friends. He was active in the Gainesville Meeting. His hobbies included wine-making and gardening.

Ken will be remembered as a sensitive haiku poet with an eye for the ironic. He began publishing his haiku about 1986. In addition to haiku, he wrote long poetry and other Asiatic forms, such as tanka and ghazals. In February 1994, when he was elected Southeastern Region Coordinator of the HSA, Ken founded *South by Southeast* as a journal of the Region, and the first issue carried "A Southeastern Haiku Sampler"—one haiku from every haiku poet in the Region he could find. Ken passed *SxSE* on to Jim Kacian and took over the editorship of *Frogpond* beginning with the spring 1995 issue. He continued in that post through the end of 1997, and during his tenure the number of haiku and other poems included in *frogpond* (he liked the lowercased spelling!) more than doubled, and a great many new poets' work was published. In his own work, Ken often celebrated the environment in which he lived, a live-oak forest in north central Florida, which supplied the images for his 1990 chapbook, *alachua*.

Oleno

The postbellum North Florida gambling hell, the Town o'Keno on the Santa Fe River, the gamblers run off by crusading clergy, rechristened the Town o'Leno, disappeared in its newfound respectability from the face of the earth, the forest taking over until Roosevelt's CCC built a state park there. Pennywhistle in my belt, I cross the swaying wooden bridge.

autumn woods
dissolving
in river shallows

The trail leads through villages of cypress knees, some near, some far from the mother trees lining the river and the ponds.

above my ankles
the water blooping blooping around cypress knees

The knees stand singly or in groups in their villages, in each perceivable a separate personality. I fantasize a Druid community. The mood is one of archaic sadness. We all need cheering up.

a merry tune
piped to the cypress knees no one dances

The trail passes ponds of tannin-brown water in which the cypress gold is tarnished, and leads to the place where the river goes underground. Instead of the half expected mighty slurp into the recesses of the earth, I find an algaed pool in which the river flotsam has formed slowly revolving islets.

evening sun
turning the pool from green to green

On the way back to camp, I hear a crashing in a palmetto thicket. I stand stockstill.

sensing no enemy
an armadillo
ambles by me

Hōryūji

By bus from Nara to the southwest, to the town of Hōryūji, which contains the oldest Buddhist temple in Japan, founded in 607. Through the imposing Nan-daimon (southern Great Gate), past the five-storeyed pagoda to the Kondō (Main Hall) where, on the central altar, are the triad of the Buddha with two attendant Bodhisattvas, and, of course, the inevitable guardians in the corners.

four fierce warriors
guard the serenity
of the Buddha

In the Treasure Hall, the Yumechigai (Dream-changing) Kannon. It strikes me that although modern Kuan-yin and Kannon representations are unmistakably female, and often known in the West as "the Goddess of Mercy," the early Chinese Guan-yin and early Japanese Kannon images are at most androgynous in aspect.

Then, walking to the Hōrinji Temple, I am delighted to find myself in the countryside; the road leads past cultivated fields, and by old, well-kept country houses with sturdy traditional tile roofs, and often with magnificent stone lanterns in the front gardens. Partly due to inadequacies in the walking map, which ignores some jags along major through highways, the promised 10 minutes extend to about 45. At one point, my halting *"Gomen nasai, Hōrinji wa doko desuka"* brings from a young lady arranging flowerpots at her gate detailed directions in excellent English. At last, the first sign of the temple.

over the crest of the road
the top two storeys
of the pagoda

Among the treasures in the Kondō, a 7th century Yakushi-nyorai ("Healing Buddha") smiles radiantly; a 10th century Jūichimen (eleven-faced) Kannon Bosatsu sees everywhere.

Another country walk, this time on a straighter road, leads me to the third of the Hōryūji triad: Hokkeji Temple. Because all the buildings are closed, the old lady at the gate refuses my money, but lets me wander about.

Finally, to Hokkijimae bus stop and a long wait for the bus to Nara, during which I learn a new fact:

vending machine–
melon cream soda
isn't bad at all!

Paul F. Schmidt

Paul F. Schmidt, emeritus professor of philosophy at the University of New Mexico, died of pneumonia in Albuquerque, New Mexico, on February 1, 2008. Inspired by Bronson Alcott and Henry Thoreau, Paul began writing a journal while at Penn State University, and amidst detailed observations of birds, accounts of long solitary hikes and speculations on science and society, he wrote in February 1943, "I seem to find only the career of professor awaiting me. I have always thought I would enjoy this, teaching psychology or philosophy." Philosophy, along with poetry and nature, became Paul's passion.

After World War II he studied English and philosophy at the University of Rochester, receiving his A. B. in 1947. He completed his Ph. D. at Yale University in 1951.

Visiting India in 1957 as a consultant on General Education, Paul lectured to faculty, taught classes and met informally with students. Equally valuable, he encountered and responded positively to the beauty of India's people, the land and the magnificent temple architecture and sculpture. When he moved to the University of New Mexico in 1965 to initiate the doctoral program in philosophy, Paul was excited by the challenge to build a well-rounded department. He also began to explore the rich, culturally diverse American Southwest and neighboring Mexico.

Kyoto Temples

On the east wall of the next room hang two ink-brush scrolls of the lunatic Zen monk who gazed too long at the moon and became moon struck. A strange smile plays over his face, a mysterious combination of serenity, silliness and profundity. For some time I have gazed at him and only now begin to sense his enlightenment from lunacy.

What might happen to me as I sit in meditation, zazen, each morning from seven till eight in Chotoku-in, one of the Zen Temples making up the complex of temples called Shokoku-ji? Zazen begins with the "ting-ting" of a small bell calling me to the meditation room, zendo, where are placed square flat firm pillows with a small firm circular pillow on top to sit on. I assume a half-lotus position, flex my neck, bend my back to side and front, letting my spine come to rest in a balanced vertical position. Our teacher enters, we make a small bow, he plays the two gongs and bell, begins to chant a sutra on negating, not-this, not-that, not-A, not-B, etc., etc., end in clapping wood blocks and lighting an incense stick. A long silence ensues of concentration-on-breathing meditation, broken midway by the bell and wooden clappers. At the end of this hour I carefully uncross and unbend my legs, flexing them slowly, rise and go to breakfast.

Sohaku Ogata, Abbot of Chotoku-in, awaits us. He is an old man now, no longer able to walk without help, no longer able to conduct morning zazen. His eldest son Yugi, future abbot, does so. But his mind is still bright and humorous. He delights most in telling and commenting on old Zen stories. If the conversation turns to chit-chat he is likely to doze off in his chair. His life is now wholly devoted to translating into English *Ching Tê Ch'uan Têng Lu, The Transmission of the Dharma Lamp* (in Japanese *Keitoku Dento Roku*), a lifelong dream. In August 1972 he is at work on scroll eleven out of thirty scrolls. Ogata-san passed on at the Spring equinox, 1973, a balanced day.

We live in a *tatami* mat room. Each such rice-straw mat is three by six feet by three inches thick. The size of any room is a multiple of tatami mats which can be arranged in various geometric patterns, an art as seemingly simple, yet as complex as flower arranging, kabuki composition or rock garden design. Great subtlety in utter simplicity is the result, the essence of this Japanese aesthetic. What a joy to slide back any wall of your room and unite into one whole whatever is beyond it. Rice-paper panels slide open walls on gardens, joining outside to inside. Our east and south walls are *fusuma*, paper on both sides of the light wood frame. Each of the four sliding panels making the wall is the size of a tatami mat, and has a painting in ink-brush of bamboo or grass. Open, they unite the room beyond. The west wall slides open on to a veranda, one mat in width, a rock and moss garden beyond, each stone placed with great care. A bamboo border sets off a few small palms. Half the north wall is a *tokonoma*, a recessed alcove in which hangs a beautiful calligraphy scroll. On one side are flowers rearranged every few days, on the left a wood carving. These set on a rise six inches above the mats.

Aesthetic simplicity is further expressed in the room furnishings. These are minimal, hardly noticeable, a floor mattress for a bed that is rolled up and put away in the daytime, a low table, some pillows to sit on. I use the low table as a desk, sitting lotus posture before it. These are Buddhist rooms, sparsely furnished, serving multiple purposes. Our temple room is a unity of aesthetic simplicity and diverse uses that brings nature inside and takes you outside. Here is an architecture of the One. Kyoto has a thousand temples, each with gardens, gardens such as I've never seen, of raked gravel, rocks and moss, ponds and trees. In the vast Daitoku-ji Zen temple-complex we contemplate our first garden of raked gravel and rock at Daisen-in, a sub-temple. You will not find flowers in the southeast garden. Instead, there are two conical piles of fine gravel and a single tree on a perfectly flat surface that has been raked into two-inch contours. The cones and tree seem randomly placed while the contours curve past the cones. In such simplicity the Japanese Zen garden manifests the Tao, the indescribable way. Or the garden shows the contingent as absolute, a chance arrangement that must be.

Another garden consists of three groups of rocks and a shrub-tree, the gravel raked in horizontal lines except for concentric circular patterns around each group of rocks. I feel the contrast of concentricity and horizontality combined with the motion and rest of the eye moving from rock to rock. The garden is a resolution of contradictories, a harmony, thoroughly Zen. We pass several hours easily looking upon such a garden.

Across the city at Honen-in you knock three times with the big wooden mallet on a thick square of wood hung by ropes. Soon you hear sandaled feet, and a priest ushers you to the Buddha Hall where Amida Buddha awaits you. The Jōdō sect believes that complete salvation can be achieved by one enlightened utterance of his name. Left alone, we see an altar rivalling any Catholic altar. In the center sits a six-foot Buddha, Amida, surrounded by beautifully carved candlesticks, vases of fresh flowers, fruit offerings, carved gold-leafed flowers, painted scrolls. Round and round our eyes travel enchanted by our freedom to inspect each item.

> "Amida Buddha"
> Honen taught people to say
> Simple salvation

In summer, day after day, the sky may drip with rain but that makes a moss garden all the more beautiful, as a thousand jewel drops glisten on a moss bed. How can each garden seem superlative? Is it because the absolute is harmonious in the contingent as the Buddha-nature is in everything?

Many think the perfect garden creation is at Ryōan-ji Temple. Twice I've sat for several hours in contemplation of its three gardens. The famous one is raked gravel in which are placed five groups of rocks, each group encircled by a small moss border. Passing through the entrance room you view it from a veranda along a long side of its rectangular form. You cannot step into this garden but you may sit in contemplation of its arrangement and forms. Iconographical interpretations vary: the rocks might be mountains or ships or islands; the raked sand the sea. A Zen story tells us that when you first begin to meditate, mountains are mountains, later on, mountains are no longer mountains, finally mountains become just what they are. Just so, this garden. As you turn the corner to your right at the end of the veranda a second garden appears. It is constructed of a thick moss bed backed with slim maple trees whose autumnal colors jewel the moss. Turning the next corner reveals a small stream flowing over a tiny waterfall into a still pond surrounded by shrubs and rock. From the silence of the first garden to the flowing watercourse of the way, we have three movements in a musical composition. Ryōan-ji gives you the history of Zen gardens. The first is not alone.

> Gravel, moss or pond
> Dry gray, cool green or goldfish
> Ryōan-ji gardens

> Velvet smooth green moth
> Wind tips the maple bow down
> Turquoise butterfly

I find a penetrating aesthetic integration among aspects of the Japanese garden, Noh play, haiku, scroll painting, flower arranging, tea ceremony and tatami floor mats. Each creates with a very limited medium, each manipulates that medium according to a restricted set of moves, each move clearly accented; each confines itself to a precise boundary; each achieves a powerful simplicity that contains a harmony of contrasts; each moulds the contingent into an expression of the absolute. As I explore each of these arts I sense striking parallels. Does the farmer design the contours of his rice paddies according to the same aesthetic ideal?

> Tea ceremony
> Threefold flower arrangement
> Tatamitexture

Temple floors and Japanese homes are covered with tatami mats of rice straw, soft yet firm, nothing more comfortable to walk on, kneel on, sit on. Room sizes progress in regular square and rectangular sizes beginning with a two-mat guard room of six by six, then six by nine, the four-and-a-half-mat room of nine by nine, then nine by twelve, twelve by twelve, twelve by fifteen, fifteen by fifteen, and so on, the larger the room the more creative possibilities for arranging mat patterns. The four-and-a-half-mat tea room and the eight-mat chamber are classic forms like the haiku and waka. Plato in the *Timeaus* displayed a similar geometrical aesthetic in the ultimate forms of the elements using several right triangles, the square and the pentagon. Set a child to arranging mats and you may have an architect.

At five in the morning early dawn light and songs of birds wake me. My eyes open on the moon-struck monk scrolls. I like to lie still in the glory of the new day. Half an hour later bells ring for zazen from the neighboring temple. After three gongs someone begins to beat a rhythm on a tight-skinned drum, shifting to the wooden drum and bass drum. Hardly noticed, the sutra chant begins, swells, replaces the drumming till the tingle of the tiny bell signals the beginning of silent meditation.

> Terse Buddhist drum beats
> Many voices sutra chanting
> Rain begins and ends

In Kōryū-ji Temple you will see the most graceful Buddha in Japan, a carving in wood of Miroku Bosotsu. So many Buddha figures are lifeless, others merely representative, but this one shows the most subtle curves, delicate proportions and soft texture. Were it not a Buddha you would agree it is a beautiful woman whose hands, fingers, back and torso are deftly turned.

> Most graceful Buddha
> Soft Miroku Bosotsu
> Bewitching vision

Tucked in a rice-terraced valley northwest of Kyoto lies Ohara, a quiet farming village with two enchanting temples: Sanzen-in and Jakko-in. In the garden of Sanzen-in you will be blessed on your travels by a sculptured Jizo, protector of children and travelers, of whom there are more images than all other Buddhas combined. Every cemetery, every road, every trail has many Jizōs to give help, many dressed in a red cloth bib or apron, unfortunately often covering fine stone carving. Even the butterfly feels safe perched on his head.

> Dancing butterfly
> Alights to rest on Jizō
> His red bib missing!

My friend Jerry Tecklin arrives from Antai-ji, a Soto Zen temple where he has shared their religious life. We talk about their heavy emphasis on zazen, making it almost the exclusive vehicle for enlightenment in Zen. To do so, I think, distorts the person and the Tao because it singles out one approach, zazen, as the approach. To select one route exclusively divides the undivided. To divide the One misses the Tao. Equally questionable is the immense strain, physical and psychological, of a *sesshin*, intensive zazen, a strain that desires relaxation afterwards in saké or cigarettes. To strain is to force, to compel, to achieve through domination. Thus the self may be forced into a constrained enlightenment, but I wonder if such enlightenment is genuine and lasting. When and if it happens is beyond the realm of force; it is effortless, self-sufficient. Strain is not the way. The way is effortless, a joyous balance of aspects of the world-divided-one, a harmony that may reach beyond or create the One. Insofar as any sect selects some aspect to emphasize to the exclusion of others, it cannot be a way to the One. The ascetic and aesthetic blend into unity.

A steady light rain falling on the moss garden. I have slid back the rice-paper screens of my room so I am in the garden but not in the rain. This is the perfection of the Japanese home. You are in nature, the garden enters your room, there is no dividing line, no wall of separation. You participate in the raining, your existing is a rainy living. Your alienation from nature is overcome. I sit reading on the tatami, the rain gently falling next to me. I can reach out and touch it. The softest breeze I feel on my skin yet I am never cold. The rocks glisten in the wet light. Why not build a home like this?

On top of Mount Hiei lived the warrior-monks of Enryaku-ji Temple who sometimes swept down on Kyoto to intercede in political affairs, attacking the other monasteries to insure the dominance of their sect. I find this history despicable, not Buddhist in any sense. May they all inherit the bad karma of their deeds. Midway between the eastern and western precincts, where tourists rarely walk, I came upon the unusual moss and rock garden of Jōdō-in where the moss undulates over small mounds, giving motion to the still garden. New monks here practice an austerity called "sweeping hell," six hours of sweeping each day for three months. Even during a late afternoon service, I see in back of the temple a monk sweeping Saicho's tomb, built by the priest Ennin in 854.

>   Sweeping life away
>   He seeks his liberation
>   Leaves forever fall

To seek the aesthetic, avoid the spectacular, leave the big-name places to the tourists, let the tour buses park at Tōfuku-ji while you walk to the sub-temple of Taiko-in on the west side. Here you will find intimate harmony undisturbed, from the ceiling lamp in the zendo to the mountain profile garden. Look at the screen of painted birds, the small statue of Hyakusai by Komachi, and the tea room built in 1599 by the eleventh abbot, Ankokuju Ekei. The seemingly haphazard tea room, its ceiling of three levels in three different materials, the odd-shaped windows in odd places, one of its four-and-a-half mats replaced by a wooden floor, and a single off-center vertical thin column, illustrates the aesthetic of incongruity. The east garden of rocks and moss beyond the pond mirrors the silhouette of mountain ridges to the east.

>   Raindrops on stone bridge
>   White butterfly on green moss
>   Careless I wander

There is a deep affinity between pigeons and temples whose roof shapes and eaves provide ideal places to roost. Many temples have constructed elaborate chicken-wire screens to keep the faithful pigeons from meditating near Buddha. Where such screens are not in place, beware a pigeon greeting. Perhaps they also deter the uninterested tourist.

> Buddhas sit and sit
> While tourists gawk and gawk
> Pigeons shit and shit

I do not believe in reincarnation as a literal metaphysical event but, I do think it guides your reflection to a consideration of the moral value of your actions when combined with the concept of Karma and, further, it lets you connect your present life to the lives of others for whom you feel deep sympathy and identity. Reading Thoreau's Journal and his biographies has always aroused in me a sense of identity that I cannot explain. A similar feeling came to me in the Kyoto Museum when I saw some scroll paintings of Bodhidharma, an Indian monk who brought Buddhism to China. I sat and stared at him for more than an hour. Somewhere back before Thoreau I felt an identity with Bodhidharma. I couldn't help noticing his big nose, his bulging hanging eyelids resting on his upper eyelashes, the wrinkles spreading into his cheeks from the corners of his eyes, his hairy chest in his faded red robe:

> Faded torn red robe
> Eyelids bulging over eyes
> Huge nose and ear rings
> Smile wrinkles on his cheeks
> Bodhidharma stares at me

Katsura Garden, an Emperor's villa, turns the Japanese garden into an extravaganza. Leave its artificial and contrived complexity to those who seek the footsteps of power. Walk through the back streets of Saihō-ji, the moss garden temple, for shadows and sunlight filtered through trees onto undulating moss and carp-rippled pond. Follow the path in both directions because each corner holds its revealing vision. At the tiny outlet from the pond, running clear from cloudy water, ponder why

> No carp swimming out
> From Saihō-ji garden pond
> No trout swimming in

You may hear a strange periodic thud along the path. Look around and you will see a piece of bamboo teetering on a hinged stick, filling with water from a tiny rivulet until the increased weight tips it down, pouring out the water and teetering back with a thud when the end strikes the ground. This thud may awaken you. I stood entranced, filling with water, teetering, making my thud.

> Bamboo tube teeters
> When water slowly fills it
> Falling back it thuds

Suppose you met a tiger who never took his eyes off you! At Sangen-in in Daitoku-ji there is such a tiger painted on the wall screen. You can begin at one side of the room constantly watching the tiger's eyes, walk across to the opposite side; his eyes follow your every step and his head seems to turn as you move. A haunting painting, an unceasing unity of you and tiger.

> A tiger whose eyes
> Follow you from side to side
> Fixed yet turning head

At Ōbai-in in Daitoku-ji the gravel in the garden conveys a vivid sense of the undulating motion of the sea. The gravel has been raked in a flattened sine curve. As I sit in contemplation the gravel surface begins to move, gentle swells about the rocks. Soon I am the waves, rhythmic diastole of the pulse of this garden. I begin to breathe in unison with it. And what are the temple buildings now but ships that sail on land, the curved-up corners of their tile roofs bows that sail in four directions. This upward curve creates a feeling of lightness, buoyancy; floating arks that may ferry you across.

> Soft gentle sea waves
> From undulating gravel
> Temples sailing free

Edith Shiffert

Edith Marion Marcombe Shiffert is a Canadian-born poet and translator of Japanese haiku masters. Her books are inspired by the natural and human worlds, and the aesthetic, philosophical and literary traditions of Japan. Since 1963 she has lived in Kyoto. Initially invited to teach English at Doshisha University, after five years she accepted a position as a professor of English at Kyoto Seika University where she taught until her retirement in 1983. She married Minoru Sawano in 1981. In Kyoto she has steadily published poetry and collaborated in multiple translations.

Her first collection of poetry written abroad was *The Kyoto Years* (1971), which contains poems influenced by Buddhism and her studies of Japanese literature. The same year she teamed up with Yuki Sawa to publish *Anthology of Modern Japanese Poetry* (1971) and *Haiku Master Buson* (1978), the first book in English to feature writings of Buson. Stimulated by exposure to Buson's writing, Shiffert put out her fourth set of poems, *A Grasshopper*, published as a chapbook by White Pine Press in 1976. This was followed by *The New and Selected Poems* (White Pine Press, 1979), *A Way to Find Out* (Raiju Press, 1979), *Kyoto Dwelling* (C. E. Tuttle Co., 1987), *When at the Edge* (White Pine Press, 1991) and *Forest House with Cat* (Unio Corp, 1991). Two of her most recent works include *The Light Comes Slowly* (Katsura Press, 1997), and *In the Ninth Decade* (Katsura Press, 1999), which feature illustrations of traditional ink paintings by Kohka Saito, a renowned artist of the genre. In total she has published some twenty books of poetry. She is currently 100 years old and resident in a rest home in Kyoto.

Yama-Biko: Mountain Echo

> Forty years looking
> up at the eastern mountain
> not high, not far, here!

For forty years I have lived directly below Mt. Hiei on the east side of the ancient city of Kyoto. Twenty four of these years have been shared with my husband, Minoru, hiking nearby and in the Japanese mountains, both of us writing poems, short and long. We traveled yearly overseas for several months visiting my family and seeing new places. Aging, we continued to walk along the streamside path known as the Philosopher's Walk. Here we enjoyed being with the birds on the Takano and Kamo rivers, feeding the pigeons and sparrows. We spent hours with the elegant herons and the tame seagulls which gathered here for the mild winters. Our lives were full and thoughtful. Then, when I was eighty-six and Minoru ninety-one, our wonderful life changed. Minoru's developing Alzheimer's and my osteoporosis meant we could no longer care for ourselves. A retirement home was found in the historic and scenic area of Ohara on the other side of Mt. Hiei. Since August 2002, we have made our new home Yama-Biko, or Mountain Echo.

> Roofed with heavy clouds
> and veiled in the shifting mists
> Mountain Echo home.

> Stillness comes out from
> solitary depths inside
> steep cedar forests.

The small mountains all around us are mostly covered with cedar trees. We used to hike in them but now we cannot even step off a paved path. Flowering trees and shrubs keep the slopes colorful more than half the year. Plum and cherry blossoms, azaleas and rhododendrons, hydrangeas, morning glory and wisteria.

> Those flower petals
> from roots in earth, stems in light!
> Self too roots and lifts.

From the first we were aware of a pair of hawks in their lookout tower by the rice fields and vegetable farms bordering our complex. We feel they are conscious of us and share our existence.

> Abiding with hawks
> we also know the long rains
> and when sunrise comes.

> After the typhoon
> a bird chirping and chirping
> where none was before.

> We too watch darkness
> slowly descend over fields
> and silence widen.

> Hawks from their tower
> above deep snow this morning
> soar up, swoop down, up.

I am conscious of all the changes of day and night, and the seasons, and do not feel lonely, even though there are no English speakers among the residents and staff here.

> The way of those hawks,
> we watch and when they fly up
> it seems we do too.

In the winter there is snow almost every day but it usually melts by mid-morning. Beautiful to look at or have falling on us.

> The plum flowers bloom
> in the snowstorms's new whiteness
> though I have not changed.

> Like heavy snowfall
> piled fragrant along branches
> flowers melt away.
>
> The Buddha body
> growing in my own body,
> in that cedar tree?

In season we are attentive to insects and frogs. Bright green frogs, the size of a fingernail, settle onto a balcony flower box and several even come inside for several days. Sitting on our balcony we watch evening fading to darkness and the darting flashes of many fireflies. The pleasure and interest we feel sharing our lives with all these non-humans, even a tiny firefly, is sufficient to ease our sorrows. We feel fortunate to be here though it is not the lifestyle we would have chosen. No more travel to Hawaii, Hong Kong, California, Alaska, Macao, or even the Japanese mountains and shores. But it is quiet, peaceful, safe, and we are content. We know who and what we are even while we endure our final mental and physical transformations. I have sufficient solitude to realize whatever can be known is what I have sought as a follower of the Asian hermit poet tradition.

> As if conversing
> the harsh voice of a lone crow
> comes from the forest.
>
> These solitary
> silences I sometimes find
> give satisfaction.

Yama-Biko has several paved paths I can still manage to walk on, taking no more than a twenty minute walk. But to walk daily throughout the seasons is to witness endless changes all interlinked with the time, my condition, and the facts of existence. It becomes an experience of the interconnection of all things, their cycles, the accidents, the evolving evolution on, under, and over the earth's surfaces, and beyond. My husband and I are confined but there are no barriers to our experience of the most simple and varied things.

> Tree of my spirit
> within me all my lifetime,
> can its roots still spread?

This winter sunlight on the tallest cedar tips, on the small mountains.

> On Mt. Hiei
> the New Year snow has fallen.
> Cold and silent night.

Even before the snows end there is a succession of tiny flowers covering the ground. Little blue veronica opens its ground-covering patches of tiny flowers, morning after morning for months, often surrounded by snow. The trees and shrubs, in the garden and in nature, succeed each other in waves of colorful, sometimes fragrant, blossoms.

> Their meditation
> or mine, clustered blue flowers
> of hydrangeas?

> The color purple–
> Hydrangeas from June rains
> dripping while they glow.

> These still red thistles
> where butterflies perch in mists
> and white moths have feasts!

> Each one a quiet
> meditation–purple blue
> wet hydrangeas.

Here the wildflowers are blooming out in the countryside but I just know their English names. The same varieties as over much of the earth. How could I become homesick during two years in Alaska when the dandelions suddenly appeared everywhere?

> Two months we have watched
> for plum blossoms to open.
> Now already gone.

Bitter wind today
but an early violet
January's end.

Dark and light, sweet sounds
from crickets and soaring hawks.
A hundred eons?

These flocks of small birds
suddenly arriving here—
did they have a plan?

As we wander through
the eternal loneliness,
its births and its deaths!

Haiku poets, as all poets, should feel free to use the haiku in whatever way seems appropriate to their creativity. There never were any rules, just fashions and preferences. To be somewhere and write about it, that is what haiku is. You may write one hundred in a night or one in a lifetime. The history of haiku and its poets, as with many things, is endlessly fascinating but is no substitute for the creative response to the moment.

White veils on the hills
appear and vanish again.
Ohara spring mists.

The whole landscape goes
and then breaks thru from the mists
pouring down Mt. Hiei.

Still the same mountain
but now from the other side
as I near ninety.

In the great emptiness of my 88th year
plum flowers in a snowstorm, and I find
I'm not lonely or afraid.

At lunch that hum? A resident snoring?
Wind in a ventilator shaft?
A Buddhist priest chanting a sutra?

With whom shall I drink this tea;
the cat, Li Po's moon, or just myself?
We are all pleasant company.

In all directions
small mountains hiding the view
while being the view.

September 15, 2003

Rod Willmot

Rod Willmot's bio in his own words: "I set out on the naked path in 1948, in Toronto. My first mistake was not getting that nurse's phone number. Things started going better in my teens after I landed in Quebec, where I played the flute and papered the walls of a tiny room with freshly written haiku. For the next twenty years or so, haiku was my voice. I should also report that for another twenty years I was a bird on the wing, a speed skater I mean, mostly on wheels, on risky roads. I would give anything to be so again. Now I live in Montreal with my wife, a Québécoise, and make my living as a translator. Lately, strange stories have been making me write them down."

Excerpts from The Ribs of Dragonfly

One day I thought of writing a haiku for each rib of my canoe. The idea led further than intended, for in time there were characters before me, with a story, told in the 9 month season in which (where I live) a canoe can be put into water. The haiku had doubled, accounting for both the ribs and the spaces between them. The result may be considered a novella with haiku; it is a form of what the Japanese call haibun.

> musty shed
> winter light
> on the overturned canoe

the prow

Mid-March . . .

The lake is ice-bound still. There is almost not a sky, but a shroud neither high nor low, featureless, unmoving. Nor an earth, but an ivory deceit where no one goes without portable solidity to move on: hickory, fibreglass, or ash and babiche. And only to return where they started.

Shut-ins must be on the brink of despair, now that the frost is off the windows. The eye detects only absence, absence of change. Yet to be blind and gifted with folly, to stumble outside into the snow with outstretched naked hands—would be to know that Winter is rotting. The snowbanks crumble at a touch. The air, after all these months of arrogant virginity, is moist and wanton.

Today I went on snowshoes to the mouth of the river. The lake-ice there has been carved into the shape of a bowl, where the river pours itself out imperceptibly, a broth of transformation. Amid the unrelenting whiteness that has so long been all there is to see, that small, dark pool has become the focus of all life: a band of early geese, ducks that have overwintered, and crows, pecking at the very ice between their feet. Tracks of an ermine along the shore.

When I returned to the house I looked at my skis and thought of the trails dipping and climbing maddeningly in and out of slush, ice, corn-snow, klister-catching powder–in the north slope woods where there will still be pockets of snow in May. I went back to the rivermouth with the axe and a few boards, and chopped away the undereaten rim of the ice some twenty feet off shore. Then I resurrected the canoe.

First stroke of the paddle . . .
No longer the soaring of will on skis . . . a long drift toward the centre. Across the bay the ducks and geese took off with a muffled splash, then passed overhead on their way upriver. Ethereal. So brief, the whistle of their wings, yet enough to change everything. Like a crack in glass.

Silence.

On the horizon, drab sketches in olive and sepia of conifers and cottage woodlots. Ice-huts here and there, too distant for motion to be discerned among them or in their tiny plumes of smoke. The ice impassive now, no longer apprenticed to the rhythms of cold as it boomed and sang responsively. Master of silence in its death. The water, at times wholly reflection, at times pure darkness, at times more silvery than ice. And over everything, the shroud.

Stillness, even in me: a void between each breath where I linger heedlessly, accepting. Yet movement. A fragrance of melting. Movement I could smell.

Eventually two men on snowmobiles came from down the lake, swerving and gesturing to each other before they passed by, as though they had thought I might be one of them, in danger. For two have lost their lives just here, the past month, after straying too near the river in the dark.

The very power of their craft is its frailty, the fragility of mine its strength. This fish-thing, insect-thing made mostly of emptiness–ribs, slats, canvas–Dragonfly that engulfs my head like a shaman's mask when I lift it to my shoulders, becoming Raven: in this, though the unfound corpse may float up beside me, I am as safe as Orpheus returning from below.

Getting out was harder than getting in. That dread of the ice giving way: I slipped a couple of times. Absurdity of portaging a canoe through snow, my knees giddy after their doze in the cold. Now Leila calls it a 'typical foolhardy adventure,' and slams the bathroom door. So I'm to risk my life on skis instead?

I am.

It's snowing again.

> under clouds
> the snow
> a shrike waits in the elm

***

the keel is unseen

Berrying after rain.

'Good luck to eat the first' Purple drupelets cupping a dying-day.

Blue flutes, a rose perfume.

The next hits the bottom of the pail with a grandiose boom.

Thereafter the notes become higher, fainter, until the plucking hand conducts more subtly. Perfunctory whispering of berries, onto berries jostling. Clicketings, clicketings, until a dragonfly stills them in the net of its wings. Dogmatic bees, discussing isms. (Avoid the violins–they're sopping.)

When I get halfway around the patch, a measured rustling traverses the undergrowth from the side where I began. One of the cats? The Persian? The rustling stops near my feet and returns to dozing.

Raspberries. Hugeous clusters at arm's length. Wet foliage, spiderwebs trembling precariously gemmed. I press in deeper, stretching, while the coolness washes over my forearms, fusing into the fabric of my clothes. There are bluets by the hundreds! Brilliant blue piccolos, silent, rising and falling among the canes. My hands move in and out of the music.

Was there once a season of austerity, when the Reverend Wool held sway by Celsius decree? Churchmouse theology—I don't believe it. Saint Fromage and the Hagiophage! Morning after morning I stroll outside, saluting the sun-drummed patio with slapping sandals, greeting the breeze with billowing chemise. And while orioles chirrup and a catbird caws in a secret bush, I gather my breakfast in the light with hands that are still reflecting over the artifacts of night.

Rasp, straw, blue, black—all berries in the end, and each a world of plenitude, a glance of willingness, unblushing, nude. The strawberries a love long gone; the blackberries tight and pale and still taboo: from flowering to fruiting the days succeed one another, flowering once again in the garden of the mouth or fruiting finally beneath the crock's lid. Swaying, ripening, fondly detaching from the wind's vine, women and men go pleasuring in the sun until the last remaining rondelets of untanned flesh, discovered, are a treasure to recover. Our very fingers believe themselves berries, juice-stained jostlers into others' hands.

Now like sprouts in the garden, friends arrive, from around the hill and across the continent. The foliage of days luxuriates, desultory branches browsing through the afternoons, while the barbecue performs its sword-dance fire-dance sizzling shows. Splash the living spirit over ice-cubes! Leaves upon leaves while the talk goes gadding it through the trees with laughter yapping after, an abstraction or two to smoke the mosquitoes out, Savonarola citronella. And from the garden, petticoat lettuces, the secret of existence in their overlapping frills: tapwashed, torn into tatters, tossed among mushrooms, tomatoes and shallots. And once consumed, reassembled, pensively, to root again, with the aid of a cheroot or shreds of latakia; coffee; a drop of Amaretto; mints.

Was it beer or champagne the girl was sipping? A lovely dress, with those thighs. Champagne! White lace over Leila's breasts.

***

We are out in all weathers now, adventuring, seeking out waves to unfurl within us. Leila before me, swaying in the bow in a flowered bikini while the prow lifts and plunges throwing spray into the wind. Strong, my wife! But slim, suppler than a mink. Adroit maneuvers in a summer gale.

On calmer days I play guide to our visitors, some of whom take to the canoe as to a new romance. Others I find unsettling: so determined to stay upright they convey their own nervosity to the craft, which then sets the very lake aquiver. Still others, seeing the waves overtake us from behind (in a following breeze), despair of getting anywhere. 'Ignore the waves!' I urge, expounding the stillness of the surface film: the dust, chaff, pollen, feathers, damsel-fly nymphs and belly-up fishes; iridescent trails of swirls and bubbles, like slime-trails of slugs, slug-motorboats that troll in inverted forests; fishermen's floats, red plastic, red and white. Only bobbing.

When you find your movement, look to the waves again.

**

Cloud-forms, changes in the wind. Rumblings: a dump truck on the hill? It can be tricky, trying to judge how far you can go before the surfaces sunder. Leaden sky, sky-lace on the waves, tossing to exchange positions. Hag-fingered lightning, startling the young folk with a glimpse of what she knows.

Today I was caught out when the storm came up, and sought refuge under a stranger's eaves. Necessity mothered well, though; I was soon in comfort, distracted from meteorology by a lady of a certain age with a gift for languages and raspberry turnovers, who served a fine coffee of her own invention (roots and grains). She had carved *Quo vadis?* into the endmost plank of her dock.

I'd forgotten to phone home, however, and apparently Leila was convinced I was drowned or lightning-skewered (it was a hell of a storm). Or soaked to the bone at least, on a hostile shore. In expiation of my sins I had a tough paddle upwind to get home, on a full stomach. Singing, *Mon pays, c'est l'hiver*, for some reason. When I reached our little bay the wind fell off as abruptly as it had risen.

> raspberry canes
> hand probing the shade
> of her open jeans

***

second thwart

A thin, pulsating bar, colourless. Perceived along the plane of formation, the sum of waves across the entire lake. Or not waves, but waveness. Vaguely journeying beyond arrival, indeterminately everywhere and nowhere, like heat-shimmers over highway. To shatter the bar into patterns of crest and trough, like colours out of white, would require . . . a prism: a schism between oneself and the thing observed. So learn to walk on water.

Gelatinous here; I'm up to my neck in it. Weed-matted, lugubriously flat. And the air over the surface deathfully busy and foul-smelling, with swarms of jigging midges making smoke-like wreathes in and out of which the dragonflies go clipping like ambiguous angels. No reeds, leaves, blossoms, except the unseen in submarine tombs. None of the marsh's pondweed poking up its pink fingers, as though to test the world for some long-meditated pearl of the slimes. I loathe it here. (Only this: the yellow bauble of a bladderwort held up, hypocritically, dry and clean.)

Dredging the bay of its filth. An operation properly done once a year, with floats, weights, ropes, chickenwire maybe, and pulleys anchored to trees; not this mucking in deep with a hayrake and my own cold body.

A day gone wrong.

This morning I opened the door over a garter snake sunning itself on the hot cement stoop. Not bothered, I just stepped over it and went on—without thinking of Leila. And from this: bitter words and grudging replies, a quarrel that became a spinning raspy thing, plucking at every loose thread in our lives. Jealousies, belittlements, suspicions:

threads becoming worms, knots in a nest of vipers. You'd think you could snip them with a gesture or a gentle thought, or disentangle them with words. 'What I meant was—' 'And what does *that* mean?' The disentangler tangled, the white knight unhorsed with a 'fucking bitch' and a clank. Before lunch I escaped in bathing trunks to do battle elsewhere.

Through June, as algae infiltrate the shallows, circles of clarity remain where the sunfish fan their nests. But in the depths of summer the aquatic weeds further offshore, unseen the rest of the year, burgeon into a swath of suffocating vegetation: motionless reeking stuff that trammels the canoe, propeller-torn rags of it haunting the lake to enshroud, maddeningly, the hooks and lines of fishermen.

The heft of a tool, a weapon of a kind, the sturdy rod and the arc it will inscribe across the sky, the teeth it will garner from the sun. Hawk-beaks plummeting.

First splash—the water scurries with catfish. The rake emerges draped with dripping algae. Swing again. *Clack-clack*, a courtly craw daddy, CLACK embarrassed in ribbons of eel-grass. And later, littler ones, cream-colour thumbling grave-diggers that I toss out tumbling to the deep. Swinging, each overhead sweep like a dawn-to-dusk transit of the sun, compressing time: a backlog of maunderings retrieved from the underworld.

Clots of rotting algae, floating about like turds. The water seems filthiest of all as its sudden cold pokes into my bathing trunks. Then my inhibitions dissolve. (*Who are you, slimy and amorphous Thing?*) Slogged up splashing onto the beach it shivers and names itself: naias-weed, crisp and serrated, prickly with the resentment of one too soon awakened. Tape-grass, transparent almost, a garland for imaginary Christmas trees. And bladderwort, a million tiny purses speckled through its ins and outs like flea-traps in a weasel's castle: unclasping to ingest, with imperceptible sucking-sounds, invisible protozoans.

The mud, now and then, is slow to release my toes.

By chance, I discover that with my arms held out to either side, my body reaps better than the hay-rake. The strings and foliage, the floating and the submarine, amass against my chest and thighs, and clinging to each other and to me, languidly let go their roots. In a relentless arc I plod across the bay, crouching under the weight as the bottom rises, to stagger ashore at least quadrupled in size, my swaddling greens aquiver and astream like the nervous flesh of a newborn monster. And wade back in, repeatedly, until my toes can barely graze the insubstantial muck and the bliss of open water is only a man-length away. Then I swim out with the rake and up-end it, gathering and turning, tangling the last weeds around my body.

Poling shoreward . . . Certain of my progress, I try now and then to touch bottom, without finding it. Again, poling, and thrashing, and slowly drifting back, exhausted.

Held fast, I rest there with my mouth just out of the water, looking at the diaphanous bar pulsating from one end of the lake to the other. Then push the encumberment down as though it were soiled clothing, and float free in the clear circle. Half crawl, half swim, over the edge and out, leaving the end to go on beginning.

As I stumbled from the water I saw Leila at the kitchen window, stiff-looking, as though she had been watching. Pretending I hadn't noticed, I turned to survey the product of my toil, but then wheeled back looking nowhere, mortified. The bay was like a cesspool.

I hosed myself down, fetched jacket and shoes and worked on, trundling my six-foot heaps of gleanings to the compost. With every load more sodden than the last, I resolved a dozen times to let the stuff dry till morning. But kept on anyway, until I could barely see what I was doing, or had done.

***

Duckweed.

Washed into inlets, sunlit, a lime green spot. Into nooks where a boulder is a mountainside, and pebbles, great boulders. Wavelets wafting a drifting thing, out through the crowds of pickerelweed blue, around and under the arrowheads' three-petalled white, and over the perches, yellowing in the haze of striped shallows. Yellow waves, green waves, orange under the outleaning sumac, red waves, purple waves . . . blue.

Plantlets of duckweed, the tiniest. Two fused together make a cap for my little finger. They winter on the lake-bottom, strangely. Things of light. Returned to the waves, they float unsinkably.

Last night we woke amid a wild billowing of curtains. After a few uncertain minutes, each wondering if the other was awake and trying to gauge the distant thunder, we both jumped up at the sudden spattering-in of rain. Separately, we hurried about the house shutting windows, until in the dining room we came together at the one that invariably sticks. The telephone clattered eerily; then there was a tremendous crash. We let the window down slowly, blinded by the brilliant arc-light of the transformer by the drive shorting out. Then blackness. Thrumming of the rain, yet . . . quiet. Two snails in one shell.

Later we set a fire in the fireplace, and made coffee and hot cereal. In the twilight before dawn we notice peculiar, egg-shaped rafts on the lake, drifting rapidly with the northward march of the waves. We did not know then that they were colonies of duckweed that the storm had released from the beds along the marsh, nor that later, when we pushed out in the canoe, marveling at the bay's unequalled clarity, we would find the rafts scattered and duckweed everywhere, glistening on the crest of every wave and dancing in every trough.

We stood at the window, steeped in its dimness, seeing so much that was inexplicable. There is no certainty anywhere, except in this ebb and return with which we answer one another.

            curtains billowing
            her hand
            spreads rain down my arm

        ***

the sternman's seat

A brush hesitant on a full palette: the paddle, dipped into water. The prow remains steady, like a painter's thumb erect for the measurement of vision. I see her now on the backdrop of sky: the girl who is the island, lying on her side with knees drawn partly in, and turned at the waist to look upward. A girl with blond hair, the near white of beech-leaves. A touch of scarlet at the wrist, the sumacs; and something olive-green, a belt, a purse, the cedars. For the rest, her colours are like worsted, an indivisible texture.

What am I seeing? The sky so fearlessly clean that I drape its nakedness with an illusion. But if the air itself pretends at colour, scattering the white of the sun to render blue . . . who is the worse illusionist?

The prow begins to sway, placidly, like a near-sighted herbivore testing the windless air.

From this far away the island shares the eye with sections of world: the ragged shores, a half-built mountain, a gull inspecting the vacancies of a gently flawed mirror, drifting away undecided.

Now there is just the island. For a moment I taste it in the air and am almost, recklessly, swollen with the pungent fullness of dying. Then the cloth unweaves and in every strand there is a triplet of colours, green by the petiole, to yellow, to orange at the tip, repeated on each of uncountable leaves: green, écru, vermillion; green, limegreen, chestnut; limegreen, straw, to crimson.

More deeply delving, I divide to impossible chromatics where a molecule of pigment is itself complex, shifting and toned, a crowd of orchestrated photons daring to be split. In one crisp leaf upon a raven pool . . . (*A stone, a stroke of wood? On the leaf-smudged bottom, silver, obsidian, mahogany; my cold-whitened hand reaching out.*)

When I look around, the canoe has come to rest in a narrow channel under the trees, and there is nothing to be seen but the island from within, huge and incomprehensible. And later, paddling out again into the lake's now ordinary stillness, I resist the urge to turn and catch the illusion coalescing once more; while behind my eyes the Island Lady steps from form to form, now jade, now ivory, now flesh.

***

Another day the same, and yet a third, but indulgently warm and hazy. It is Indian Summer, now if ever. In the full light of noon I risk a visit to the duckblind, in the sparse reeds opposite the mouth of the river. Neither birds nor hunters are about in weather like this. Their goddess sleeps beneath the mirror: she of the tousled hair and tantrum eyes, most beautiful when most tragic. With wind and clouds the Canadas arrive, stitching the rumpled sky about her limbs, and blacks and teal and goldeneyes come jetting to braid her hair and settle into sequins on her breast–whereupon she rips off her clothes. Then the hunters hurry with their drums, and boom, and boom, who knows whom they are placating, her or the higher gods, or if the circling birds are harpies at her neck or attentive maids.

(The first dawn of hunting season: roused in a panic, our first autumn here, by the sudden volley of explosions, and later, half-asleep, dreaming of shotgun pellets in the meat of roasted pheasant–a boyhood memory–the dream confusing them with peppercorns and pushing them, as though into liver paste, into the oil-paints with which I'd later tried, with the chance success of inability, to reproduce the bird's feathers.)

Letting the paddle knock the gunnel as though upon a door, wanting to be certain that no one sleeps within, I scrape the canoe through the many-postured reeds. Through the drapery of boughs I confirm that the blind is empty, and look for the hinge that allows one end to swing aside. With the amused awkwardness of someone trying on a costume, I guide the canoe in sternwards.

It is quiet. A net of delicate shade, lambent upon everything. Cigarette-butts, floating, nuzzle the piles, pine-trunks nobbly with congealed resin. Outside, the sky's brilliance attenuated, a helicopter kisses the horizon to the lyric hammering of a cottager on his roof, and a truck rumbles down to caress the shore. You could wait here forever, as though the warmth you had drawn around yourself were a net that had caught the world; or as though, through dense capillaries in silhouette, you were looking out peacefully from within the flesh of another.

***

First, Bellatrix. Then the ember that is Betelgeuse, out of the murk along the horizon. Gradually the belt of three with 'String of Pearls,' Alnilam, in the centre; and then bright Rigel, the Nebula, and Saiph . . .

A mouse sitting on a stump watches Orion sit up in bed and stretch, sniffing the universe for prey worth hunting. The Pleiades fly before him in a tight little flock, no longer women to his eyes, but sparrows. The mouse huddles down beside an owl-pellet, inwardly scornful, knowing that the night's true eyes are not owls but his own breed, kinsmen of stars.

Who comes, no owl or fox, but one of the two-legged tall ones of the naked path. It stops, and for a long while gazes upwards. Then– suddenly–it bursts into applause–waits a moment, as though transfixed–then turns and goes back the way it had come.

The mouse is astounded. What had he missed that the other saw? Did a mouse-star fall? Could Orion in truth be–a dancer? His reflections become more exalted and more passionate as the stars wheel on, until the real explanation (something to do with a skunk toddling up the road) becomes a pretext of little importance. And finally not even true.

***

How long can this weather last? This evening in the gold and copper haze a heron comes to perch heraldic on the duckblind. As I gaze through the binoculars, with the last sun burning in the windows of a farmhouse high on the opposite shore, he squawks, shits majestically, and takes his leave, trundling low toward the river.

> the roofing-tar that humid afternoon
> is good now
> in smoky tea

Note: Originally the final haiku was this: "hermit thrush / weeds, unidentified / evening mist on the meadow". *Writing it, I kept thinking that a similar poem had been done by someone else, yet it was my experience, the most magical of all during my time in that cabin. A few days later I found the answer, on page 41 of "The Ribs of Dragonfly" (1984):* "thrush all evening / pages of a botany / turn to forest". *It was one of the few haiku in Ribs, if not the only one, that wasn't drawn from my life at the time when Ribs was being written. I wondered what to do. I was also troubled by my inclusion of the hermit thrush. It was* specifically *a hermit thrush I heard that evening, but how many readers have a clue what that means, how many will ever have a chance to hear such beauty? We are fixated on our gadgets, gliding through the endless flatness of technology, unaware of all that has been destroyed so that we can be distracted. With these thoughts I went to bed, and later was awakened by what came after, on that and several other evenings, so many years ago.*

Unanswered Questions

Around 1970 I lived for a few weeks in a tiny log cabin that Eric Amann* built. When he and his friends (they were all doctors) came on weekends, they stayed in a trio of hunters' shacks some distance away. Eric was amazed at my reports of wildlife, things he hadn't seen on his own land: the bear, as frightened as I by our meeting; the deer in the meadow, the grouse (thumping like a pump starting up) in a thicket; the porcupine, whose craving for salt was evident wherever sweaty hands had touched.

>   porcupine hesitates
>   until
>   we both leave

In a lean-to beside the cabin, someone had left a pair of surgical scissors, delicate things, splayed-open amid rusty tools and gnawed wood. I had a deep respect for tools, learned from my father. I admire those scissors each time I use them, as I often do.

>   porcupine licked.
>   transient took.
>   scissors *snip*

Modern devices. Logically there must have been a well with a hand pump, or I'd be dead. The wood stove I remember thanks to the bird, a black bird, that woke me one morning like a nightmare, crashing and scrabbling in the stove pipe. It could only escape by falling into the stove, from which I released it–relieved that it was a bird. I've never forgotten how it flew: straight, straight, out the door and across the meadow, the most determined thing I've ever seen.

>   something is right
>   about being off-balance
>   in a sea of poison ivy

Besides the stove there were two crude oil lamps whose wicks needed constant trimming, their glass chimneys daily polishing. With them I read into the night: Stendhal's *Le Rouge et le noir*, Faulkner's *The Sound and the Fury*, and a glossy introduction to wild plants. Stendhal was an escape to a romantic past, Faulkner a trap in the past present. The longed-for Caddy, her name repeated obsessively, reopened my wounds from the summer before, a girl named Camille.

> Caddy! Caddy!
> the lamp-wick chars
> glass burning hot

Between the cabin and the shacks there was a forest, with an almost path that led unwillingly through, or not. One had to set off before twilight. On one occasion, in the full light of day, I strayed somehow and for several moments was in a panic, dashing from side to side till suddenly the path reappeared. I was too ashamed to recount this to Eric. I the nature boy, handy with an axe and so on.

> silence in the forest
> then
> silence

Once in my childhood I was wading in a creek, then flailing uncontrollably, over my head. By chance my feet found the edge of a sandbar, and I got out as my friend said (laughing uncertainly) "I thought you were drowning." Then as well I was ashamed and said nothing. After years I've learned the solution, though I suppose I've practised ever since I was born: get off the path, and stay off.

> lost again
> long drink of water by the road
> feeling good

My sojourn in Eric's cabin was a moment of shelter in a journey of risks. In the worst of times my friend of friends was the passion for botany I acquired that summer. Till then my country had seemed a beige place, a place of browns, greys, featureless green. But the meadow between my cabin and the woods rippled with swaths of orange hawkweed, whose fiery eyes opened mine. Plant after plant I brought back to introduce to the little book I'd found somewhere, which all too often merely said, "They're your friends, not mine."

> at last I light the lamp
> the dark and stillness
> deep inside

Note: Eric Amann was one of the early proponents of haiku in Canada. From the late 1960s he published Haiku *magazine, followed by the more ambitious and influential* Cicada. *He had an eye for quality, and an openness to exploration.*

Section II: Contemporary Writers of Haibun

Melissa Allen
Cherie Hunter Day
Lynn Edge
Judson Evans
Chris Faiers
Charles Hansmann
Jeffrey Harpeng
Ed Higgins
Ruth Holzer
Roger Jones
Gary LeBel
Tom Lynch
George Marsh
Michael McClintock
Beverly Acuff Momoi
Lenard D. Moore
Peter Newton
Jim Norton
Stanley Pelter
Dru Philippou
Richard S. Straw
Bill Wyatt

Melissa Allen

Melissa Allen grew up in Connecticut and has an undergraduate degree in Russian language and literature. She has lived most of her adult life in Madison, Wisconsin, where after stints as bookstore clerk, freelance journalist, home educator, and librarian, she now works as a technical writer at a software company. She began writing haiku and haibun in 2010 on a whim that quickly became an obsession and has now published widely in both genres. The author of the poetry blog *Red Dragonfly*, she also is one of the editors of the journals *Haibun Today* and *Bones*. She has an adult son and enjoys working in the fabric arts, singing (badly), procrastinating, and daydreaming.

https://haikuproject.wordpress.com/

Where We Live

It's a tiny motel: four rooms, two tacked on to each end of our house like the spreading wings of a Southern plantation. But we're the opposite of a plantation, we're the site of endless uprootings. Poor soil for weak vegetation. The less successful variety of traveling salesman, in cheap suits, bearing leatherette briefcases and expressions of bewilderment at how fruitless their lives have turned out to be. Men who've been kicked out, out of the house by their wives and aren't quite sure yet whether they can go home tomorrow. Drifters who've scrounged up enough money somewhere to settle down in one of our nineteen-dollar beds for the night, often leaving behind them the evidence that they had enough left over for a good-sized bender. Even hippies sometimes, though there aren't a lot of them in this blue-collar, conservative town; maybe they're just passing through on their way to someplace more congenial—a commune, a city squat, a rock festival. They arrive, unlike most of our customers, in clumps, too young yet to want or need or have to be alone. Most of these people don't stay long; the wind blows them to us and then blows them away.

Then there's Miss Knight. June comes and so does she, in her blue VW bus, crammed to the ceiling with everything she owns. All summer it sits in front of the motel, down by Room 4, which is her home for the summer and always has been. (As far as I know, anyway; my "always" isn't very long.) She fills the room up quickly. She's not the kind of wanderer who travels lightly, who pares down her possessions. She likes things. Not luxurious things but things that are her own, that make her feel at home. Her room feels like nothing so much as a nest, lined with bits of fluff and feathers and string, trifles that seem worthless on their own but make excellent insulation. She wears layers of clothing too, shapeless skirts and sweaters draped around her tiny thin body, even in the heat of summer. She coddles herself, but she thrives this way. Nothing blows her away; she's rooted.

We don't know how old she is. Seventy-five? Eighty-five? Her hair is pure white and scant, her spine bent, and sometimes her mind, to us, seems to travel on illogical paths—but maybe it's our minds that are at fault, too limited to follow her flights of fancy, her mental travels into the less explored regions of the universe. She's energetic, her eyes sparkle, she takes good care of herself and her dog, the Chihuahua that goes with her everywhere: so whatever age she is, it isn't too old. We're not inclined to be critical anyway; the place seems entirely different with her around, less like a dreary way station for the desperate, more like a bucolic paradise, a fit resting place for any respectable elderly woman who spends the year driving around New England in a VW bus. It never feels like summer until her bus arrives, to remind us that we have an acre of land out back, filled with fruit trees and shade trees and flowering bushes. Miss Knight takes daily constitutionals around it, looking at everything with appreciation and curiosity.

She's friendly, even ebullient, but guarded. She looks hazy-eyed past questions. We don't know her story, her past or her future. It's as if she only exists here and now, in the summer in a small motel in Connecticut. The only indication we have of her life away from us is the one postcard that arrives every spring, in advance of her own arrival, letting us know to be on the lookout for her. It sits propped on the dining room table for weeks, while the weather grows warmer, the school year wears on, our other customers come and go, our own lives mutate and progress inexorably. It's our surrogate for her; we read it over and over, day by day, until she pulls into the driveway again, and then we put it away in a drawer with the ones from every other year.

The year it doesn't arrive, we all start wondering whether we're any more real than she is.

> summer solstice
> how much of my life story
> is invented

Post Office

The main post office on Gorky Street in Moscow. A line of squat beige phones—a line of people in thick coats to their ankles standing beside them. Staring at them like half-boiled pots, waiting for them to ring. Waiting to hear the voice of someone from the other side of the Iron Curtain.

You've filled in the required forms. *When do you want to talk? Whom do you want to talk to? For how long would you like this conversation to continue?* Be careful: they'll give you exactly the amount of time you ask for, no more and no less. But the phones are ringing, your mind is buzzing, you can only make awkward, half-thought-through calculations.

Not long after our phones ring and we lift the receivers to our ears like stones, we realize we answered all the questions wrong. The conversations should have been earlier or later, longer or shorter. The people we are talking to are not people we really know. We've forgotten the languages they're speaking. We live in different countries for what we now know is forever, though we meant it to be temporary. "Wait—" we say. "It's about to end—"

The phone makes a noise that means my life has returned to me. Everything goes silent until it's the next person's turn. Down the line, feet shuffle, stirring the hems of coats.

    melting snow—
        letting go
  of what I meant to say

Wave and Particle

You know how it is: time is on your side. Then it isn't. You cartwheel down the sidewalk one day in spring and watch yourself drive by, ten years older in the passenger seat with your head on your boyfriend's shoulder, twenty years older in the driver's seat carpooling to your son's soccer game, thirty years older in the back seat of the lead car in your father's funeral procession, your mind emptier than it's been in years, turning your head to follow the progress of the little girl cartwheeling down the sidewalk. You never noticed her before.

> the mistakes in my mirror image of myself

Well, but why should you have noticed her? Maybe she was never there before. And then again, why shouldn't you have? Is a little girl really a less permanent feature of the landscape than the house behind her, the one that looks eerily like your childhood home? Houses fall down, streets cave in. Even hills, like this hill your car is climbing to the cemetery, even hills wear down over time, don't they. Yes, someday someone will pick up this hill without thinking and put it in his pocket. And give it to his little girl when he gets home.

> seismic movement my errors in judgment

The stars are coming out now, it's that late in the day, the dark comes early now that it's winter, though surely it was spring earlier today. You step out of the car and join the stream of your father's mourners, all of you shrinking and fading as you move toward his grave in the darkness. Stars, you think: now they're eternal—and then one winks out as you glance at it. Yes, it had a good run, but it's cold and dark now, and everyone living on the planets that spun around it winked out themselves long ago. Time flies like an arrow, only faster. You've wasted time, but no need to get so upset about it, everyone does. It's there to be wasted. And then it's not there anymore; or more precisely, it is, but you're not. You're not.

> eight minutes later the truth finally dawns

Melissa Allen

Misdirection

It's winter dusk—a faded, in-between sort of time—and my mother and I are standing in a wallpapered hallway—a faded, in-between sort of place—accompanied by a large man who is wearing a dark suit and fluttering with apparent anxiety. We can't take long, he tells us, and shows us a trolley on which is lying something human-shaped, covered with a sheet. His implication seems to be that this is my father, but I'm not fooled by this story; it's the usual magician's patter, a way to distract us from the sleight of hand being performed. I'm curious, though, about what will be there, exactly. A raft of rabbits, a drift of doves? A float of pink carnations? A thousand bright silk handkerchiefs?

in and out of winter ready or not

Abracadabra!—pulling back the sheet from my supposed father, we find him transformed into a doll, a puppet, a cold and eerily motionless replica of himself. The likeness is astounding. The things they can do with mirrors! I put a hand to his cheek. It feels as if it were made of some very soft, pliable sort of clay. Magician's clay, perhaps they call it. I picture the page of the compendium of magic tricks in which this one is described. The Victorian illustrations, the magician wearing a handlebar moustache and a cravat. The diagram of the secret panel behind which the living man is concealed. The rotation of the chamber to present the mock man to the audience. A flourish of the wand.

lily stamens
reading a thin pamphlet
about the future

Through the hall window the sky has deepened to navy and the moon has begun to shine dully. The features of the father-doll recede and blur. The magician flutters at our backs. It's time to go, he says, the show is over. This, too, doesn't deceive me. The grand finale has yet to come—the restoration of the living man to the stage. We allow the large man to draw up the sheet, to push the trolley into another room. Soon he'll bring it back and let us pull away the sheet again. My father will climb smilingly down; we'll all applaud while the dark-suited man bows, no longer anxious but proud of his skill at concealment and misdirection.

                last bus out of town ice moon

We'll all walk together out of the hall and out of this stiff, formal building, discussing magic and its mysteries. Perhaps my father will tell us how the trick is performed, or perhaps he has been sworn to secrecy. He'll smile at us mysteriously, tell us we should volunteer ourselves someday, agree to be replaced and then restored. *There's nothing frightening about it, after all,* he'll say. *A little boring, maybe. You just lie there for a while, listening to voices and sensing the growing darkness. I might have dozed off for a while there,* he'll say. *But I enjoyed the rest, I admit. In fact I don't see why you had to wake me at all,* he'll joke, looking up, as we leave the house, at the first bright star in the blue-black sky.

                morning star
                a blaze consumes
                what's left of him

What Was His Is Mine

The desk I work at was once my father's desk. In my father's desk there are many drawers. In the drawer where I keep my passport, he kept his cigarette papers. In the drawer where I keep my secret chocolate, he kept his canceled checks. In the drawer where I keep my unfinished novel, he kept his very well-kept ledger books. In the drawer—the top drawer—where I keep everything else, he kept everything else. Throughout my childhood I opened this drawer regularly, to inspect its nearly unchanging contents.

>subclinical
>waiting for the rain
>to start

There were pencil stubs in here, matchbooks, old business cards, and various office supplies that were more or less interesting. But what I was most drawn to was an old pair of glasses, black and squared-off: old-fashioned, discarded eyes that my father never looked through anymore. I sometimes took off my own glasses and looked through them for him. I didn't think the world looked much different through those old glasses, though. A little bit smaller, that's all, and a little bit farther away.

>distant thunder
>tobacco isn't what got him
>in the end

Cherie Hunter Day

Cherie Hunter Day edits the journal *Mariposa* and is a staff editor for The Red Moon Press Anthology of English-Language Haiku. Her most recent e-chapbook *sting medicine* is featured on the website for *Bones: journal for contemporary haiku* (http://www.bonesjournal.com). Her second full-length collection of haiku, *apology moon* (Red Moon Press, 2013, 2016), received a Touchstone Distinguished Book Award for 2013. Her work is included in *Haiku 21* (Modern Haiku Press, 2011), *Haiku in English: The First Hundred Years* (W. W. Norton, 2013), and *Where the River Goes* (Snapshot Press, 2013). Her award-winning tanka book *Early Indigo* was published by Snapshot Press in 2000. A responsive tanka book, *Kindle of Green*, with David Rice, was published by Platyopus Books in 2008. She also has won multiple awards for her prose poems and flash fiction with publications in *100 Word Story*, *Mid-American Review*, *Mississippi Review*, *Moon City Review*, *Quarter After Eight*, *Quick Fiction*, *SmokeLong Quarterly*, and *Wigleaf*.

Fifth Floor

Todd points to the fifty-five gallon drum in the corner and says, "That's *para*-dichlorobenzene. If you start to feel dizzy or nauseous, leave the area and get some fresh air. Did you bring latex gloves? The specimens you requested are very old and were processed with arsenic, which is easily absorbed through the skin. I'll try to check on you later to make sure you're alright."

The hall is immense and lined with tray upon tray of bird skins reaching from floor to ceiling. Birds devoid of bones—just skin wrapped around cotton batting. I'm here to reanimate the heads with life-like eyes and draw nineteen species in flight. "Sorry about the temperature. We don't heat this part of the collection."

Todd gestures with a sweep of his right hand. "All of the tropical *Oceanodroma* and *Fregetta* are located in this area. *Puffinus* is just around the corner to your left. If you have trouble finding what you need, let me know and I'd be happy to help."

> twilit spruce trees—
> storm-petrels miles out at sea
> turn for home

Inclement Weather

thunderclap–
the darkness
between us

"July 1960" is stamped on the back of the Kodacolor print, each corner stained a glossy amber from old tape adhesive. Three names are written in blue fountain pen–Mom, my sister, and me. We are outside the backdoor of the old farmhouse when it was painted grey. Mom and I are in summer cotton dresses. My sister is wearing a dark navy swing coat and she is holding a large handbag. With the other hand she grasps the cuff to straighten the outfit underneath. I can almost see her shrug her shoulder just after the shutter clicks. She and Mom are locked in eye contact. They are the same height in heels. From the slight drop in the angle of their heads and the tension in both jaw lines there is heat between them. Mom's slender body leans away from my sister towards me with her weight on her right foot. She drapes her arm around my neck and her hand nestles under my chin. Her left arm hangs limp at her side.

My birthday is in July and so was my parent's wedding anniversary but this isn't a party shot. My sister is leaving. She is dressed for inclement weather: the yelling, the weeping like heavy rain.

Boo

She was in high school when I was in grade school. The school bus used to pick her up at her house, but she actually missed the bus more than she rode it–her mom waving from the porch for the bus to go on without her. She was the girl who dressed in thin cotton dresses in the middle of winter, came to school barefoot, and wore a heavy Icelandic sweater when the weather turned warm. She was the girl with leaves in her long brown hair, bruises under her eye, and scratches on her long legs. Gangly and awkward as a crow, she was shy and kept secrets like ashes in her mouth. Something happened in her family and she came to live in the two room pump house of the dairy farm next door. My mom gathered up some things for her: a lamp, a red vinyl hassock, a few dishes, and a chenille bedspread. I was cautioned not to visit her, not to pester her. She needed her privacy. She stayed only a couple of months. A farmhand found her sprawled on her bed with an empty bottle of pills. In the middle of the night I saw the flashing lights of the police car that took her away. I didn't know what a psychiatric hospital was; all I knew was that she didn't graduate with her class.

>   diary entry
> the intermittent light
>   of fireflies

Aftermath

Lightning blew apart the old English walnut tree in our backyard. It happened so long ago I can't pinpoint the season. I didn't know yet about voltages and watts. Resistances. Before the strike the storm raged and rattled the dormer windows of my bedroom. Hard to forget the nearness of destruction or the quickness of the elements in the middle of the night. In the aftermath I don't recall the tree ever being whole.

> fairy tales
> the swift descent of darkness
> in the sound of wings

Soft Landings

Scrub jays toggle blue in the sunlight. They fold that brilliance next to their bodies when they land. We hear each small thud on the wooden deck—the rhythm fits into the conversation like a heartbeat. A scattering of millet and sunflower seeds is enticement enough for them to come close. For us it's the ritual of loose leaf tea steeped until the leaves completely unroll and release their astringent and slightly sweet floral notes. Our ears are still tuned to soft landings, when the conversation shifts to the latest lab results and paperwork for two new clinical trials. Refractory is the word chosen over stubborn, wayward, contrary, or difficult. The latter terms would more aptly describe a truant child, not cancer. Does clarity have a color? Something on the prismatic scale next to indigo or ultramarine. Outside the jays leap from the balcony railing and unfurl their sun-brightened wings.

> thistledown—
> a fugitive
> at flight's end

Lynn Edge

Lynn Edge lives in a small farming and ranching town in South Texas. She obtained a degree in Elementary Education and a certification in Library Science, but preferred to raise horses and work in her home. She has been married for 48 years and has two children. In 2002 she was introduced to haibun by taking classes on the internet. She entered a WHO haibun writing contest and placed. She was encouraged by that recognition and it led to her work being published in the then new journal, *Contemporary Haibun Online*. Her work later appeared in *Modern Haiku*, *Haibun Today*, *Frogpond* and other journals.

Midnight

In a beat-up Dodge truck, my husband and I drive the desolate West Texas Highway 285, no cars in front or in back. Not even a light from a ranch house breaks the darkness. When we round a curve, I glimpse the twisted arms of hanging chain cholla caught in the beams of our headlights. We travel on to Fort Stockton where a neon "no vacancy" sign greets us at every lodging except one rundown motel. Inside a swamp cooler dampens the stale sheets, and from the sink comes the steady drip of a leaky faucet.

>   moonset
> did we ever love
>   one another?

Glory Days

The steak house is decorated with antique tack, so while we wait, I run my hand across a western sidesaddle. The suede seat feels smooth, soft, yet grainy beneath my fingers. The sensation whisks me back to my former life: raindrops on a yellow slicker, the scent of fresh alfalfa, the black mane of my favorite mare, a galloping horse beneath me. For another moment, I move my hand in a circular motion over russet leather, then the hostess ushers us to our table.

winter twilight
the dutch door swings open
on one hinge

Trucker

We kept in touch even after she moved to El Paso and started driving an eighteen wheeler. Once she told me of roaring down I-10 to New Orleans with a load of flowers. She accidentally took a one-way street in the French Quarter, and ended up driving over a hotel lawn. Another time she described a winter haul to Minnesota, something she vowed never to do again. A few years ago, we planned a meeting at a truck stop. We hadn't seen each other in thirty years, but when she swung out of the lavender cab, I recognized her immediately. Last week she called and said she was scheduled for heart surgery.

late frost
she leaves her ex
thirty dimes

On My Mind

> weathered bones
> on my mind
> a wind pierced body
> —Bashō*

My life becomes sepia. Only the Sacramento Mountains of New Mexico remain clear, a visible form of grace.

> Valley of Roses
> daffodils line
> the chapel path

These mountains gave me the joy of one foot after another on the Cloudcroft Trail, sun streaming through tall ponderosas with the Tularosa Valley below. Why did it take so long to appreciate my legs?

Trips from Texas to New Mexico blur. Instead of years, I remember seasons. An elk and her calf dashing across the road and up the mountainside, pebbles rolling in their wake. The scent of dusky blue spruce. Fuchsia aspen leaves in early autumn. Wedding white of new snow.

> summer sun
> plum-red chilies
> drying on porches

I lie in bed with my visions: bright sunlight, a house near the Rio Hondo—not mine, but one I wish were mine. An adobe with a stained glass door above steps painted blue.

> evening . . .
> the old gristmill powered
> by city water

---

* Bashō's quote translated by Robert Hass

Frida and Me

The cookbook falls open to a black and white photo of young Frida Kahlo: thick eyebrows almost touching, dark hair parted in the middle and slicked back, a bulky pre-Columbian necklace around her neck, and a rebozo crossed over her breast.

>Dia de los Muertos
>a long tiered skirt swirls
>around my ankles

Her favorite recipes are arranged by months. November features Chicken in Pipián Sauce. On the next page is a complicated recipe for Tamales in Banana Leaves.

>chili peppers
>cooking in a clay pot
>autumn heat

For almost half of her life, Frida was bedridden, looking at a mirror above her head, but when her health allowed, she loved to cook. I think of her when my back aches.

>mortar and pestle
>a faint scent of garlic
>lingers

Judson Evans

Judson Evans is a member of Boston Haiku Society and is Director of Liberal Arts at The Boston Conservatory, where he teaches courses on utopian societies, ancient Greek literature, and Japanese poetry. He has published haiku & haibun in many journals over the last fifteen years and writes back and forth across the frontier of haiku forms and contemporary lyric poetry in English. He was recently chosen as an "emerging poet" by John Yau for the Academy of American Poets, and won the Philip Booth Prize from Salt Hill Review 2013.

Work, Labor, Play

I never thought of what my father did as "work". That was done by those we called "the men". These "laborers", to use my father's phrase, dug nursery stock, bound shrubs in burlap, loaded trucks, planted trees; watered, hauled, and sweated.

Each year I became more self-conscious of the uselessness of my books, and games and plays. I invented acts in the enormous freedom of afternoons while "men worked". That odd look an outsider, an idler, always has around those working, those with authority to be truly still. Although my childhood was probably typically middle class, I was paralyzed with guilt and self-disgust, in first inklings of class war, caught in reading and watching B-movies like *Anastasia*, I recognized myself in Marie Antoinette, the last of the Romanovs.

That fall I worked for him and didn't go back to school. I hauled railroad ties and timbers, boots soaked in creosote; laid brick, Dutch block, sprayed water through candles of pines until the red clay bled through burlap; always fretting and threshing words, repeating lines of Keats' *Ode to Autumn* until I'd taste the syllables—September, the milky sweat of rhubarb and rye grass; October, the walnut blue shellac, the flayed red leaves of sumac, into November, carving sod like dirty glass from frozen pallets . . .

> September morning
> green hay steams
> against my chest

Window Washer

It's the job I've always wanted—ladder and chamois, buckets and blades, high above the Monday morning traffic. Before I found this niche, or aerie, I suffered the belatedness of cities, dreams already sub-let, area codes exhausted, every inch pre-strung with webs of wires and clotheslines.

Secure the swing stage, strap the harness, set the controls on "glide" . . . Who says there's no advancement, no future in my work? Even if there's nothing to show but shine, every day's a branching out, another set of stories to scale. The fluid world flows back beneath my blade. Sometimes I see myself on hands and knees, kneeling in the stream you can't step twice in, the wet skin of sky that floats powerlines and billboards. Only so many practice runs: steady the squeegee, circle the wrist for the broad unbroken S-sweep down the glass, then for years it's all patience, entering the distraction, the blur and clear and blur and clear made up of those awakenings when a whole ensemble lies before you like a shiny museum case. You open it and touch everything and nothing can be broken.

> a whole city
> soluble in fog
> only the antennas

Soundings

This morning I notice the micro-sounds of things, a deep amplified resonance–objects touching objects, scraping, ringing, as if I were listening to Toru Takemitsu pick up a bell and brush it with a perfectly designed plectrum. A ceramic coffee mug placed on a granite bonsai stand not quite level gives off an unbalancing grate that see-saws up my arm, –the scrape of the leg of a wooden chair against the hard wood floor–itself a complex bowing of the room against its tangents. A large ceramic vase carried to the sink to rinse after the flowers, the sallow swill at the bottom starting to reek. Cautious for all the bowls I've broken in this operation, including the heavy cut glass punch bowl that sliced my right hand so deeply I still feel electricity each time I pull a sweater off. I treat the vase like a delicate instrument, turning it under the lathe of hot water, hearing the gush–and then, despite my care, the tang of a curved edge against the porcelain . . . a deeper, more oblique glass harmonica Monteverdi in his underworld might have amplified.

>   listening more carefully
>   wasp nest
>   in wind chime

Windswept Style

Near the Kyoto railroad station two women in such short skirts they seem almost naked and such high heels they are hobbled in the awkward struggle to wrestle a neon sandwich board over the threshold of a chain restaurant. An old man with a cane stops to watch. Strikingly determined, powerfully coordinated despite the self-imposed impediments, they wear their sexy outfits like construction-workers' uniforms. In this culture of the geisha, where manga and schoolgirl porn froth over into street-styles of thirty year old women and even, yesterday, a sixty year old man in school-girl drag, female sexuality stays hard for an outsider to decipher. But, here, style is at stake, which is always a kind of oppression. More hair-shirt than Victoria's Secret, those skirts and heels are brands of a fiendishly modern self-control.

> training the bonsai
> with copper wire
> windswept style

Backpack

1.

"weary from my ancient bundle . . ." (Petrarch)

Spasmed to the tugged cords of my scapulae, antibody backpack triggering spider web alarms at each slackening—daily bundle of scrap and sundries for various moody weathers of the mountain—sunglasses, knit wool cap, gloves, sweatshirt, maps, French dictionary, notebook—core samples, and exempla. Later, down from the heights, it would gather a set of antique keys from Arles. A vague plan for a wind chime or mobile—dangling from bonsai wire, four keys to guard the compass points—four celestial kings or protective deities. Then, the Avignon book store the beautifully worn bilingual edition (French and Japanese) of Bashō's *Oko no Hosomichi*.

> first edition—
> black marker dedication
> bleeding through the flyleaf

2.

Receiving the transmission through my body—distant pings of a sunken aircraft, the book with his inscription sending its black box message. Throughout the night in a fever of words I ripped off t-shirt after sweat-soaked t-shirt grabbed from the stack in the partly packed suitcase. Had I dreamed the book, had the book existed? The passionate dedication of one man to another. I stood in the bookstore trying to translate: for my friend—or was it lover? —in poetry and insomnia . . .? A whole cherry orchard burned. Graffiti heart pierced by three black daggers. Lost coordinates neither in nor out, above / below, the way the laurel torn from its once–human branch can't be grafted—phantom limb . . .

> idly broken off
> in the toast
> stem of the wine glass

Chris Faiers

Chris Faiers (cricket) was born on Hamilton Mountain, Ontario, Canada in 1948. He and his family emigrated to the southern U. S. when he was six. Although a Canadian citizen by birth, Chris became an anti-war activist in Miami, Florida, attending demonstrations, organizing a campus group and publishing an underground newsletter.

Around 1968 Chris began writing haiku poetry under the tutelage of Eric Amann, the publisher of *Haiku magazine*. Chris is internationally respected as an early English language haiku poet. He left the U. S. forever in June 1969 to avoid conscription for the Vietnam War.

Chris lived for two years in the largest commune in the United Kingdom, the derelict Eel Pie Island Hotel in Twickenham. *Eel Pie Dharma: a memoir/haibun* tells the story of his explorations and adventures in the late '60s and early '70s. After three years of street-level poverty Chris returned to Canada. In 1987 Chris was the first recipient of the Milton Acorn People's Poetry Award for his book *Foot Through the Ceiling* (Aya/Mercury Press).

After his retirement from library work, Chris founded the Purdy Country Literary Festivals (PurdyFests) in Marmora. Chris bought a small piece of land on the upper Moira River. Chris renamed the riverfront retreat ZenRiver Gardens, and many of the annual PurdyFest activities were held there.

Chris continues to have his poetry widely published with. Chris has been the poetry editor for Quinte Arts Council's tabloid, *Umbrella*, for a decade.

http://riffsandripplesfromzenrivergardens.blogspot.in/

The Day We (Sort Of) Met George Harrison

It was late summer. A bunch of L'Auberge regulars decided to take a Sunday trek to see George Harrison, who was rumoured to be living in a little village named Esher. We hopped on the double-decker bus in Richmond, and after an hour or so of riding we arrived in Esher. The ten of us were a scraggly lot, all would-be hippies trying to grow our hair long, the girls dressed in shawls and long skirts and granny boots.

Our goals were the standard ones in 1969-California Jon, Canadian Peter and a couple of other guitarists had made a tape, and wanted Harrison's opinion of it. I had a copy of my just printed haiku chapbook, *Cricket Formations*, and I hoped to get up enough nerve to present my poems to my idol. And of course we all wanted to meet a real live Beatle!

Harrison was my favourite Beatle, largely because he was the one closest to me in physical appearance, with his craggy face and dark hair. I had modeled my haircut and clothes on Harrison for some time. I also thought he was the most interesting Beatle because of his enthusiasm for Eastern mysticism.

Someone had gotten good directions, for we actually found Harrison's house without a lot of trouble. Located in a very staid, upper-middle-class suburban neighbourhood, the house stood out like a psychedelic advertisement. A high fence bordered the large lot, and the house was painted a myriad of colours, like something out of the movie Yellow Submarine. We were all entranced to be setting foot in a sacred preserve of Beatledom, and after knocking on the door and receiving no answer, we boldly began surveying the premises.

"MICK & MARIANNE WUZ HERE!" was spray painted on the front wall, and this further consecrated the property. Our rock heroes actually lived here, visited with each other, slept together, and had probably done these wild paintings on acid trips like our own. We were all strengthened in our faith as true believers in hippiedom.

Some of the group camped by the front door, and the guitar players started scratching on their ubiquitous instruments. I wandered around, and found a pair of George's jeans hanging on a clothesline. For a fleeting moment I was tempted to steal them, to see if my hero's jeans would fit.

> Manicured lawn
> would-be hippies wait
> for a Beatle

A touch of the Beatles' famous ironic humour was present in a large wooden cross leaning against the back fence. I even had the nerve to peek in the draped windows. On the window ledge of one room was a collection of seashells. Miracle of miracles-there was even an apple tree-how appropriate for the founders of Apple records. If there was a heaven on earth, this was it for Beatle fans.

> Seashell lined window
> apples rotting in the yard
> suburban fences

I rejoined the group on the front lawn, and soon a mini-car came scooting up the drive, quickly followed by a luxury sedan. The driver of the mini got out, and a not-very-pleased looking George Martin confronted us. He wanted to know what we were doing, and while we all sat there stunned, George and Patti Harrison disembarked from the sedan. George wasn't really very prepossessing at all, but Patti was a vision of beauty, a psychedelic queen who smiled on us and calmed down the two very aggravated Georges. She knew that we were harmless fans come to honour Beatledom, and while she smiled her guileless smile, we felt like we were in the presence of a divine goddess from another reality. Canadian Peter recovered first, and awkwardly handed George Harrison the tape, mumbling something. I followed suit, even more awkwardly giving George my thin booklet, and saying I hoped he would enjoy it.

An invitation inside was not forthcoming, although I believe Patti wanted to ask us all in. We were all so enthralled at meeting George and Patti, awkward as all involved had been, that we decamped and blissfully headed back in the dusk for the bus to Richmond.

Several weeks later, a few members of the entourage went back to pick up the tape. Apparently a record contract wasn't immediately offered, but Canadian Peter did have some good news for me. George Harrison told me to tell you that he really liked your poetry. I was thrilled, even though I now realized that Harrison was a mere, awkward mortal, and I was no longer in his thrall. As a postscript, I note that George Harrison's first solo album, All Things Must Pass, had the lyrics printed on the sleeve like poems. I like to fantasize that maybe my booklet had some subtle influence, but that's wild hope and speculation . . .

Meeting Eel Pie

> "Out of college, money spent
> see no future, pay no rent
> all the money's gone
> no place to go . . ."
>   –Abbey Road, The Beatles

I nervously wandered off the curving streets of Richmond into the offices of the local newspaper to ask for a job. I was surprised when I was taken seriously. As a test assignment, the editor told me that a group of hippies had started a commune in an abandoned hotel in Twickenham, the next village along the Thames. The directions were fascinating-the hotel was called Eel Pie Island Hotel, and it really was on a little island in the middle of the Thames.

I caught the double-decker bus to Twickenham, and quickly found the arched footbridge which led to Eel Pie Island. It was about two hundred feet across the little bridge, with a beautiful view of the Thames. When I had reached the island I felt I had entered a special place. A footpath lined with neat little cottages wound through the centre of the island. There was no missing the old hotel at the end of the footpath. It was derelict, and I just walked in where the grand front entrance had once been.

Without any problems I quickly located the founder of the commune. Cliff was an artist, cartoonist and an anarchist. He was living with his American girlfriend, Ame, in a large room on the second floor of the hotel. Cliff was a big bear of a man by English standards. He had long, strawlike brown hair and an unkempt beard. With his granny glasses he looked like a professor gone bad. Ame was an All-American girl fresh-faced and clean limbed with glasses-a professor's wife gone bad.

Cliff's easel and layout table and supplies spilled over one half of their large room, and in the other half was a big old mattress on the floor covered with quilts and blankets. The scene was artsy and cozy and there was the musty smell of Thames dampness pervading.

It looked like an enticing way to live, very bohemian and independent and countercultural. As I introduced myself to begin the interview, I was compelled to say, "I'm really a poet, not a reporter."

"What kind of poetry?" Cliff wanted to know. "Mostly haiku poetry, it's a Japanese style," and I dug into my dolly bag to give them a copy of *Cricket Formations*.

"We want to build a commune of artists, especially politically conscious artists," Cliff explained. "Why don't you pick out a room to use as a study and you could live here as part of the commune. Only a couple of people have moved in so far. You'd have your pick of rooms."

This was too good an offer to resist. I dashed around the hollow building. Too Much! There were no flats available in the Greater London area. I had been turfed out of two bedsitters in a week, and here I was being offered a room of my own in this picturesque setting. Thoughts of the interview were forgotten. I was a poet again.

EEL PIE ISLAND

At first there were only a handful
of hippies in the derelict hotel
and I got a room
instead of a story
when I said I'm really a poet
not a reporter

Two years of my life
sleepstoned
hiding from the clammy Thames fog
only our black and brown hashish
smoke holding up the crumbling walls

It's all so trite ten years later
so far out and away
from the foggy decay
of spunksoaked mattresses

Dougie, Crippled Eddie, Lorna
Scotch John, Seamus
Angie-Dominic
Where are you now
as the world discos towards 1984
to lift my head off the floor
hand me a fuming chillum
to kiss me tonight

The Buddhist Monastery

Mark Valiant at first seemed an unlikely person to have a deeply religious side. He was an ex-cop, and the story goes that as he was becoming more and more sympathetic towards the youth rebellion, one day he took the plunge, and took it in a big way. Mark took a strong dose of STP, a psychedelic even more hallucinatory than LSD. He tripped for three days, and after that experience he was a changed man. He quit the police, grew a beard and took to hanging around L'Auberge Cafe.

Mark was one of the regulars in Martha's crowd, sort of an older brother for Martha and a surrogate son for the Holmes. He had been the unofficial "elder" who took charge when Martha's parents left on their holiday to Ibiza, the one I ruined with the flooding bathtub.

A couple of times Mark led Sunday expeditions to a Buddhist monastery several miles away. It was always exciting to get up early for a change, and to watch London slowly coming to life from the top deck of a double-decker bus.

A path led down a lane to the monastery and the temple beside it. The service consisted of all present sitting in meditation in the comfortable chapel for about a half hour or forty-five minutes. It was very relaxing, and the meditations were led by a monk, who sat in front. The layout of the chapel and pews wasn't that dissimilar from a Christian service- with the notable difference that no words were spoken, no hymns sung. It was up to each of us to make our peace with the world.

One morning a cat found its way into the chapel, and halfway through meditation it let out a yowl, and decided it wanted to go elsewhere. It was amusing to see the startled look on all our faces at this unexpected interruption, but the monk calmly got up and let the cat out to wander off, and we resumed meditating.

My impression of these mornings is of a tranquil blue atmosphere. There was a subtle presence of blue energy always present after we had begun meditating, and my feeling was that the monk was pleased with the aura, which I'm sure he was very aware of.

After the meditation session we would gather in the vestibule of the chapel, and drink tea and discuss religion. Everyone present was offered an equal chance to speak, either to pose or to answer questions offered by the others present. Not surprisingly, after the relaxing effects of the meditation, most of us didn't have much to say, the words would have just come between us and the immediacy of the experience of sitting calmly in the blue atmosphere of the chapel.

One Sunday morning in early winter, when I was making one of my last visits to the chapel with a couple of other Eel Piers, it began to snow. Many years later I still clearly remember the experience of walking down the narrow lane, crunching the white powder under my scuffed boots, when this haiku popped into my mind:

> Walking to meditation
> through fresh snow
> Twickenham Cemetery

I got a letter in the early winter of 1970 from my parents informing me that 'for my own best interests' they were no longer going to send me any money. I held out for as long as I could, and then when starvation became a real likelihood, I began working for temporary manpower agencies. A day or two's work would supply enough money to last me for several weeks, and then I'd head out in the early morning dark for another menial job, usually with another Eel Pier also on the verge of starvation.

The winter and the spring passed in this manner. My temporary assignments included work in a book depository, cleaning a filthy flooded basement on a downtown office building, organizing office files and a stint sweeping floors in a textile factory.

It was a hand-to-mouth existence, but it didn't bother me too much, because at least I was alive and not dropping napalm on civilians in Vietnam. One of the L'Aubergers commented to me one day that I should get a job, as I seemed to be becoming more and more spaced out by the hippie lifestyle. Roy had been talking about applying at the Twickenham Cemetery, and so I decided to accompany him. Somehow I managed to get up early for the visit to the cemetery, but Roy didn't. I decided to go ahead with my plans, as I'd already ruined a good morning's sleep, and I might as well go for a walk on this beautiful June morning.

The Twickenham Cemetery was several miles away, and I enjoyed the early summer walk. To my great surprise, I was hired on the spot, and a pair of garden shears were handed to me and I was told to clip the grass around the graves in the plot by the entrance. I realized that this was a test, and I bent my back and went to work. It was peaceful in the cemetery, and very relaxing stooping among the trees and gravestones, many of which were a hundred years old or more.

The morning passed pleasantly, although I was beginning to feel faint, as I didn't have any money for food, and I hadn't eaten. I hummed Rolling Stones' songs to keep my mind off hunger, and by the end of the day I'd clipped my way through half the plot. Just as I was finishing, two of the local schoolgirls appeared-Lesley, of Eve of St Agnes memories, and her pretty girlfriend, Carol. They had gone to visit me at the Hotel, where someone had told them that I had gone to the cemetery to find work. The two nubile girls must have made quite an impression on the other workmen, and I sailed off at five o'clock weak with hunger but accompanied by my two sexy friends.

And so began my induction into the working class. To be at work by 8 a.m. required that I get up by seven, and that meant getting to bed before midnight. No more all night dope sessions. I bought a second-hand bicycle, and the three mile ride each morning was just about enough to wake me up before I reached the cemetery.

The days fell into a pleasant routine. A couple of hours clipping the dewy grass, and then into our shed for ten o'clock tea. A quick flip through the daily tabloids, and then back to the grass and birds and flowers until lunch. For lunch I'd bike into the nearby hamlet and have bacon and eggs at a workers' cafe. Some days I'd bring a bag of nuts and raisins and a juice, and spend a relaxing hour lounging in the sun in the park-like setting of the cemetery:

> Breaktime
> coal smoke, thermos tea
> tabloid ink

The fifty or so acres of the cemetery were surrounded by a low fence completely overgrown by a privet hedge. There were five of us working full time, so the grounds were immaculately gardened.

George was the foreman. He took his job seriously, but he was an open-minded and tolerant boss, and so long as we did our jobs, he didn't interfere.

Fred was a rough–looking character. He had a ferocious look about him, like a living caricature of an axe murderer. His thick black brows almost covered his sunken eyes, and his body was ill-shaped but extremely strong looking. Fred was a gravedigger, and he looked as if he didn't wash off the dirt from his labours for weeks at a time. I soon learned that under his coarse exterior beat the proverbial heart of gold, and Fred wouldn't hurt a fly.

His mate was Tom, a sly character with whom I never established any rapport. Lanny was our other mate. He was simple minded and lazy, and the story was that he had never been the same since his father had been blasted to bits right in front of him during the blitz in World War Two. Lanny was amiable enough if you left him alone, and very quiet.

As the days fell into a comfortable pattern, so the year itself took on its seasonal changes. After a few months I was promoted from full time headstone clipper to part time grass mower. As a teenager I had earned pocket money mowing neighbours' lawns, and I had always enjoyed a Zen sense of fulfillment in the work.

The long London fall was spent raking and burning piles of leaves. We'd load up the hand-pulled cart, surely a relic from another century, and then the lucky assigned person would pitch the leaves and wreathes and dead flowers onto the bonfire. It was pleasant to work in front of the roaring fire and keep warm while enjoying the aromatic smoke:

> Fall bonfire
> crackling leaves
> and dead flowers

In winter we had fewer chores. The grass stopped growing, the leaves were all raked, and our main chore was the planting of trees for the spring:

> In the dead of winter
> planting trees
> in the graveyard

Spring comes early in London. By late January the first bulbs, snowdrops, are pushing through. Quickly they are followed by the many coloured crocuses. By mid-March the daffodils and tulips are up, and spring is in full bloom.

A grammar school was across the road from the cemetery. One of my spring highlights was the day two of the young mini-skirted beauties wandered over on their lunch break to look for rabbits. One girl was a gorgeous brunette, and her girlfriend was a blonde. They were all of fourteen years old, and they were as interested in meeting the cemetery "hairy" as I was in flirting with these beautiful distractions. It became a custom for the three of us to meet on our lunch and talk.

Spring was also the signal for the neighbourhood gardeners to begin work. The area was a poor, working-class district. Most of the local houses were council row houses without gardens, but a plot had been set aside behind the cemetery for allotment gardens:

> Behind the graveyard
> senior citizens digging
> allotment gardens

Summer brought a couple of summer student workers. They were looked upon as a necessary nuisance by the older workers, and so George assigned me to be their "ganger". We had a great time. Tony was Anglo-Indian, and an accomplished folk singer who had performed gigs at the Hanging Lantern Cafe in Richmond. We would trade lines from Bob Dylan songs while we worked, and the days went by more quickly than ever:

> Summer students
> shouting Dylan
> across graves

Working in the cemetery was almost vacation enough, although I did take a month off that spring and fly to the Balearic Islands off the coast of Spain. These adventures are told later.

Eel Pie was also entering its final days. The junkyard landlord had repeatedly tried to get us out, but to no avail. However, natural processes were destroying the "commune" both physically and spiritually. Floor boards had been ripped up for two winters, and the very foundations of the hotel had been weakened. Lead had been stripped off the roof and sold to metal dealers. While Eel Piers were slowly demolishing the building bit by bit, more and more wandering hippies, musicians, runaways and finally junkies and bikers moved in.

Most of the original Eel Piers moved on to more secure squats in the heart of London, but I stayed on. The bikers took to throwing stones through all the windows, and syringes could now be found littering the dirt-packed floors.

Finally I packed it in too, and my final months at the cemetery were spent boarding in a crowded rooming-house for Irish navvies. I had spent the full cycle of a year working in Twickenham Cemetery. It was time to take to the road, to find the romance and excitement that had sustained me in other places, with other people:

> Green garden hose
> spouting
> a rainbow

> Dewdrop
> in spiderweb
> on graveyard gate

The Three Fishes

Pub life in London reflected the British tendency to divide into classes and areas of interest. There were upper class pubs, right wing pubs, Irish Republican pubs, working class pubs, and one unique pub where all the regulars were very short, young males who only listened to Eddie Cochran on the juke box. There were skinhead pubs and of course hippie pubs.

The Three Fishes was a hippie pub, located on the corner next to the Kingston-Upon-Thames rail station. The lights were dim, the music blaring rock'n'roll, and the clientele longhairs of both sexes. At that time in Britain, kids as young as fifteen could get away with going into pubs, although the legal drinking age was eighteen, so there was the expected quota of schoolgirls and boys.

It was just the sort of atmosphere I loved after a hard day of digging graves. On one of my first visits, a gorgeous young girl of about sixteen came and knelt before me, as if before a medieval knight. She clasped her long hippie shawl about herself, and even I found I couldn't take advantage of her, and offer the expected walk home through the park:

> Young girl
> in an old shawl
> kneeling

One summer evening I made the long ride into Kingston on my bike after work, and had a pint or two at the Three Fishes. It stays light very late in Britain in summer, and so dusk was just turning to dark when I left after 9 p.m., and began undoing my bicycle lock.

In the half light I noticed something very strange. There were several police vans parked outside, and more arriving every second. In the dark I made out the shapes of several dozen policemen, and I realized that a raid was about to take place.

I wasn't drunk, only stupid, and some sense of hippie brotherhood won out over common sense. I walked back into the Three Fishes and began yelling "It's a raid!-It's a raid!"

The officer in charge followed me through the doors, and I was the first one grabbed. "You're nicked," he snarled, and passed me to another bobby. Bustled back out the door, I caught a glimpse of the pandemonium as drugs were dumped under most of the tables. I was pushed onto a bus, much like a large tour bus, which the bobbies had requisitioned for the occasion, and soon I was joined by thirty or forty other longhairs. Then the bus and several vanloads of miscreants were taken down to Kingston police headquarters and booked.

I didn't get to sleep that night, as it took the police all night to process so many of us. In the early morning light I found my way back to my locked bicycle, and slowly wound my way back towards Twickenham.

Our case didn't come up for a month, and the courtroom was a mob scene. When my turn came, I pleaded "Guilty, Your Honour" to the charge of interfering with the raid by warning everyone, but I added, "I don't feel guilty, though." The courtroom burst out laughing, both at the oddity of my charge, and at my unusual plea. I was given a fine of thirty pounds, which was then my wages for about three weeks.

>   Hash aroma
>   and stale beer
>   under the table

Hare Krishna

Martha had a redhaired friend named Jill. I always had a thing for her, and as I was in-between girlfriends, I decided to look her up. Through the grapevine I learned that she had joined the Hare Krishnas, and so one afternoon I headed downtown to their main temple with a young hippie guy who was passing through Eel Pie.

The Krishnas greeted us warmly, if a little absentmindedly. They were blissed out, in a robotic way. While we snacked on the light vegetarian food they offered us, one disciple kept repeating, "George Harrison is a member. He helps us." Over and over he name-dropped the Beatles, like a mantra.

The Krishnas ushered us into a second room, where the devotees were kneeling on mats. An incredibly ugly old man with a shaved head approached me. "I know you. We've worked together in other lives," he intoned. He seemed sincere, but I felt a little displaced. On the wall was a chart listing all the qualities of a good devotee of Krishna. Near the bottom was the word "poetic". I had always understood poetic to mean being free, to being one's own person, but the Krishnas were very dogmatic. They were better, perhaps, than the acid fascists who were taking over Eel Pie, but not by much.

Soon it was time for prayer and dancing in the chapel, a larger adjacent room. The young hippie and I followed into the chapel, and the devotees began chanting and dancing in rhythm. We joined in, not wishing to be poor guests. The effect became hypnotic, and the blue presence was in the atmosphere, just as it had been in the Buddhist Temple:

> Two longhairs
> among saffron & shaved heads
> dancing blue phantoms

We chanted and danced for several hours, and then returned to the smaller sitting room. This alternated all afternoon. It put the two of us on a high. When we finally left in the early evening, after four or five hours of chanting, dancing and discussion, we felt very high. The blue presence was still with us, and we both wondered if the Krishnas had put small doses of acid in our vegetarian food. Although I had gone there for reasons of the flesh, I had enjoyed the afternoon, although it was too regimented for my spirit.

Years later when I received a Krishna pamphlet in Toronto, I was startled to recognize the ugly old guy with the shaved head and the cosmic memory. He was the founder of the movement, and I had been highly honoured to have had him approach me.

Charles Hansmann

Charles Hansmann has published haibun, haiku, fiction, and poetry in dozens of magazines and a half dozen anthologies. He is the author of five poetry chapbooks and has won the Apprentice House Chapbook Award, the Clockwise Chapbook Award, and the Willet Press Poetry Prize. A native of rural Wisconsin, he lives with his wife in Sea Cliff, New York.

Low Tide

On the shore of the inlet we stalk a firefly strobing a bush. Up close we catch short breath: it's caught in a filament of web, and the spider is on it, embossing the wrap with diligent thread. Smooth as silk, the last glint of day on the ebb.

        moonrise, crickets quieting
          our footsteps

Birthday Hike

My bottle filled with mountain runoff chills me suddenly new to old skin. The uphill ache sets in. Snow fell the winter I thrilled to be twenty. Its melt I ford these decades later. Time for a breather.

        scuffed boots on polished stones

The rest makes me cold. I spill through these woods for their bounty of kindling. Where else to warm my heart but at the campfire story it's my turn to tell?

        silhouette in the hemlock all ears

Camouflage

A neighbor had taken a bus trip Out West, and for not saying no I put up with the squawk. "In for it now," her bird kept saying with prophetic inflection, and I jotted it down. I was keeping a journal of cockatiel wit, and not just for amusement. I thought it would show how easy it is to find meaning where none is intended.

> lit room, the window
> looking back into it

I had a postcard from the cockatiel's owner, a textured drawing of a pepper tree with dark red berries traditionally used for toothache and wounds, depression and pest control. On the verso she had written in gothic script: "Tucson, Arizona—101 at 1:01."

> clouds piling
> the darkened puddle

She had signed it The Searcher, with Irma in parentheses. I knew she believed that the world is encoded, has a message for anyone privy to its signs, but she didn't have to travel so far for such paltry coincidence: early last week my former bank's electronic billboard showed 92 degrees at 9:20. I took this in stride, hardly worth noting, but a man at the bus stop asked if I believe things happen for a reason. He started opening vials and pouring his pills to the blistering sidewalk. "Because if they don't," he said, "then why do they?"

> rain brightening
> the far-off thunder

For camouflage, I thought, as I glanced through the cage at the outback plumage. The bird's feathers were gray, clipped at the wing and pearled in a pattern that looked like marble. "In for it now," the bird said again, and I found a dark towel to drape over its cage.

Contact

I went down to the esplanade and sat on a bench. As I put my arm across the backrest a woman sat down and leaned into it. She jumped up from the touch, as if I had groped her, and I stood up too, equally startled. We smiled to acknowledge our mutual embarrassment. Then she turned and walked off. It was merely an accident of timing.

> afternoon shadows
> tracking the sun-bather's towel

Flip-flops and sandals: the sidewalk applauded. When had the esplanade become so crowded? I felt a gnawing at my innards as if my stomach were teething on an iron tine. It was beginning to feel like hamburger time.

> gull cries, the seawall
> rising on rock

I went over to the Hab-or-Nab to have a quick bite. "What'll it be, Stranger?" I always sat at the bar and the barmaid always called me that.

"Medium rare, pepino solo."

"And an order of rings," the woman who had sat beside me on the bench said as she took the next stool.

She started fumbling through her purse. "They have a beer menu here but I can't find my glasses. Are those for reading?"

> sky at moonrise
> closing the kiosk

I took the Cary Grant repros from the neck of my shirt as a strand of her light brunette hair slipped down to her dark brunette eyebrows. "Two point five," she said, adjusting the glasses on her nose. "I'm an excellent judge of magnification."

> sand at low tide
> a placemat fading

Our conversation was a series of overstrikes. By last call I felt imprinted in an old-fashioned way like paper slowly working through a typewriter. "Phyllis," she said, "since you'll want to know my name." She took me by the arm as if batting left-handed. "I knew you were nice when you jumped off that bench. I bet you open doors."

We turned up my walk and inside my apartment I draped a towel over the cage to keep the cockatiel quiet. Phyllis was thirsty, and as I gave her a glass I wondered if she had to take a pill.

> banyan root, the tucked
> leg of the wading bird

She drank the water in the bathroom and wouldn't let me watch. When she opened the door dim light floated out toward the couch where I was waiting. She was wearing just a towel wrapped under her arms like a strapless dress. "I want to make love without taking it off. You don't have to know why."

> eyes in the dark
> thicket of night

She pulled the bathroom door shut and went over to the window to widen the blind. Partly blocked by the slats the streetlamp looked like a lunar eclipse.

"A moon like this," she said, stroking the bands of shadow and light.

Rash

The beach was out of the question today because of the sun, because of the rash that had spread on my cheeks like butterfly wings. I looked it up on the Internet and found it most common in teenage girls with red hair and fair skin. This described her to a T.

                scattered petals
            scattering the sparrows

Her letters were coming addressed to a name that only sounded like mine: Nick Knocked. I'd been getting them all week in envelopes the color of a bruised peach. Today's had a Liberty-Bell Forever Stamp angled to the corner, and humidity blurred the red ink of the postmark. I knew it was local, like all the others, a privacy envelope with the flap loosely sealed, as if all she could spare were a dab of saliva and a passing lick. I slipped a finger inside to open it. Her message hadn't changed, but today she tacked on the suspense of ellipsis: "I'm still waiting . . ."

                lapsed wind
            the tall grass righting

She recounted a night exactly like the one I remembered, an almost hostile ardor, fierce and impersonal, Hessians just doing their job. She even got in the identifying mark: two linked rings, "in epidermal blue," tattooed above my sternum.

              all night breathing
              the ceiling fan

Like the letters before it, this one ended on an ominous note: "As and for a first cause of action, Nick Nacht knocked me up." The first part of that sentence was obviously cribbed from papers she had seen in some lawsuit. The second explained her little pun.

             pebbles splashing
            the flooded quarry

It was one of those parties where without even speaking we went out the side door to the sand. A few weeks later as I was walking down the street she hailed me from a table on the sidewalk. "Sixteen candles!" she called, putting a finger to her lips, "but I'm willing to hush." She was sitting with friends deceptively young, tilted back in their chairs and flagrantly smoking. As I turned to walk away I heard one of them shout, "We know where you live!"

shadow of the nomad
shadow of the uprooted tree

I was possibly the target of attempted extortion, possibly the perpetrator of a statutory crime. The threshold to shame is trampled with moral ambiguity. This was a crime you could commit by mistake.

I set the letter down for a cathartic backbend. Facing away from the window, I kept on going until the sun was in my eyes.

Jeffrey Harpeng

Jeffrey Harpeng has had a number of haiku, tanka, haibun, tanka prose, sonnets and short stories insist that he write them. His everyday life is shallow water. His writing wades out into the river, out into the ocean. That said, the sky is in his eyes though not in the colour of them.

Horse Tale

a wild horse
galloping toward me
granddad's fingers

The mantle clock chimes as if it were an omen in a fairy tale. The opening notes of a slow waltz. Blue notes. How beautifully the mermaid dances on pain made out of daggers. How the tin soldier's lead heart is heavy as ammunition. How the beanstalk winds toward heaven lithe as smoke from a smelter's chimney. How I listen as my fingers gallop toward my granddaughter, off the table and on out the window.

Outside the almost laughter of a kookaburra, the supernatural quardle of magpies and her answering the "h-h-h-oo" welling from the hearts of the doves.

The Ghost in the Haibun

In the dream Uncle Fred is dead, is a skeleton floating against the ceiling. My dream understanding tells me he is not floating, rather it is the ceiling or some thought beyond that holds him.
This dream recurs every few years. I still haven't caught what Uncle Fred says as he bonily expounds. The unease of that dream, a dream I first had in my early teens, is again with me.

   shade of English Oak   in the Jewish cemetery   a heavier silence

After breakfast I walk to work with that dream in me. Walk past old St Mary's (I keep a nail-holed shard of roof-slate for all the prayers risen through) round through the Domain (some mornings are fog, and in the fog grounded seagulls), out the gates and past Auckland General

   (hospital   chimney   meditation)
   across Grafton Gully bridge (the far pylon among grave stones).
   graves   down the slope   a black koru uncurling

I nod to the faces I have nodded to, and am nodded to in passing the past. I glance back to see them gone. I arrive, and the work day is a desert island, and nothing as simple/as complex as that.
Sometimes after work, I catch the bus, chat with the midget at the stop. She has such a sexy mind, and in her sideways glances there a seraphim's glint, a succubus hallows her wink, yet there's no god in her phrase-book. Conjoint we spark a jest about how Africa and South America could fit snugly together. Amazon and Congo flow muddily to the ocean between them. Mid-ocean the Sargasso turns slowly.
Other days it's a walk home through the campus,

   which is heavier   these clouds   this avenue of trees

down Constitution Hill, up Parnell Rise, and Parnell Road, round Birdwood Crescent, and down the stairs. Walking home, the hangover of that dream lifts.

Down the stairs, in the flat below street level, in the kitchen, over a cup of tea with grilled cheese on Vogel's bread, over the distraction of her

'Girls are not Chicks' T-shirt, Gwenda tells me her grandfather visited today. "Just a brief call," he said, to tell me, "Never forget, yes I know you know how much I love you."

She pauses then adds, "Later I got a phone call from the rest-home. They said that early this morning he quietly passed away."

  left   no footprints on the cement path   grandfather

There is never direct sunlight in the kitchen.

Birdlings Flat

A spit of greywacke, gravel and stone ground round as river-rock, infilled with sand and further inland soil, stretches south from the underbelly of that burst volcanic boil, Banks Peninsula. This stony spit landlocks an inlet, endstops gray water: Lake Forsyth.

On the lake old car tyres carved to garden ornaments have transmigrated, come back as black swans: small submarines, their conning towers necked with question marks. An old railway embankment dykes the lake's north shore, and terminates at Little River. The end of the line is all that is left of the line, the old station has been reinvented as a cafe, stroke souvenir shop. The platform is still out the back, a wagon on the tracks.

>   iron buffers
>   end of the line
>   we journey on

This narrative turned off a couple of clicks back, hung a right to Birdlings Flat.

The following photo is not in the family album. The shot is four-fifths sky. The sun has sloped below the distant Alps and blue diffuses into black. The sky is getting set for a comet or a falling star to wish upon.

Star light, star bright, first star I see tonight,
I wish I may, I wish I might wish upon this . . .

The photograph is four-fifths blue. A hand pokes in from the right of the frame, reaches toward the moon which is high and just off centre. In the hand, g-clamped between thumb and forefinger, a stone, which is dark or just dark against the sky. The held stone is posed to partially eclipse the moon. In the bottom fifth of the photo is a lump of hill. There is no annotation on the back of the photo, no entitlement for posterity. The horizon in the picture is out of kilter. Out of shot there are voices, how the sound of this one tilts me this way and another tilts me that, one child and another, and the woman's voice leading them back to the car, tilts me which way.

Jeffrey Harpeng

The Mitsubishi is parked over there, where soil has been rollered hard to top the shifty substrate.

We have spent a few windswept hours on the beach, hand mining wet stone for green, for ferrous faults: fate lines. We settle for some rounded quartz, abraded cloudy by sand. I find my white stone. It fell out of the book of Revelation, the stone with my secret name underneath. Both obverse and reverse are without text. A poem plays around in that idea for a while, for a few years, for a lifetime. If the stone were a minimalist sculptor's reading of my heart its every turn would show another's name written in invisible ink.

Down at the rock gurgle, shush and rush shore my daughter stepped out and back, sashayed with the sea, and in parting said, 'I'll come and play another day'. The pockets of my son's hoodie are potbellied with stones.

Back in the car we backtrack past the baches* that hug the back of the stony dune. Most are footnotes rather than grand tales. One or two are reverting to the shambles from which they were cobbled together. Browning decay of iron and timber leach together and slump against the salt spray wind.

We take the main drag (more drag than main) to its turn around end and turn around in front of the house of a friend we came to visit and missed. We leave a note.

<blockquote>
on his doorstep
stepping out in hiking boots
grow forget-me-nots
</blockquote>

Across the road a thick-branched bush bears no bloom, no green. Branches end in hands as if hands were in the gloves worn to direct the wind. A grimmer rendition, told, has those gloves as grabbing hands. The wit of an artist comments. Boundaries of old squatted properties along this stretch are fuel for feud. Now, statute is to descend and hammer argument into pegged out plots.

>   where dirt forks
>   from gravel a wind-plucked tree
>   wears forty gloves
>   winter comes ashore
>   just to shake hands

In the lee of the stony dune, his back fence, and his house, my friend has grown hedge walled rooms. A hammock hangs in the bedroom. Day and night and the seasons are the ceiling. This autumn shooting stars, to wish upon, chalk the night. Beyond his gate, in a slightly wider sky, a comet passes on a cloudy night.

The face in the moon is made of fallen wishes, think craters, which is one way of saying it. Moonlight ghosts a high ceiling room, no curtains drape the tall windows, faint sound of children's laughter, fades to ballroom music, a projector sound flickers in the cinema of dreams. How a place can be a ghost. And a ghost can be another way we see we hear ourselves. And our children are where our bodies forget what it is like to live in our bodies.

Craning at the rear window as we drive off, the kids wave back to the tree.

>   the day fading
>   we drive toward
>   the stony moon
>   beside the moon
>   a dying star

---

bach: A New Zealand name for a beach hut or cottage, often established by squatting.

Seven Teas–Sixth Tea
–Hamasa Yukki Bancha

Candy floss at a fairground, the buttery tang of popcorn, trampled grass, hay-bale seating in the beer tent. Bancha nudges me to remember those notes and the rustic tune they compose. Bancha provokes me to remember what it is not. There are stories, tatty as backpackers' paperbacks, carried by pilgrims and fellow travelers.

The second cup, are we there already, is waiting for a fish grilling over charcoal. Then I unwrap the leaves wrapped around my small-treat rice dumpling with sweet red bean filling; every mouthful is a note-perfect duet.

> ant on the page
> Buddha doing what ants do
> not being Buddha

There is an island of froth on top of the third cuppa, a chain mail of bubbles, a slaked off hide of transparent fish.

There is reincarnation and eternal recurrence in Bancha. I share a brew with Nietzsche* who is drinking from a moustache cup. He says, "In a strong cup of tea there is all the happiness we need." He says he'll edit that later.

In Bancha there is a sweetness as sweet as a kiss. When we speak of sweetness in a kiss we speak tongue in cheek. There is the salt of a kiss. There is less than that in Bancha. Two grains in a wooden bucket brimming with rain water. Bancha, as the salt of a kiss, is but a rumour in the mouth.

> lip to the cup's lip
> a holy jazz of things about
> to be told

Bancha is an inscrutable psychogenic. It quickens the heart, calms the mind. By those measures it alters the way we feel the world. Now consider the meditations of Zen monks who have taken a lesson from that cup.

Bancha is a pilgrim's conversation, belief pressed to the lips. A story that is true as it travels by word of mouth, as if ink would stain the facts. Then said again it is a sleeping draught for daydreams, and in those daydreams there is a sadness. The weight of nine or ten feathers rest on the heart. Quietly, Bancha tells you there is always some sadness, some weight upon the heart. Perhaps many feathers. Bancha announces tea as the holy water for funerals, drunk in a grieving as long as, no longer than the Yangtze.

> wind in the palm fronds
> a magpie swoops
> to sing where it lands

Note: Friedrich Nietzsche, Ecce Homo: "Nothing should be eaten between meals, coffee should be given up-coffee makes one gloomy. Tea is beneficial only in the morning. It should be taken in small quantities but very strong. It may be very harmful and indispose you for the whole day, if it is taken the least bit too weak. Everybody has his own standard in this matter, often between the narrowest and most delicate limits. In an enervating climate tea is not a good beverage with which to start the day: an hour before taking it an excellent thing is to drink a cup of thick cocoa, freed from oil. Remain seated as little as possible, put no trust in any thought that is not born in the open, to the accompaniment of free bodily motion-nor is one in which the muscles do not celebrate a feast. All prejudices take their origin in the intestines. A sedentary life, as I have already said elsewhere, is the real sin against the Holy Spirit."

Liberation

On the *mani* stone by the pathway is a Buddhist prayer for the peace and liberation of all beings. A couple with dogs on leashes pass by. I am following the Avon down to the daffodil lawn where I said goodbye to her, five years ago. On top of the stone somebody has twined supple pine branches and set in feathers and a cone to form a kind of crown. For the once and future king.

Om mani padme hum, the prayer is written. The sky is frosted blue. There is a giddiness in me as if I had just filled with my breath a hundred balloons for a child's party. Under the grass daffodil bulbs await the spring sun.

> a frosted blue balloon
> drifts into a vacant lot

Ed Higgins

Ed Higgins' poems and short fiction have appeared in various print and online journals including: *Monkeybicycle*, *Tattoo Highway*, *Word Riot*, *Triggerfish Critical Review*, and *Blue Print Review*, among others. He and his wife live on a small farm in Yamhill, OR, USA raising a menagerie of animals including two whippets, a manx barn cat (who doesn't care for the whippets), two Bourbon Red turkeys (King Strut and Nefra-Turkey), and an alpaca named Machu-Picchu. He teaches writing and literature at George Fox University, south of Portland, OR. He is also Asst. Fiction Editor for *Brilliant Flash Fiction*, an Irish-based flash journal.

So one day

So one day I'm finally dead, torn to pieces by the perils of old age and the ravages of forgotten depravities and I'm classically floating above the hospital bed happy as a helium balloon saying CONGRATULATIONS! bouncing and twisting off the white acoustical tiles while looking down at my weeping wife kissing my pallid forehead goodbye with glistening tears I can clearly see, anointing the back of my right hand she had been holding, in rivulets and small globs of sadness rolling off to stain the wrinkled bedsheets as I'm, ironically maybe, thinking if only I could get her to look up at me floating here like some Cheshire Garfield wanting to say it's all right, and where else can you get this much comedy with me thud, thudding against this ceiling in a kind of light musical thrumming that may or may not be my soul, because it certainly isn't my heart anymore, when the cloud-like tiles suddenly blink open in a beckoning adventure letting me float lightly through.

passing seaward
under Golden Gate Bridge
above clouds colliding

The Letter

You know how it is, one day a good friend sends you this long or short distant note of sorts telling you how-the-hell they are or aren't getting along in the frigging world and you realize someone's sent you something quite lovely or maybe lonely or likely both about how what's not been divulged or actually related and isn't even the point anyway but rather asking how much you're paying enough attention to just listen out there wherever you are at that moment. And suddenly you're writing back to her, oh yes it's her in this case, about something or other too, ok something certainly, and while all the while you're still listening and writing into those same empty spaces you've been proffered trying again for the same kind of attention I've just now been trying to tell you about.

>   risked words
>   cupped lightly
>   from the lake's edge

Ida's Parmesan Cheese

The recipe, Ida says, goes like this: You first talk to the goats and pat their udders coaxing out flavors only goats know about. And you must feed only excellent quality hay, alfalfa is best but first-cut clover or timothy will do. Ida takes out some of the colostrum, essential for the new-borns, and mixes bits of, yes, hay or straw in a teaspoon or two of her own saved grated parmesan. She ties this up in a cheesecloth sack letting it hang to dry as a starter. After about three months it is lardish and spreadable. This way the cheese is incredible.

hand milking
white foam
flecking her pail

Ida then pours nine to ten quarts of warm goat's milk straight into a black spatterware kettle and stirs in two teaspoons of her special concoction, mixing thoroughly. The curd sets in about half an hour. Ida cuts the curd and pours it into cheesecloth draped carefully over a large blue bowl. Naturally she saves the whey for ricotta later. Next morning she scoops out the drained curds pressing them lightly into an old wooden mold. After draining again overnight Ida presses more curd into her wooden mold, pushing down firmly. Then the mold is set to drain over the large blue bowl for eight or nine days.

When the cheese loosens from the mold Ida rubs salt all over the round and hangs it in a string-net bag for six months to cure. Parmesan, she says, will last and stay delicious for four to five years. But Ida's parmesan cheese couldn't possibly last that long.

the tongue's memory
lingers
lightly

He drank

Excessively. And this worried her, of course. But in WWII he'd been a tail gunner in a B17 Flying Fortress. He completed seven sorties over German occupied Europe. Over France he was shot down and declared missing in action, presumed dead. She spent most of the government insurance money then moved in with her parents in Bangor with her two young children.

> noon's summer sun
> line-dried towels
> rubbing her shoulders

He had been wounded earlier in a Bremen raid, struck by flak twice in his right leg. So he had bad dreams when he came back from the dead. With shrapnel now in his back also, from German Focke-Wulf 190 fighters that shot down his Flying Fortress, shooting parachuting crew members as they drifted down over French hayfields. He also beat her up occasionally when drunk.

> all these wars
> both inside and out
> the shifted earth

Mostly nothing terribly serious, some bruises, a black eye now and then. Once matted blood in her hair from a large cut when he shoved her against the door frame as she was coming out of the locked bathroom where she'd retreated to escape his rage. She thought he was gone but he had silently waited in the hallway for her to come out.

When he grabbed her she fell backward cracking the back of her head sharply against the door moulding's edge. Her crying and the blood stopped his anger as he helped her up and back into the bathroom daubing the bleeding gash himself with a wet washcloth, repeating how sorry he was. She forgave him. The seven stitches left a scar and a slight bald spot.

All scars are areas of fibrous tissue replacing normal skin after injury or disease, and have inferior functional quality.

> remembering once
> she spent the night
> crying in his arms

Forging a Fishmonger's Knife

At his forge in the city of Fukui, bladesmith Masaji Shimizu produces the five-foot-long maguro-hocho, or tuna knife, prized by Tsukiji's tuna dealers. The painstaking process entails heating iron and steel bars to 900 malleable degrees; the gold-glowing metals fuse under precise hammer blows. The blade is scrutinized for flaws by master Shimizu-san smiling in the fire's liquid glow off his gold-capped teeth. Honed on a wheel, the blade showers sparks that leap in arcing curves like schools of startled tuna fleeing a predator.

> off the horizon
> turning away—
> a school of bluefin

Ruth Holzer

Ruth Holzer has been writing poetry in both Western and Japanese forms for a long time. Her poems have appeared in a variety of haiku, tanka and haibun journals and anthologies. Her longer verse has been published in *Freshwater*, *California Quarterly*, *Earth's Daughters*, *Southern Poetry Review*, *Off the Coast*, *Journal of New Jersey Poets* and *RHINO*. She is the author of three chapbooks, *The First Hundred Years*, *The Solitude of Cities* (Finishing Line Press) and *A Woman Passing* (Green Fuse Press). A multiple Pushcart Prize nominee, she has been an associate editor for *tinywords* and a co-editor of *Haibun Today*.

Cefalù

Protected by its overhanging rock, the town spills down to the sparkling sea. Boys dive from the jagged cliffs, daring one another to leap from riskier heights. Their thin bodies slice through the air like swallows. The blood that quickens them is Sikel, Greek, Carthaginian, Norman. After the wars ended, this strategic headland lost its importance and turned into a backwater. Again and again, the boys fling themselves into the Tyrrhenian, shouting as they go.

> vase painting–
> a man hacks at a tuna
> today

Dinner at Timmy's

>the beggar halts
>at a wayside inn–
>before my time

Sick on a journey–that punishment of poets, now mine to endure. In a featureless hotel room I'm chilled and feverish, far out of range of anyone's concern. Weak with hunger at day's end, I wander into the chain coffee shop in the mezzanine. The vividly illustrated menu boards turn my stomach. I just want a plain sandwich. I ask the young counterwoman about the different sizes. "My dear, the small is this big," she measures a few inches with her hands, "and the medium is about this big," her hands moving farther apart, "and the large is like this, and the super-deluxe, like this," as she extends her hands even farther apart. I order a small one. "Oh, but we're out of all of them, my darling. We're out of everything."

>a hard pillow–
>I'd even drink sake
>if they had any

Gros Morne

We're talking billions of years here, the primeval ocean, continents drifting and colliding. The earth's mantle thrust up from beneath the waters to form these tablelands. We're talking plate tectonics, granite cliffs surrounding landlocked fjords, Ordovician fossils, glacial scouring. Bare orange mountains loom through the rain, their mineral-rich soil hostile to vegetation. In the shallow hollows of my eyes, an ache. I can no longer care for any of you.

    purple mouth of the roadside pitcher plant agape

Niklasstrasse 36

Arise from the sofa of dreams. Onto the sill. Out of the window. To throw himself out of the window was what he wanted, to go flying or falling five stories, coming to land on the pavement in front of the elaborate portal or in the pool of misted light under the streetlamp. The river, the bridge, the toll-taker, unchanging, his last view. The observer with his longing for solitude and panic at marriage. His longing for marriage and panic at solitude.

        no children of his own   up in smoke

The elusive embrace, desireless and comprehending, was what he wanted. One that that would release him in the end without blame. His mind jumping between fear and indifference.

        the collapse of empire   Dear Max burn everything

Smoking

The children are asleep in the back seat as the countryside rolls by, Dad driving, Mom riding shotgun. He's contentedly inhaling. She turns away from the view of hills and fields to let him know that if he only had the sense he was born with he'd stop smoking, it's ruining his health, or at least he could do it for her sake, she can't stand the smell in his hair and on his skin, or he should think of the kids, who'll need him to be around as they grow up, plus there's the cost of his filthy habit, they'd easily save hundreds a year if he'd quit. He continues silently concentrating on the road. Suddenly, she nicks the cigarette from his lips and throws it out of the window. A long spray of glowing ash and it's gone. Then she wrests the pack from his breast pocket and flings that out too. The car veers, soars and comes to a halt, wheels up in a ditch.

          dum-dee-dum
   something something something
         Burma-Shave

Roger Jones

Roger Jones was born near San Francisco and lives in Texas, where he teaches in the MFA poetry program at Texas State University in San Marcos. He earned a PhD from Oklahoma State University in 1986. His poems have appeared occasionally in journals over the past four decades, and he has published four collections of poetry, including the most recent, *Familial* (Finishing Line Press, 2015).

His haiku, tanka, and haibun have appeared in various journals, including *Frogpond*, *Modern Haiku*, *Haibun Today*, *Contemporary Haibun Online*, *Eucalypt*, *Heron's Nest* and *Acorn*. In 2012, his haibun manuscript *Goodbye* was selected for the Snapshot Press haibun e-chapbook award. He posts regularly on Twitter, and parks published and unpublished tanka on his blog, *Red Candles*.

http://califraction.wordpress.com.

Global Warming

July 29. 4 pm. Temperature 104.

Katydids loud in the treetops. A hint of breeze.

The sky blue, relatively cloudless (occasional wisps), reflects my laggard imagination and lack of ideas. I'm content to let the world go on today unremarked.

>   tap tap tap
> woodpecker waits–
>   no response

Everything looks withered, dry, heat-stressed, droopy. As the climate heats up, experts warn of more radical droughts, higher heat, stormier storms to come . . .

>   butterfly
> leaving its shadow
>   on a sunlit wall

Yosemite Recollection

His family stopped by a clearing in the park, set up their picnic baskets under some tall fir trees, and unpacked the food. The phrase "vernal light" kept coming to his mind. He reached into the basket and pulled out a roast beef sandwich, and a black cherry soda. This was before pop tops, so he had to fish around a little more for the "church key" opener, with which he made two triangular holes in the top of the can, *psshht!* Bright sunlight made an aura atop the fuzzy seed-heads of nearby meadow grass. In his memory, he sees a deer step out of the shade of the tree and venture cautiously into the grass towards them, though he can't be certain years later that this part isn't some imaginary embellishment.

> clatter of a stream
> on sunlit stones
> the agate I saved

Galveston, 2010

We've checked out of our hotel. I'm on my way to the car with one last suitcase when a sea gull out of nowhere swoops in front of me, arcs upward, and smacks full-speed the concrete overhead crossbeam of the hotel's front awning. Its impact makes a dry crunch, like a ball of husks. It falls straight down, landing upside down a yard or so in front of me. Maybe a foot twitches once or twice, but there's no doubt: dead as iron.

Across Seawall Boulevard, the constant white noise of the Gulf.

It's the summer of the year my parents died a month apart. In my mind, a split-second montage of the dead—parents, friends, relatives, various pets. I feel a new wave of grief. But there's little time to react. Almost at once, a concierge is on the scene with broom and white plastic bag to sweep up the still specimen and make the driveway clean again. New guests arriving soon.

      umbrellas
    along the beach
an empty row of chairs

Publish or Perish

Flying over heartland, pitch-dark, the red-eye flight from Newark to Houston. 3 a.m. EST. Few lights on in the cabin. Attendants passing out pillows and blankets, like a big sleepover.

I'm coming home from a conference, having flown sixteen hundred miles to deliver a paper that seemed to impress no one, and elicited no response. Headed back home, my usual window seat.

Out the glass, across the cover of night, occasional isolated ganglia of mid-continent small town lights along a nerve system connected by a few streets, lamps, county roads—a far cry from the east coast's glowing celestial mass.

Hours later, back on the ground, call a friend and hitch a ride to my parking lot—one sleepy hour more of driving home. Late snack, then an unmade bed. This scholar's life definitely not my cup of tea.

> bachelor pad—
> bills on the table,
> empties

Calling Home

"Happy birthday!"

"Well thank you!" my mother says; "And who am I talking to?"

"This is your son."

I have to remind her who I am three more times as we talk. But her voice sounds good today.

"Has anyone else called to wish you a happy birthday?"

"Oh yeah, Ray writes pretty regularly now," she says, misunderstanding. "A lot better than when he was in the Navy."

I don't remind her that Uncle Ray died years ago, his ashes long since scattered at sea.

        winter night
        half-moon blowing
        behind torn clouds

Gary LeBel

Gary LeBel has been making images in words and pictures for many years. After beginning field service in 1988 as an industrial consultant, he started to write haibun. He credits Bashō's work in particular, as do so many others, for the impulse to begin.

His first few western-style poems appeared in the early nineties and his first short story, "Fresh Bread," in 1996. Modern English Tanka Press published *Abacus*, his first collection of short poems, haibun and prose poems as an eBook in 2008. His haibun and tanka prose have appeared in *Contemporary Haibun*, *Haibun Today*, *Kō*, *Kokako*, *Lynx*, *Modern Haiku* and *Skylark*. His haiga have appeared in *Haiga Online*, *Modern Haiga*, *Modern Haiku* and *Reeds Contemporary Haiga*. His tanka prose has been included in *The Tanka Prose Anthology* (2008) and in *Modern Haibun* and *Tanka Prose* in 2009. His individual tanka have been included in *Modern English Tanka's* journals as well as in anthologies such as *The Dreaming Room*, *Ash Moon Anthology*, *Atlas Poetica*, *Landfall*, *Streetlights* and *Take Five* as well as *In the Ship's Wake*.

Bridge

I had not returned to my native Maine in a number of years. Although I'd misplaced my recollections of mustard yellow and teal blue cape houses spread out along the hem of a white-capped sea, the heady sweetness of pine and spruce finds me immediately as I leave the plane. The strong, muscular beauty of this place explodes in a sudden rush of scent and color.

When we return to where we grew up, we look for bridges by which we try to join the shores of past and present. The crossing bridge over which my years seem to touch in indefinable ways was built by the cries of loons.

Those moved even once by their cry carry its echo wherever they go. Few birds have this hold on the psyche. It's said that the health of a body of fresh water can be known by carefully observing its loon population. If they leave, the waters are either too polluted or crowded. A lake they've departed would be unimaginable.

My sister and I have not had a swim together since we were teens, separated as siblings are by state lines and telephones. There being no boat traffic, we head for deep water at the center of the channel. The lake water has a delicious taste—dense, clean and full of minerals.

A few feet below the surface, the sunlight dulls to a soft green. You can feel the layers of increasingly colder temperatures distinctly as you dive deeper, adding greatly to its pleasure.

> a pine-wind rises
> between the shores of a lake
> two hearts remember

Suddenly about ten feet away, a loon has surfaced. I'm astounded by how large it is, having never seen one close up. Its hard-edged patterns of pure white bands on luxuriant deep indigo plumage make one imagine how soft but firm it must feel. Raising its equally black bill toward the open sky, it sets free a long, yodeling cry that pierces the air like a javelin. The loon isn't at all afraid and remains with us for some time. Its burning eyes are dark and impenetrable, lenses to a far younger earth.

I dive; the loon dives. An excellent swimmer, it's little more than a blur beneath the surface, as agile underwater as it is in the air. Now surfacing, it rises beside me maintaining its safe distance as my sister remains transfixed, treading the cold water. As we continue our interplay for several more minutes, I wonder about its reason for remaining with us. Is it simply curiosity? Is there a nest nearby? Though renowned for its secrecy, the loon remains close for several more minutes until it dives suddenly and disappears.

On the morning I'm to fly home, loons from far down the lake nudge me from my sleep. As the sun's thin light begins to brighten the white curtains of the little cottage, I listen to their cries as they interweave themselves with my thoughts and memories—a boyhood spent waking up on this same squeaky bed and the sheer wonder that almost nothing has changed here in nearly thirty years.

After the last of their music falls away to nothing, I rise and busy myself with the details of travel: clothes for the day, a suitcase made ready, the warm circling arms of aging parents. On the back porch I pause to take a deep breath of the woods and, in treading its three steps to the walkway, both end and begin a journey.

> the loon's shrill cry—
> but what has the morning lake
> whispered in return?

Note: In memory of Robert Spiess, a man I never knew, yet a man who changed my life profoundly.

Circuit

Attracted to the splash of color on the little seaside gallery's walls, I go inside and strike up a conversation with the owner. We talk of the great shows we'd seen over the years: Renoir, the Vatican Collection, the opulent museums of Russia she'd visited, a place that seemed as far away to me as Andromeda.

"Who did you see in Russia?" I ask.

"Oh, Vuillard," she replies in a swoon, releasing a flood of tears at the very taste of the Frenchman's name.

I wanted to tell her how I'd once stood spellbound before Caravaggio's life-sized *Entombment*, how the shoeless room and all the scrambling world outside the painting suddenly froze as a great, phlegmatic current began to flow invisibly into the gap between Mary's cry and the awkwardly laboring arms of Nicodemus, that it moved down through the sagging body of Christ with an achingly slow velocity whose magnetic fields blew on the hairs of my skin, before it inched its way up my spine, leaving a trail of icicles where each nerve had been pricked and helplessly fired . . . but my little spark couldn't hold a candle to a tear.

palms on canvas
and shimmering through a window—
island sunset

Machinery

Laughter runs amid the trees that encircle the little beach—swimming late at night when the state park forbids it is delightful mischief, especially when naked. How beautifully soft and supple are human bodies when smoothed to the simplest of contours by a bright, full moon! Like those candle-lit faces in Georges de la Tour, they glow as if the radiant machinery of the soul inside were showing through.

At last, the water begins to chill, the hour is felt, the stars grow more distant. As talk recedes into a dribbling quiet, we're left with nothing but a deep, plush sky as toes grope shyly for the stones of the beach.

> Eridanus tonight . . .
> every inch
> a lake

Noisy Things

I ring the doorbell to pick up my son. Behind me on the family's large estate, the pond at the edge of the hayfield teems with a high-pitched, ethereal sound. An old woman comes to the door and I introduce myself saying why I've come.

Snapping the brittle awkwardness of waiting with her in the doorway, I say that the sounds of the frogs from the pond are nice to hear, that they're lucky to have them in such abundance to enjoy each spring.

"What?" she asks crabbily. *"What* frogs?" I look down toward the pond, pointing. "There–can you hear them? They're called spring peepers, Ma'am," I say while gauging them with my thumb and forefinger to give her an idea of their size.

She listens a moment, shrugs. "Oh, **those** *noisy* things. I'll get your boy."

> Almost home
> the lights of our kitchen
> one street away

Watermelon

At the old Wormsloe Plantation's museum near Savannah, Georgia, hangs a watercolor painted by an early settler some two hundred and fifty years ago, the picture of a watermelon. Intensely bold with the childlike simplicity of folk art, what comes through immediately is the artist's love of color and zest for form, a verisimilitude sought and achieved that captures both the object's is-ness and its pleasures, feats which are never possible when only the mere likeness of a thing is traced and color halfheartedly added: I stand transfixed, enjoying its boldness, its irrepressible flatness and luxuriant flesh, its intricately mottled rind, the indigo seeds each so carefully painted,

and with a small leap in imagination you might sense the artist's pride when, with the last stroke having been made, he sets it aside to dry, moving back a step or two to appraise it, his young bride looking on approvingly as it joins, as Borges might say, the world's sum of things,

and she may reach for his hand, leading him thru the open door and past the study's window to the garden, her free hand's fingers floating dreamily thru the young corn's silken tassels to the patch they'd planted together beside the pine-woods, always sunny, where the watermelons, like her belly, are just now starting to bulge . . .

twilight . . .
the path her dreaming cuts
thru the buttercups

(The artist: Philip Georg Friedrich von Reck (fl. 1736-c. 1790) in Ebenezer, Georgia)

Gary LeBel

Tom Lynch

Tom Lynch is an English professor at the University of Nebraska, Lincoln, where he teaches ecocriticism and place-conscious approaches to literature. He is the author of *Xerophilia: Ecocritical Explorations in Southwestern Literature*, and the co-editor of several volumes, including *The Bioregional Imagination: Literature, Ecology, Place and Artifacts and Illuminations: Critical Essays on Loren Eiseley*.

He is also a co-editor of the forthcoming volume *Thinking Continental: Writing the Planet One Place at a Time*. And he serves as editor of the journal *Western American Literature*. In the last few years his academic writing has taken him away from the writing of haiku and haibun, but he considers those genres essential for understanding the role of nature in literature.

Thunder Season

In the desert the days are usually blue-skyed. But in summer months the monsoon winds curve up from the Gulf of Mexico, rise over the dry mountains, curl into dark clouds, obscure the sun, and pound thunder down the arroyos. Sometimes it rains. Usually it doesn't. When clouds build and rumble, but dissipate without raining, the Tohono O'odham Indians of southern Arizona say "as t-iatogi." That is, "they just lied to us." Every summer afternoon my dog looks worried, her ears pricked, anticipating the first rumble. Even when it doesn't come, thunder defines the rhythms of these days.

> night's dark sleep–
> thunder
> flutters the curtains

White Sands Dunes

Glittering in the wide tularosa basin between sheer-cliffed mountain ranges, white gypsum sand spills across the landscape. The huge dunes are spiked with yuccas. Stark light and crisp shadows define the landforms. Hill beyond hill of soft clean sand makes a perfect terrain for kids, tumbling and shrieking down the dunes. Overhead, missiles and jets from White Sands Missile Range and Holloman Air Force Base trace the blue. When kids stop laughing you can hear, sometimes, the rumble of invisible jets. On the northern horizon, the first atomic bomb was detonated. This place, a giant sandbox for my boys, makes clear the fragility of innocence.

>   clean dune face
>   I decline
>   to walk it

A Beginner's Mind

> In the beginner's mind there are many possibilities; in the expert's there are few. —Shunryu Suzuki

Recently I moved to Las Cruces in the southern part of New Mexico. My new home lies in the Mesilla Valley of the Rio Grande, as it courses muddy through the Chihuahuan desert, North America's largest but least celebrated arid land. The Organ Mountains rise to the east, serrating the dawn's liminal blue. In the first few weeks of my residence, I made some tentative contacts with the landscape on a series of short hikes, toting my 16 month old boy, Riley, in a backpack.

The "beginner's mind," the elusive skill to look without preconceptions, to perceive originally, is an ideal in Zen and in haiku poetry. Moving to a new place, especially one so different from prior experiences, can nudge one toward that ideal. Of course I've read about this place, even passed through a time or two, so it is not entirely new, and I am certainly burdened with preconceptions, expectations, fears; but still, I am a neophyte, greenhorn, scurfed with innocence.

Yet, while haiku poetry nurtures a beginner's mind, it also does so in a landscape that is familiar, not exotic. Traditionally, the audience for Japanese haiku knew the look, sound, and scent of each plant named, each animal mentioned, each landscape traversed, and had read hundreds, thousands of haiku on the same subject. Can the allusive form work here? The intimate haiku of plum blossoms, bush warblers, crows, and crickets—will it get lost in the vastness of basin and range, the vocabulary of bajada and playa, piñon and nopale, ocotillo and arroyo, acacia and mesquite? Can it speak in the prickly dialect of desert words, so remote from the verdant Japanese diction?

***

viii/21/97
southern edge of Jornada del Muerto

Hiking midmorning with, as usual, a baby on my back and a border collie trotting ahead. Temperature in the low 90s. Jeep trail off the interstate—scattered debris from beer bashes: smashed bottles, faded cartons, yellow shotgun shells in sandy soil, the copper glint of spent cartridges. I can imagine it all. Drink a six-pack, load a six-shooter, see who can drink the most and shoot the straightest. Concussion and shattering glass, whoops and more beer tops popped. Desert party in the wasteland, gunfighter heritage of this too little loved land.

Today, I-25 murmurs in the distance, bees hover, ants scurry in grit.

> arroyo sand–
> brown bottle glass
> glints morning light

> ant mounds–
> shotgun shells
> filling with silent sand

Where the sand is fine, numerous lizard tracks from the night before criss-cross—prominent in the low-angled light shadows. So many, more than you'd imagine. Excited to be out, and unfamiliar with the climate, my dog runs ahead the first quarter mile, then slows.

> mesquite shade–
> trotting dog
> pauses a moment

It's the rainy season, the monsoon, humid and not that "yes, but it's a dry heat" one hears of. A desert greener than I guessed and a vast scatter of flowers brimming the Jornada del Muerto basin—creosote bush yellow, peppergrass white.

As of now, only the most obvious plants and animals do I know: mesquite, jackrabbit, red-tailed hawk. Is it true that "the names of things bring them closer" (Sund, 1969)? Is the sensation—the primal touch—enhanced or diminished by knowledge? Does my field guide, as I flip through for the matching flower, lead me toward or away from intimacy? Suzuki (1970) says, "So the most difficult thing is always to keep your beginner's mind." But what of the old-timer's sense of familiar comfort? When will I be able to say to this tree at hand, "Mesquite, my old friend, I greet you again today"?

***

viii/22/97
night storm

Creosote bush, disdained shrub of the desert. Vast flat valleys stuffed with creosote bush, spaced decisively across the red sand. They whiz past the car windows as we, going someplace else, hurry through. Wretched plant of wretched wastes. To live here and evade desiccation, their leaves are coated with a water retaining resin, at the touch of rain dissolving aroma into the breeze, borne miles ahead by the storm's wind.

Tonight, I lie in bed as a storm approaches.

> Distant thunder–
> curtain swells
> with the scent of creosote bush

***

viii/25/97
The Rio Grande

A stroll along the great river. Camino Real came through here, conquistadors and ox carts, billowing banners northward with empire. Now a gravel road atop a levee.

> rio grande–
> yellow butterflies eddy
> over the coursing current

> muddy river–
> tamarisk shadows
> cool the water

> river's sound–
> a tumbleweed turns over, over
> in the languid current

***

viii/28/97
La Cueva Trail

This trail leads to a small cave, occupied from at least 5000 B.C. Later, Apaches, no doubt, rested here after raids on travelers below—La Placita de las Cruces, where stones and rude crosses covered victims. Las Cruces, a town built on graves. And then a local legend:

> El Ermitano (The Hermit of La Cueva)
>
> Italian-born hermit Agostini-Justiniani spent many years walking through Europe, South America, Mexico, and Cuba. After wandering the Western deserts, associating with the Penitente Brotherhood in the Sangre de Cristo range of Northern New Mexico, he moved south into this very cave. When warned by locals of the dangers of staying there alone, he supposedly replied, "I shall make a fire in front of my cave every Friday evening while I shall be alive. If the fire fails to appear, it will be because I have been killed." He gathered herbs and healed the sick. One Friday night in the spring of 1869, the fire failed to appear at La Cueva. Antonio Garcia led a group up the mountain to find the Hermit lying face down on his crucifix with a knife in his back. He was wearing a penitential girdle full of spikes.

The hermit, I wonder, did he love this landscape, these birds so numerous, the trill of canyon wren, the filter of breeze through lacy acacia, impossibly jagged mountains beyond?

Every plant here bethorned—acacia, mesquite, yucca, prickly pear, barrel cactus—and snakes, wasps, scorpions, biting ants, too. His own spikes tortured his flesh, did these add? Was each thorn a penalty for his body's delight? He crossed the world to this place most remote from temptation, but he could not escape a cool breeze on a hot day caressing the flesh. Was he home here, or in exile from this and any place, from his very incarnation?

The knife in the back, another and final thorn to gouge desire.

> hermit's cave—
> wasps buzz in sand,
> acacia shadows flutter

In the cool of the cave, growing out toward the sun, sacred datura's green leaves and white funnels of flowers. Jimsonweed, psychedelic and deadly.

> cool white—
> in the cave mouth
> sacred datura blossoms

Did the hermit nibble datura, envision a cactus huge with fleshy pink petals, a yucca spear yearning toward sky, a cloud's crisp outline against cosmic blue, wind tossing a million grama grasses? These mountains, for once, seen.

Riley sits in the cave shade, sifts sand from clenched hands, happy just to watch the falling, falling. We depart, trot back down the trail.

> beyond the yucca spears
> red-tail hawk wheels
> in sun brilliance

> sun—
> each thorn distinct on the
> prickly pear shadow

> speckled mesquite shade—
> baby lifts to me
> a cool rock

***

ix/11/97
Baylor Pass Trail

> last night's rain,
> pooled in the rocks
> glints the hot sun

Riley in the pack dozes as we hike. These scents—wet sand, sun-dried rocks, Apache plume, creosote bush–and these sights–yucca, quivering cactus, abounding boulders–forever exotic to me, but, archetyping his place on earth, they seep into his psyche.

>spreading acacia shade–
>boulders worn smooth
>by hiker bottoms

>dung beetles
>swarm across coyote turd–
>a breeze dries my sweat

***

ix/17/97
Baylor Pass Trail

Hot and still morning alive with birds: loggerhead shrike atop a yucca, cactus wren, black-chinned sparrow, Inca doves, evasive sparrows I can't decode.

As I pass up into the bajada boulders, rock squirrels yelp alarm, grasshoppers shoot off with red wings clicking. Sweat beads sting the eye, intent ants cross the trail. Atop a boulder, against blue sky, a roadrunner cocks his head, watching me, immigrant, human.

In the shade of a grey oak, where arroyo descends the boulder strewn bajada, we sit on rock ledge in shade. Dog laps water, Riley holds a rice cake. I scribble notes, sweat-soaked back cooling in a casual whiff of wind.

Trudge back down the arroyo. Whiptail lizards dart away, and the red-winged grasshoppers clatter, and that one, there, a pale blue surprise. As I alternately flip through Peterson's guide and peer through scope at bird on the acacia branch,

>baby in the backpack
>repeats
>"birdee, birdee, birdee, birdee."

***

x/2/97
Rabbit Ears Plateau Trail

At the trail head, the BLM "w ld rne s stu y a e" sign, hard to read for the spatter of bullet holes. A mile up the trail—a rough jeep road—old stone mine house gradually whittling to dust. Amid shotgun shells and cigarette butts, shattered glass sparkles. Mine relics rust a sun's redness. Shafts with rigid doors open into mountain's inner dark, a distant Bud light can flecks the verge of blackness.

Back down the trail in the bright, bright, squinting light: gilded flicker undulates over boulders, rises to cling to yucca shaft, squawks twice. Ruby-crowned kinglet hops on acacia branch, swallows something leggy. Indifferent, these seem, to human detritus, at home regardless.

We pause on the trail, gaze out across the boulder-strewn landscape. Layers of distance recede. I look, Riley looks: between our parallax, the emerging dimensions of a world.

> atop a rock
> 2 rock wrens hop and twitter–
> feathered stone

References

"*El Ermitano*." (n.d.) In J. Baumann, R. Calderon, C. Carrillo, & H. H. Ramli (Eds.), *La cueva trail guide*. United States Bureau of Land Management and the Nature Conservancy.

Sund, R. (1969). *Bunch grass*. Seattle: University of Washington Press.

Suzuki, S. (1970). *Zen mind, beginner's mind*. New York: Weatherhill.

George Marsh

George Marsh was born in London in 1946, educated at Selwyn College Cambridge and trained as a teacher. He has taught in all kinds of schools, prisons, colleges and Universities, but spent most of the time in teacher education, specializing in the teaching of poetry.

He has written a book and has a couple of websites on the subject.

In retirement he enjoys verbal tennis with his grandson (that's what he calls our banter), badminton and sailing. He leads a Zen group locally, and edits the magazine New Chan Forum. These entries were posted online in *Haibun, Poetry by George Marsh*.

http://darkislands.co.uk/category/haibun/
http://www.haiku.org.uk/

The Higgs Boson

"Expanding, contracting, killing, giving life–such is its subtle function."
—Zen Master Yuanwu,
Author of The Blue Cliff Record

At the Large Hadron Collider they accelerate particles round and round a seventeen kilometre tunnel to meet each other coming the other way in a kiss throwing out a starburst of fizzing debris. They want to find out what is hidden inside. There must be something else. They think it will be the Higgs boson. This, dear one, is our Anniversary Metaphor.

The Higgs boson has revealed itself to the Collider's detectors, but in a teasing flash of thigh. The Higgs is laughing at them, balanced between Supersymmetry theory and Multiverse theory, where it should not be, where it confirms neither theory, and where it should be unstable. Could the whole subatomic realm collapse?

> O the sun burns!
> This mountain was syrup
> flowing under my feet

Imagined numbers explain the laws of nature to us, but we don't know if we discovered mathematics or made it up, whether it is out there or in here.

> Always roaring
> the echo in me
> of the wind between the stars

The Higgs refuses to reveal whether the universe was born, or born again and again, or inflated as a bubble in a multiverse of infinite bubbles.

> Beginningless kalpas of time perhaps
> to the Big Bang
> of this ripe nectarine

Gravity is weaker than the delicate tension in finger and thumb pulling skin off a ripe peach. Like Higgs, it is not the power it ought to be, and won't fit into the theory. Perhaps it is not even a force, just dimples in space. And perhaps the exploding universe is really sitting still. While space inflates. Maths gives us the speed and strength and size, but of what?

>   Fractals in sand
>   the ebbing tide
>   knows how

At the Hadron Collider nature is being mysterious. You have got the best answer.

>   For the unloved
>   an immense night sky
>   creamy with stars

The stars are mother and father to us.

>   Farmyard flints
>   through the soles of my shoes
>   the Milky Way

Outer and inner cannot be distinguished.

>   She licks her kittens
>   and her fur
>   as if it were all the same

We may be particles, we may meet, but there's something else hidden in or around us which may or may not be dark energy or something Higgs-like.

>   The feeling's my hand,
>   your skin, our bothness
>   and

The Ruined Church

"... for everything that lives is holy"
—William Blake

Tenacious flowers of golden weed grow from the cracks. No roof, no door, no pews, no treasure—does it still have a bellyful of love?

> entering by the arch
> a Cabbage White searches
> for what it needs

> high above
> swifts feast
> in endless blue

> from an oubliette
> in the abandoned ruin
> crawls a ladybird

> pecking together
> a chaffinch couple
> graze on the ancient stones

The church walls are blocks of yellow rock, still bearing the scrapes of the rough stone-cutting tools used to square them off. There is a bees' nest in a hole, hectic with hovering traffic.

> Bee City Airport
> helijet entrance arch
> in the broken mortar

> buzz buzz buzz
> the congregation ignore
> blackbird's sermon

The blackbird watches me with a bright black pupil rimmed with yellow. The gecko I study is also bright-eyed. A smart beetle, like my neighbour, comes from the carwash with polished metallic bodywork. From the lean-to outside the church there's a strangely insistent rhythm.

         in the thatch
    squeezing notes in unison
        a choir of sparrows

     in the heat of the sun
          a dry font
       christens everything

         I'm squatting
          on the altar
         awed by ants

I feel as old as the need for rain, here with the ancient urges of birds and bees. I just sit in the ruins, with my evolutionary company.

           I am a bee
          I am a lizard
          I am a people

Langstone Harbour

On 7th. November 1991 my father died. I walked by the shores of Langstone Harbour.

> winter wind–
> two geese turn
> a broad descending circle
> and end
> facing it
> knowing how to touch down
> lightly

At the wake my sons looked after me sweetly, talked of family memories and had me laughing. I returned to Langstone Harbour and watched the birds, and watched yachts on their moorings as fishing boats motored by.

> I lift, judder
> spin and settle
> in your wake

> water in the bay
> no trace
> of the splashy wing beats

> low tide mudflats–
> I breathe out
> tremble

> dense cloud
> the colour of ashes
> the sky is my father

One night, fascinated by the waves slopping inside a wreck with the life-force of the ocean:

> between the ribs
> of the broken boat
> rises the moonlit tide

In the New Year:

> bright cold morning–
> for breakfast let's open
> the last of his marmalade!

On the anniversary of his death I stood on the ferry pontoon at Eastney Point, tasting the windblown spray:

> grief, and breathing
> the salty fragrance
> of the deep tide drift

I revisited the Heath by the family home, where we scattered his remains:

> under my foot
> at every step
> my father's ashes

I inherited a dusty oil portrait of my father reading a book, painted in the forties, with a rip in the corner, and I commissioned a friend of mine who is a conservator to repair it, clean it and frame it.

> his portrait restored–
> my father
> younger than me

Waiting at the Ferry café

> a dog trots down
> a puddled flight of steps—
> smoke puff over the ferry

Oh these tacky provincial dumps. But I've half an hour to kill, so here goes . . .

I order coffee, and a cheap bacon sarny, served by an amazingly old man with a gentle smile. I have the impression he's in a trench as I look down upon him, behind a misted display case, shuffling from the Gaggia to the till. His eyes are washed out pale and wet, but he's still there, behind them.

His fat son looks like a comic grotesque. He tells a trite story to tolerant listeners. He is the waiter, and pauses to plonk my bacon sandwich on the formica. The old man must have been patient with him. The old man works, because he can't hand it on.

In fact, as I sip and watch the chorus of yokels, who need not be here, wrapped up in Asda fleeces against the autumn chill, trading greetings and ungrammatical family news, I am startled to see more smiles.

> a hard life
> and a simple son
> don't entirely explain

The old man gives me two surprisingly well-formed sentences of gratitude as I leave. Is this politeness excessive? Out into the wind and stinging rain.

> a drooping canopy:
> dogwalkers shelter
> giggling together

The sea has a pewter gleam and shakes the jetty. I must have mislaid something and pat my pockets vaguely, feeling isolated.

> the ferry throbs
> props blending
> this into foam

How little is left

> winter dusk
> how little is left of the moon
> how lovely it is

Getting older now, feeling vulnerable after my operation, weak as a kitten, I refuse to accept–as I refused when I lost you–that suffering is wanting it not to be so, that I wouldn't hurt like this if I surfed the convalescence, the grief. I need pain.

The sea churned all day and gulls cowered on the Common.

> after a gale
> kelp-stink in the moonlight,
> crashing waves

With a stick, I can shuffle along the seafront after dark and start to think of something other than me. Recovering now, I recall those games we won together, what a partner you were.

My favourite people are gone from me, which leaves the night, the stars, and the flirty moon winking from wisps of smoke.

> long cold night
> the silver river on the sea
> flows sideways

It is a long night and no sleep. I have to bring you to mind, and put you away again and, in the end, you're mixed up with others in scenes fading to fragments until bits loop stupidly and then I'm bored awake.

> before dawn
> the reflection of dawn
> on the restless sea

Michael McClintock

Michael McClintock lives in Clovis, California, with his wife, artist Karen J. McClintock. His poetry and other writings appear worldwide, in print and on the Web, including all three editions of *The Haiku Anthology*, ed. by Cor van den Heuvel (Doubleday/Anchor, 1971; Simon & Schuster, 1986; W. W. Norton, 1996), and *Haiku in English* (W. W. Norton, 2015). During the late 1960s, he was the Assistant Editor of *Haiku Highlights*, working with editor-publisher Jean Calkins. From 1972-1976, McClintock engaged in more editorial work as Assistant Editor of *Modern Haiku* with Founder-Editor Kay Titus Mormino, as chief editor of the American Haiku Poets Series, and as editor-founder of *Seer Ox: American Senryu Magazine*. In recent years he has worked as tanka editor for *Simply Haiku* and *Notes from the Gean*, served as President of the Tanka Society of America, and writes the "Tanka Cafe" column for *Ribbons: the Tanka Society of America Journal*. In 2006 he became contributing editor to *Modern English Tanka*, at that time the world's largest quarterly journal of tanka and related studies in English.

A seminal study of Michael McClintock's early work in "new Imagism" may be found in Barbara Ungar's *Haiku in English* (Stanford Honors Essay in Humanities, No. XXI, copyright 1978, Stanford University). He is cited as *"master of contemporary English language haiku"* in The Bedford Glossary of Critical and Literary Terms by Ross Murfin and Supryia M. Ray (Bedford Books, a Division of St. Martin's Press, Inc., 1997 and later editions).

Sea of Cortez

The cobwebs at my door I leave alone; the year grows old, I will tend to other things. Leaves on the roof have collected for a season. My yard is weeds and sticks and broken blossom. I have poems to write, letters to some friends. The sweetness on the air says rain tonight.

Even though darkness sets in before I can go very far, I'll come to where this thorn nest and snare of hooks release me, where green mountains make love to sun and moon, where sweet-pea frame door and window and hold a house in vines. I would tend to the wonder of that place.

The late summer sun pulls down into the ocean the day's afterbirth, my sense of waiting too long for something, for anything.

>   from the mud-daubed house
>   the voice of the daughter
>   who's just learned to sing

Men of Property

I let my eyes and hands run over the tools he had used—the trowel, the spade, the mulching fork. I gazed at the few remaining tin pails, enameled green, and recalled how the one got its crimped side and the other its bullet hole. I pocketed the worn canvas gloves; the man buying the place had much smaller hands than dad's, and could not wear them. But all the tools and pails and contents of the shed he said he would use, and would be grateful to have them.

I stepped out of the shed and walked onto the broad sloping hillside, only a small corner of which belonged to the property. The shed was planted in the middle of six rows of fruit trees, six trees to a row, with extra room made for the shed and open ground around it for loading boxes with fruit from the buckets: oranges, lemons, plums. I could still hear my father from somewhere in the trees calling to my brother and me, to bring him a ladder, or come get the dog, or haul out the pails full of fruit, or stop horsing around and go in to supper—he'd follow.

> hefting a plum—
> I know by heart
> my father's orchard

Raspados

The hour when the horned dog sleeps, that hour, and the moon a smear over the freeway, the electric plant, the brewery, the blocks of warehouses, suspended pale and humid, that moon at the end of the long avenue of trees and small homes and apartments, and the evening air a moist breath of voices, those voices at the end of all the long avenues, our voices, tired in the dark, the languid hour after dinner, tired from the world's canning, the world's stitching machines, the lathes and hot lights and liquid metals, the smell of grease and ozone, cement and tar, deaf from the buzzing saws, deaf from the hammering presses, deaf from drills endlessly drilling, ceaselessly laboring for that foot in the ass–

> muggy nights . . .
> the child's moon drawing
> taped to the fridge

There is an old man from Calexico, a man mute and blind in one eye, who comes along pushing a small cart carrying rainbows of color on shaved ice, syrups of orange and yellow and green, cool fantasies in sugar for a dollar.

We listen for him, his sound a tinkling of tin bells coming out of the purple splash of tree-shadow–our eyes on him, the only man in the world good for the eyes at that hour–that man selling syrups on sparkled ice, bringing his sweet, cooling, tasty raspados.

> suddenly awake–
> the dog's chain
> dragging in the dark

Koi in Winter

It's true—a snowflake screams as it enters water.

George had read my haibun about the dish at Arecibo that listens to the stars. "This is the other end of the spectrum—micro sound."

George smiled at my alarm. We were in his backyard, near the koi pool, testing the sensitivity of sound equipment he was engineering for the next Martian probe, intended for landing at that planet's southern pole.

"What do you make of it?" he asks. "I thought you'd appreciate it. Our senses are gross. Imagine a disk the size of a quarter. Lay a human hair on it. The human hair represents the breadth of what we see and hear of the world. Poets write about the human hair—that's all." He said this teasingly; he was always at me about my interest in poetry. "Of course, you're welcome to it. But for me that's not enough data to draw conclusions."

I am unnerved by what I hear. Snowflakes are falling into a shallow pan of water. Thin, insulated wires run from the pan to a book-sized electronic device, into which our earphones are jacked.

George sniffs the air, like a dog. "Perfect conditions today, just a few flakes falling." He turns to his meter. "Here, listen to this . . ."

I hear heavy panes of glass falling into a street and look at him in disbelief. There is screaming among the falling shards.

". . . a snowflake hitting this little metal plate," he says.

That was four weeks ago. I gaze over the wall into his yard, at the wind-sculpted white. I listen to the sifting shadows. A bright half-moon shines hard in the dogwood tree, a splintered wedge.

I keep going back to what George had asked so casually. I wonder what he meant when he said, "What do you make of it?"

>   do they dream?
>   the fish pond
>   deep under snow

Michael McClintock

Ordinary Seductions

Dolores rose early and, careless about buttoning up the front of her sky-blue house coat, under which she wore nothing, primped her small flower beds and mowed her rug-sized lawn, the dew fanning from the blades in a light spray that wet her legs and made a thin, tremulous rainbow in the air. The last thing she did was step to her front gate and carefully twine a strand of flowering vine from fence to mailbox post. Smiling, she then went into the house and I saw no more of her that day.

> honeysuckle . . .
> the mailman takes a sniff
> as he closes the box

Beverly Acuff Momoi

Beverly Acuff Momoi has written many forms of poetry and has a particular interest in Japanese short forms. Her poems have been published widely in print and online journals, including *Acorn*, *A Hundred Gourds*, *Contemporary Haibun Online*, *Daily Haiku*, *Eucalypt*, *Frogpond*, *Heron's Nest*, *Modern Haiku*, *Ribbons*, *Spillway* and *tinywords*, among others.

Her haibun collection, *Lifting the Towhee's Song*, was a Snapshot Press 2011 eChapbook Award winner, and one of her haibun received honorable mention in the Haiku Society of America's 2015 Best Unpublished Haibun Contest. Her haiku is featured in the anthologies, *A New Resonance 9: Emerging Voices in English Language Haiku* (Red Moon Press), *Haiku 2015* (Modern Haiku Press), and *but for their voices* (Haiku Poets of Northern California's 2015 *Two Autumns Reading*).

Recipient of poetry fellowships from The Loft and the McKnight Foundation, she is a member of the Haiku Society of America, the British Haiku Society, Haiku Canada, Haiku Poets of Northern California, Yuki Teikei Haiku Society, and the Tanka Society of America. She lives in northern California with her husband and two cats.

Lifting the towhee's song

I have been thinking about Darwin and the puzzle of survival.

>reaching into sky
>the farmer culls pear blossoms
>for October fruit

In Japan, a son mourns. When the earthquake struck, his father was in Futaba Hospital for treatment; 90 patients were left unattended. The death certificate simply states that his father died of lung cancer. No mention is made of the disaster, the chaos, the abandonment.

Forty miles inland but well within the zone of destruction, another man died that weekend, and our family still grieves. A handsome man with an easy smile, my brother-in-law was stricken with leukemia a year ago. We were shocked, but thankful when he responded to treatment. Then the temblor. He was the toughest one among us.

>California spring
>the purple finch lifting
>the towhee's song

Yellow flag

I am slowly working my way through our boxes of stuff. My husband and I save everything. We have menus of kaiseki dinners marking anniversaries; lesson plans from decades ago when one or the other of us was teaching; baby pictures of nieces and nephews who now have babies of their own; tapes of my mother telling stories for a family history project; letters from my grandmother who died in 1985; a great picture of my father-in-law laughing.

As I sort, NHK provides a running commentary on the cleanup efforts along the northeast coast of Japan. 24.9 million tons of debris. Mementos of people's lives. In Minamisoma, a man goes through the rubble of his home, methodically searching for his father's memorial plaque from the family altar. He finds his daughter's wedding pictures—beautifully serious in her kimono, more relaxed in her white wedding dress—and carefully wipes off the mud. His father's name plaque still missing, he plants a yellow flag at the door of his home to signal workers: Do not destroy. He has not given up looking.

> against a gray sky
> the brilliance of yellow
> daffodils

Holding fast

Late winter and I am leaning into my life, leaning to catch a glimpse of that flat blue line, to see just how far sea and sky extend.

    look again a cloud blossoms out of thin air

In Tohoku, the camellias have bloomed, a sudden shock of red and white. At the shrine, the camphor tree's gnarled roots reach for new saplings.

    bare branches then a blaze of green reframing everything

Assisted living

As we settle her into her new place, my mother folds and refolds the tissues. It is her habit lately. To smooth wrinkles in unwrinkled sheets, fix the creases in a letter, imprint the lines in a map. We ask her where she wants the pictures of Grandmother, if she can reach the phone from her armchair, if she is looking forward to making friends? She has just one question: How long can we stay?

wabi sabi
the solitary turn
toward age

Broken

The picture is still in its original frame, cheap metal with a worn velvet-covered back that unfolds to make a stand. The edges are tattered where it stood on her dresser for decades. The glass covering the photograph is broken, a star of shards radiating just below the eyes. Another blunt-edged star of cellophane tape holds the fragments in place.

>ghost notes
>in the early morning
>frost flowers

After he died, the photograph arrived in the mail. A soldier with unwavering gray eyes looks straight into the camera. Hat brim level. Tie well-knotted. Shoulders squared.

1942: He was 19, a private in an Army camp in New York with nothing to do but wait to be shipped out. His mother was so angry when he enlisted. The picture was his peace offering. He wanted her to see him in his uniform. To make up for leaving her alone on the farm.

He had followed his big brother to the war, just like he followed him when they were kids. Looking for a good time. Looking with those gray hazel eyes.

>cotton burrs
>and broken down fences
>Delta camouflage

I was five the first time we left him. Mom took me and my sister on a Greyhound bus to see Grandmother in New Mexico. It was a short visit. She said her daughter had made her bed, she needed to get back to it. So we came home and pretended everything was normal.

>jagged green glass
>where the TV used to be
>triggered lightning

That's what I remember. His eyes. Like granite, with yellow flecks of hardness. When we stopped speaking, his eyes were so many shades of gray, they were like weather vanes predicting storms, skittering around, this way and that, never at rest.

> last leaf
> on the dogwood tree
> past imperfect

Lenard D. Moore

Lenard D. Moore, a North Carolina native and U. S. Army Veteran, is the Founder and Executive Director of the Carolina African American Writers' Collective and Co-founder of the Washington Street Writers Group. He is former President of the Haiku Society of America (2008 and 2009) and Executive Chairman of the North Carolina Haiku Society. Moore's poems, short stories, essays and reviews have appeared in over 400 publications. He has taught workshops, served on literary panels, and given hundreds of readings at schools, festivals, colleges and universities. He has lived in South Carolina, Virginia, California, and Germany. An avid reader and listener of music, he writes about family, jazz, identity, and global issues. Currently, Mr. Moore, Associate Professor of English, teaches Advanced Poetry Writing and African American Literature at the University of Mount Olive, where he directs the literary festival. He is working on two poetry collections, a novel, short stories, a play, and literary criticism. Mr. Moore mentors several other poets and writers.

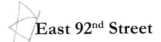East 92nd Street

After sitting nearly an hour on a bench, I pull out my journal from my tote bag. Long-haired woman in tight, black dress and dark shades; boy who cries in his stroller; pigeon pecking sidewalk; two couples and their two girls and two boys congregate on the corner. A man in a red apron wraps twelve roses. A city bus idles at the stoplight, then releases air brakes. An unseen bird chirps and chirps. The purple bike shines against the "No Parking" sign.

>   summer afternoons . . .
>   the scrape of her flip-flops
>   against the sidewalk

Manhattan Chronicle

Leaving Carlton Hotel, I weave through crowds on 29th Street. Yellow cabs clog the sunlit street. A siren blares, drowns the block with an ear-aching scream. A fire truck races past cabs and delivery trucks. I keep pace, enter White Castle as a young man holds the door open, ordering two cheeseburgers and a soft drink, sit in the front near the window. The young man sits and watches a woman walk alone on the sidewalk. He says, "You're shaking, baby." "We can work it out," he adds, holding his tiny cheeseburger. We swap a laugh. I finish my brunch and leave. I walk several yards, cross the street, and head towards the Empire State Building. I walk through the revolving door, proceed to the entrance line and visit a gift shop. After an hour of eyeing souvenirs, I buy a World Trade Center brass plate with stand, exit the towering building, and remember September 11, 2001: phone calls to my wife, daughter, mother, father, sisters, brothers, and childhood friend in Manhattan.

> wavering heat
> two cars exchange honks
> amid still shadows

A Blueberry-Picking Day

When school was out and the first day of summer was about two weeks away, we knew that much excitement belonged to us, my brothers, sisters, and me. We could hardly wait for the first hint of sunlight in early morning. We rose from our shared beds, washed ourselves off with washrags that floated in the small sink of hot soapy water. We slipped into old bellbottom pants or worn blue jeans and polyester-cotton shirts, white socks, converse tennis shoes, and straw hats. We poured cornflakes, sprinkles of sugar, and milk into bowls. We ate without talking at the kitchen table. We knew that our mother and father did not believe in wasting any food. So we ate it all, and drank the leftover milk from the bowls. I remember how we rushed out of the screened door, off the concrete porch, and dashed to the roadside to wait for the blueberry bus. We laughed and talked about how many berries we would pick to fill our homemade plastic buckets that hung around our waists with twine. How deeply we loved this time of year. Yet we watched to see when the bus would come:

> the bus one stop away,
> its horn blowing and blowing
> this summer morning

Often, as we got on the bus, we flopped in seats with home boys and home girls. We picked up others from a number of neighborhoods throughout our small town. My brothers and I marveled at the beautiful brown girls who boarded the bus. I wonder if my sisters marveled at the afro-wearing boys. I remember how we would duck down on the twenty-year-old gray bus, not wanting anyone to see us riding it. We would see the ones, who stood outside to watch our bus creep by, at the skating rink on Monday nights and the dances on Saturday nights. We waited until we were clearly out of sight before popping up into our ripped seats.

> forty miles away
> we pick our first bucketful
> in dusty sunlight

        all day long
our mouths turn blueberry-blue
      the taste of grit

       deep stillness
a dozen dollar bills rustle
before we board the bus

        back home
the last glow of day
  behind the pump

This Autumn Night

While watching the television, I listen to my decade-old house settle again and again. A stray cat screams outside. The full moon casts shadows on my upstairs walls. Suddenly the silence greatens. Then a picture frame falls from the wall. Passing headlights disappear into the mirror on my chiffonier. For an extended period, I sit up straight on the waterbed, ignoring the television. My wife returns home and darts to the bathroom. I exhale, leaning against the headboard. Slowly my hands settle on the patchwork quilt.

her shadow floats
through the hallway–
I grin

In The Owl's Claws

After leaving the D. H. Hill Library at North Carolina State University, I notice the evening deepening all around me. A hint of orange flickers in the colossal trees along both sides of Hillsborough Street. Rainwater dries on the asphalt. Not a single shadow stirs. With hands gripping the steering wheel, I drive toward home, looking skyward. Jazz slips out of the radio. I watch the traffic light. No one else is in the car with me as I continue homeward, ready to settle into my house for the rest of this evening. I am getting hungry and I begin dreaming of hot baked sweet potatoes, barbecued chicken, buttermilk biscuits, okra, and macaroni and cheese. Suddenly I glimpse something gray moving in the sky; and all the while I continue to drive onward. I begin to creep. Momentarily, the riffs of a saxophone on my car radio seem to turn to silence. Coolness settles all around me. My eyes follow the enormous gray wings punctuating the slowly-darkening sky, studying its calmness while being absorbed in its own moment.

> moon on yellow aspens
> an owl flies
> beyond my windshield

Witness a small bird in the owl's claws makes me feel a sadness for all living things. It is the uncertainty of how we will depart from the earth. A few clouds creep across the face of the moon. It seems as if that owl wanted me to see him. It is the way he swooped on the currents of Carolina air. Bonded by the natural world, I am one with this moment.

late night remembering the clasped claws of the owl	open Venetian blinds moonlight strikes the *Birds* book

Peter Newton

Peter Newton is a poet and author currently serving as co-editor of the online international journal, *tinywords*. He lives in rural Massachusetts, USA. His haiku, senryu, tan renga, haibun and other short poems have appeared in a variety of print and online journals. He is the author of several books including *What We Find* (imaginary press, 2011), *Lonely Together* (Nut Wagon Press, 2013), *Welcome to the Joy Ride* (imaginary press, 2013) and *A Path of Desire* (Red Moon Press, 2015).

A new collection of his haiku entitled *The Searchable World* is due out in early 2017. Equally in love with the ocean and the mountains, much of his free time is spent on Cape Cod and in Vermont where he was a student and is now a staff member of Middlebury College's The Bread Loaf School of English.

Cold Comfort

The deer are motionless under the low-hanging pines, easily mistaken for the trees themselves. Their sapling legs thin trunks losing sunlight. I only know to look a few hundred yards past our back fence because they've come here before. For the past few nights they have bedded down under what little canopy young pines provide at the edge of the woods. One deer reaches up to nibble a loose piece of bark. How could this ever be enough? Forecasters say single digits. The neighborhood is quiet. Everyone's inside standing over their stoves. Through bird binoculars I can see one deer fold in on itself, front legs first as if kissing the earth. Then the hind. It's like watching the closing scene of a play. No music. No dialogue. All slow, intentional action. The central character coming to terms with the gradual dark.

        tracking their every up and down ridgeline coyotes

One Thing

My friend, Jeanne, was always up for an adventure. She liked the quote by Eleanor Roosevelt: "Do one thing every day that scares you." Jeanne lived by it. She pushed the fast-forward button at every chance. Time is short. Chop-chop. Let's go. And that was just when we would head out the door to take a walk in the year's first snowfall. A tradition in our college days. A way of honoring Ann Arbor. Our crazy, carefree time together. Up early, into the quiet street, to see our breath, clear our heads. There were books to be read. Words to be written. Swings to be swung on in Burns Park down at the end of Olivia.

Since Jeanne's death in a car wreck not two months back, she's been coming to visit early just before the birds start singing. I am somewhere between waking and sleeping. And don't know whether her appearance is a dream or a nightmare or both–"Courage," she says in my face, more like a drill sergeant this morning, instructing all those she loved and left behind. Her voice is steady, like she'd been reading aloud just moments earlier.

"You have to be like that first bird," she says. "You have to open your eyes each day and sing. Sing dammit. Sing–no one needs a crybaby to carry around." Jeanne strides before us half coach, half cheerleader. All business.

"Now, wake up," she says (and here is where she stops in front of me and turns to speak the words right up in my face) "with the courage to wake the world."

>first light
>under her doll's bed
>the packed suitcase

Simple Folds

I'm here for a late lunch and to see how the mural's coming along. One of the waiters has a brother who's an artist. He's self-taught but shows a talent no one denies. He's been painting the mural in the slow times for weeks. It's on the far back wall of the Lucky Dragon. A massive scene of a small harbor and the surrounding landscape. A square-sailed boat is coming into port. Grass-roofed huts line the beach, almost expectantly. It's a tan landscape with ocean blue highlights above and below. A balance, I think, with everything that's going on in between.

High up in the hills, herons nest in simple folds. It's a portrait of calm. The artist himself paints so slowly he almost disappears. The restaurant is nearly deserted as I knew it would be and I can hear the sound of his horse-hair bristles stippling the sky. I look up again and a few stragglers from the flock are shrouded in mist.

Maybe an hour goes by. The waiter whose name I've never known brings my fortune with the check. I stand to leave just as the painter finishes a man who is wading the rest of the way in to shore, towing his skiff. There is the slightest glint of little fish in the water ahead.

spring frogs . . .
softening the sound
of traffic

My America

What this place needs are a few corner bars and a street fight or two, he says of her immaculate neighborhood with its bumped-out bungalows and cobble-stoned driveways. Sure, it's nice enough, pretty and all. But it's not real. Not to me, anyway. But my America comes from growing up in the heart of an industrial city at the height of post-World War II euphoria. People were having kids right and left. We were all growing in leaps and bounds. I mean you couldn't not find work. They were pulling guys off the streets into the second-shifts they'd have for the rest of their working lives. Whaddya got a noise ordinance around here or something. It's a Friday night.

America. Baby. C'mon. What's happened to you? It's as if you lost heart along the way. Waylaid by all this glitz. It's not like you to settle down. Get comfortable. C'mon. Let's drive south. Go west. Anything. Where's your spirit? His eyes scan the once gutted kitchen now decked out with its two-inch thick glass countertops. Installed to look like reflecting pools when the sun hits them just right.

           occupying
    a dream I didn't have
         Wall Street

The Anatomy of Hope

We are all on guard. Waiting for word. The topic is locked on the missing Malaysian plane. Thirty four days of near-constant coverage and tonight they're calling it: The Anatomy of Hope. A blatant ratings grab no one seems to mind. We are listening for the cockpit voice recorders. We are spellbound, hypnotized and desperate for that errant ping. The panel invites us to dive deeper into the mystery. During the commercial break, there's been an outbreak in Africa. A car bomb in Kabul. I am standing in my quiet kitchen, staring back at a row of windows. A soldier at lost attention. The world is in ruins and I am thinking maybe these people on the plane have gone searching. That kingdom of kindness I've heard tell about. Or was that only me talking, spreading rumors of a better world.

> mid-winter
> the drive-thru cashier's
> scripted greeting

Jim Norton

Jim Norton born Dublin Ireland 1947 where he currently lives. Began writing haiku early 1990's. Started the Irish journal Haiku Spirit which he edited 1995-8. Associated with the Redthread group. Publications include *Words on the Wind* (1997 Waning Moon Press UK), *Pilgrim Foxes* (co-authored with Ken Jones and Sean O'Connor, Pilgrim Press Wales 2001), *The Fragrance of Dust* (Alba Press UK 2012).

These have been archived by the Haiku Foundation Digital Library. He also recevied an award in the Genjuan Haibun Competition Japan 2012 (haibun Yeh Go I).

Out of the Blue

The evening is warm and clear, but something else is happening: sensing a change in the air I hurry through the streets to the shoreline. Out of the blue

> Sea mist—
> gathered up in it
> the floating world

Between the wasteland and the strand, drifting in a state dream-like but with senses heightened, feeling each droplet, turning about in wonder. Out of insubstantiality forms manifest. Slabs of concrete bristling with rusty iron float into view, dissolve. Dripping silver, a stand of teasels cards the fleecy wraiths.

> On the shoreline
> man and heron
> swallowed whole

From the mouth of the bay beyond, voicing inexpressible longing

> Cloud-wrapped
> in utter stillness
> the foghorn lows

In response the thought arises: I need go no further, say no more. Here is condensed all I have searched for, ever-receding yet everywhere at once, ungraspable yet soaking me through and through. Again the South Bull sounds, and out of the depths a sea-calf answers.

Turning for home along the track, so deliciously contrary the crunching sound I look down in delight.

> In its own time
> a snail with horns erect
> floats over the cinders

When You Need It

At intervals along the long arm of the sea wall there are little red-n-white plastic strips across the cracks. They look like band-aids. Seems they're gauges recording the stretch, the rate of rupture. Storms pound the seaward side, shipping side-wash rakes at the lee.

Feeling faint from after the walk to the lighthouse and back, I need a sugar boost fast, so recalling the eats shack I'd noticed earlier, I swing off at the roundabout on the drive back to Raytown. The shutters are up. A big guy stands outside, cell-phone held away from his ear with a look of–exasperation? –creasing his fleshy face?

Opening the offside window as much as I dare–this is dockland–I catch his eye. 'Open?' Irritation becomes resignation as he thumbs off his call and with a slight shake of the head focusses on me. I'm halfway out the car now, keeping it between us.

'What'y'want?' 'Bottle of water and a chocolate bar?' He eyes me, then decides. 'Never refuse a body water. Sail or oar, can't do without water'. And he's off through the side door.

I make to follow but faced with a plastic strip curtain and semi darkness–wuu! I see a store-room and not much beyond. Then it's– fuck it–and I'm through, behind the counter of Deke's Diner. It's a galley kitchen, everything ship-shape. On a magnetic wall-strip a row of knives and a cleaver,

'Twix? Good for a boost. Or a Yorkie bar?' Ta. Then the water. Then suddenly we're talking diabetes . . . no, had the tests . . . hypogly-what's-it . . . giving up and going back on cigarettes . . . yeh, suckin yer dinner through a tube, who needs it?' Booze. Drugs.

'My sister's young fella, comes to me an' says, if I don't give him fifty, they'll stab him this evening.

So I give him fifty an I says, don't buy what you can't afford'

Jim Norton

And I offer in return 'Yeh, there's my Da dying of emphysema and he says to me 'son . . .' so I give him the cigarette'. Deke nods. 'You couldn't not'.

I give him the €4:35–not doing me any favours there. For two Twixes and a bottle of water? I'm half surprised to see the car's still parked outside.

                      Pecking around
                a stump-footed pigeon
                        gets what it needs

Knockree

Switch off. Sit motionless a while. Drifts of mist settle on the windscreen, gather into beads, pool their weights, slide down in crooked courses, stop, start again. Others here before me, a dozen cars emptied into mountain quiet, its presence absorbing all, an absence palpable, sways and whispers. Now as then, warm moist air releasing waft and tang, spicy sweetness of gorse, aromatics of crushed bracken, pine-ooze, oily reek of sheep. Find the gap, the meadow sloping up, fine grasses yellowed early, feathery seed-heads, uncut thistles elbow high, purpling.

City children holidaying. There I am in sepia, seated on a donkey, its ears back, not pleased. No more I am myself, braving it, but her arm around me and she smiling. Happy then.

Summer evenings here the rug is spread, we gather round a wind-up gramophone, cavort, sing along: He walks the bloody tower/with his head/ tucked/underneath his arm/at the midnight hour . . .

A two-roomed cottage, loaned to us by one-eyed Uncle Jack. Turning the pages of damp picture-books while rain hammered on the tin roof. Emerging into sunlit vibrant silence.

> Drawing water
> In the clang of a bucket
> the mountain rings out.

From across the valley a soft roar, cascading between Ton Duff and Maulin. Wonder, on being told its name: O'Toole's Buttermilk.

In the cold hearth finding a nail, long, square-shouldered, hand-forged. That'll do.

> roofless
> all that was in it
> flown

Sandscript

> Lost to sight
> a seabird's piping
> pierces home

Nasturtiums crowd the porch, spilling orange light through the open door. The grass is seldom cut and snails abound. I enjoy a spacious upper room with two tall windows and a creaking floor. To walk across it is a conversation, the better part of which is listening.

> brick and lath and joist
> settle with little groans and sighs
> into what they are.

Baby William Butler Yeats was wheeled in a carriage through these streets. Young Stephen Dedalus strode into eternity along this strand. There Bloom ever wanders, ogles Gertie while his Molly plays. Which is real, who imagines?

> Herons
> mirrored in sky-pools
> ruffled, rippled

> Hand in hand
> two tiny figures
> cross immensity

The sea disappears eastward each day and comes back speaking tongues, cries of seabirds voice unsayables, the waters riddle answers in sandscript and each night erases.

> Notice to quit:
> the musician's violin
> snug in its case

A Tear of the Sun

Uvas . . . a word to savour as I push the shopping trolley around the unfamiliar aisles of a Spanish supermarket, stocking up for a week of mountain solitude, in flight from Christmas jingles. Uvas skinned and tinned, stacked high for the celebrations.

> long red nails:
> the checkout girl's a star
> peel me a grape . . .

Rake out old ash. The wood-stove crackles, settles to a glow. The iron butterfly flutters in its throat with each down-draught of mountain air. In the tiny bedroom the glassy gaze of a long-lashed doll confronts me, chubby arms out-stretched. Felíz Navidad. Unquiet dreams.
What day is it? Lose track. Shake loose. Settle.

> mountains
> carried on snow-clouds
> playing light

Perched somewhere up there among the peaks and crevices is the hermitage of San Martín, one of many such ermitas scattered in these parts, in their time little lighthouses of the spirit beaming out across the plain. And though the keepers have deserted the heights, yearly the ancient images are carried up and back from towns and villages, maintaining the delicate balance of sacred and mundane.

Et in arcadia, ego. Burden of longing, obdurate, intractable. The sweetest meat lies closest the bone. Learn stone. Read wood. Study water. Be.

A feather floats down and the load shifts, settles. Sometimes that's all it takes.

Last evening. Shower and shave the manimal, walk to the village, see what's cookin' in La Flor. She shrugs. Sí. And returns with an armful of firewood. Jabalí grilled on the open hearth. To die for.

Perhaps because of the day that's in it—New Year, I'd quite forgotten—her man has a treat for me when I go to settle the bill. A glass of his vino de paga, on the house. Holds it up, a cloudy rosé, tilted to the light. There—do I see, glistening on the rim? Lagrima del sol.

> No grapes at midnight
> but full moon over Moncayo
> is a mouthful

[The story goes that a farmer who had a bumper grape harvest brought his surplus into the town square on New Year's Eve and distributed them free to the revelers, with the suggestion that they eat one for every stroke of the bell at midnight to share in his good fortune.]

Note: *jabali*—wild boar
       lagrima del sol—tears of the sun

Stanley Pelter

Stanley Pelter was born in January 1936 in London. During the Second World War he was evacuated twice. Then lived on Europe's largest Council Estate. Attended Wallington Grammar School.

A conscientious objector to Military Service was followed by the Royal College of Art where, for three years, he was in the same small tutorial group as Ron Kitaj and David Hockney with whom he remained close friends until Ron's early death. During this period, he was also a student of J. G. Bennet who was selected by the great Master Gurdjieff.

He has been a member of The British Haiku Society soon after it's inception. Since then he has written and illustrated over 500 haibun in eight volumes.

sonata

mist eases
below a windbreak hawthorn
an alphorn grips air

forest walk. struggle. climb over mutilated trees, snap detached branches, crunch muddied twigs. from inside leaves, lighter than sun dried sounds, we hear a minor key drift of sad adagio notes grow sadder.

town based lovers
somewhere lips dedicate
to piccolo thrills

City of Gifts

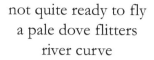

        not quite ready to fly
        a pale dove flitters
          river curve

Fancy going to Florence on Wednesday?
Where?
Florence
Where's that?
Italy
How come?
Someone's cancelled. I'll square it with school.
Thanks   *but no thanks.*
Why not?   It's only for a couple of days.
I don't know anybody. They're learning Italian. I'm younger than them.
I've got lots on.   *I don't want to.*
Most are young   very friendly   and I'll be with you.
She is 12   Square it with School.

It's your bar mitzvah
What?   *Can I sit by the window?*
Yes

They have been friendly. She is relaxed. Flight will arrive early morning. Seems to sleep; head to one side, eyes closed. Rapid first growth of morning. Pre-sun glow spreads across a clear blue light of Florentine sky. Opens her eyes. Descent follows bridged line of river Arno. Slowly we lower. Early sun shapes all colours and hues. Luminous space of a City of Gifts is compressed. Not blinking, she looks down on an unfamiliar roofscape. I know that look.

        cage glides to earth
      which we watch grow large
        she silent   wide eyed

Why didn't you tell me?
There is more

Let's walk. Go to the Accademia. Visit David

We look up at this translated marble, lit by a midday sun. A dome flows light. A frozen moment of silence dominates space a juvenile giant occupies. At first she doesn't speak. Then . . .
Who made it? David was the small one, not the giant.
Michelangelo. He does reverse things a bit. Usual image is after their battle. Michelangelo describes that moment when a childman makes a momentous decision, enters an arena of power. One act will change his life forever. See that huge veined hand, its position, sling lifted, ready to kill. Michelangelo was a little man with a broken nose. *David* was his gigantic, one-man rebellion against convention, against accepted tradition. Single-handedly, this huge Italian created a spatial, a temporal shift that had a profound effect on river flows of art.

I had said too much. Said it all wrong. She says nothing. Is still looking up at this boy who would be King. After two hard years of carving, here he stands, a technical, an aesthetic marvel. Unsurpassed. Maybe those 'Slaves' emerging from rocks. Perhaps his 'Pietà'. We walk away. Walk towards the Ponte Vecchio with its sparkling gold, shining silver shops, past the Uffizi, the Piazza del Duomo, to the Brancacci Chapel. Stand silently before Masaccio's 'The Expulsion of Adam and Eve' and, in disbelief, 'St Peter healing the Sick with his Shadow'. Walk. Walk in silence. Walk until the sun tires.

She puts her arm through mine like a grown up woman.

river view
see clouds in ways
that change everything

Always Discordant

        pitch of loud thunder
    bedtime soon dreams of a dream
          in a stranger's house

An untidy B&B trembles under threat of a turbulent train that hurtles toward an old viaduct overhanging an ancient relative's house. Any loitering light dissolves into a slag of darkness.

A hollow, ill-fitting bedroom door shakes in time to bouts of tantrums. Sometimes it is deafening. Always discordant. Mock porcelain cups, saucers, even plates, jangle at soprano height. Unclaimed bedroom windows overlook a permanent alley. Crowded bins spill, reshaping an already closed-up wall. Divided women settle into their dream of a dream shape while love movements extend into a pool of exuberant colours that press close to a shared event.

Dissolved in rain, lampposts wave from top to bottom. Only when sight of it stops can thrush sounds flourish, goldfish glow their surface, goldthread lines lead sheep in a tame walk across their dream of a dream.

Beyond rain-touched taints of a moth flicker, fingers glide into growths of old softness, new tautness, tonight's speech. Here is where thought lines stop. Some part. Outside newly co-opted shape is ice blue. Music drips from an over-strung washing line.

Inside a maybe dream, globules of honey are covered in pollen
below zero   beyond their dream of a dream   not yet sound of day
In her sleep she is sure   In his, he is not.

          just a single path
      delves between two valleys
        slow flow of juices

Stanley Pelter

Glen Catacol

      a mile   of hot summits   more hills roast

Long into the trail. It meanders; follows rises, drops with dips, turns with the sweeping bends of a swollen, sometimes flooding, rock-pitted river. Underfoot the path is less than a shoe width. Lower down, sandstone is wider, grittier. Shapes of summer heat form much of its length. Stagnant water claims some hollows. Streams from Madadh Lounie, from Creag na h-lolaire, zigzag down. Close-by, land is transformed into bog. Moths, grass snakes, frogs, remnants of wild flowers, camouflage in swathes of earth browns. Spurts of dragonflies crisscross the path. Course marram grass, heathers, head high ferns, thistles thrive. Sound of a ground cuckoo feed into the river. Where giant plates of layered granite spread, churning roars pull free of froth foam. Redirect. Other sections feed soft feet to a precipice edge.

sudden sharp pain   subterranean swells rise   as resolve collapses

To look down is to wobble each wet footstep. Adrenalin surges into addictive moves forward. Y split river becomes indecision.

         water divide   stare at a parting   of ways

Tin colour, crag clad sky. Begin to cross. Turn back. Wearing sandals, with no map or compass, the path lost in a wilderness of ferns, this is a new scale, a new fear fix.
Dressed to contour this vast, irregular circle, an archetypal hiker approaches. From distance indeterminate, closer the appearance is hermaphroditic. Even closer, more ethereal, there is yet another seamless modification to that of an alter ego, Translucent, floating, her now supremely feminine shape, covered in white, rippling materials like she is one of Botticelli's 'Three Graces', glides through me. Turning, I feel touches of the lightest of winds before, near to transparent, she fades into disappearance.
Unknown miles yet to travel over Gleann Easan Biorach before we are able to subside into the calm mantra safety net of a semi-Shangri-la Loch Ranza. Only then decide to catch the bus.

near a crest   crossover point at which   one becomes two

insideoutside

sounds detach
empty birds disappear
and buttercups close

so i will wait for U in the garden ~ sit in the garden that has just been watered ~ waiting for a buttercup to close ~ a buttercup on the grass that waits to be cut ~ the grass just watered ~ in the garden just watered where I read ~ last of the sun not ready to go ~ from nowhere a fly ~ a nowhere fly on me ~ a still fly still sits on me ~ the fly from nowhere tickles ~ i look up ~ look up ~ something is up ~ look up for birds ~ fly nowhere ~ not on me ~ birds nowhere ~ sounds of birds somewhere ~ birds not here ~ bird sounds here ~ bird sounds there ~ sounds detach from birds ~ sounds of young oak tree leaves ~ sounds of young oak leaves wave ~ sound that is not bird sound ~ they are not here ~ they are somewhere ~ waiting to attach sounds ~ their sounds in the garden ~ in the enclosed garden ~ i sit here for U ~ alone with sounds scents of breeze ~ wait for U to come ~ enclosed by greens ~ the enclosed garden just watered ~ so many greens ~ so many enclosed by so many shapes ~ enclosed with so many spaces ~ spaces are shaped by waves ~ wavy shapes ~ U live in spaces of shapes ~ i in spaces ~ wavy spaces of insideoutside ~ insideoutside meet out ~ where i wait for U is not inside ~ i go inside to outside ~ wait for U in the garden just watered ~ inside has inside scents ~ outside has breeze ~ inside scents spread outside ~ breeze blows inside scents ~ the evening garden aromas ~ U will be drunk on aromas ~ sun ends day ~ i say 'yes' ~ i say 'yes' to inside ~ i say 'yes' to outside ~ so i will wait for U in the garden ~ sit in the garden that has just been watered.

wait in the garden
wait in the watered garden
wait wait wait for U

Dru Philippou

Dru Philippou was born on the island of Cyprus, raised in London and currently lives in northern New Mexico. She received her M. F. A. in Creative Writing from Naropa University. She writes haiku, tanka, haibun, tanka prose and book reviews for *Haibun Today*. An award winning poet, her work is widely published and anthologised. In her spare time, she hikes the wilderness areas of New Mexico.

Between Peaks

At the trailhead, wild raspberries and rose hip pods turn red among the deadfall. The wind sweeps in gusts through the upright silver lines of dead trees and living pines bearing fire scars. Aspen leaves release their raiment of rain higher up, and a gurgling stream slips down through rocks. I reach the edge of a meadow and startle two grouse into flight. The trail eventually disappears through thick tufts of short grass. I head straight up slope to the ridge and sit between Flag Mountain and Lobo Peak, not wanting to revisit either of them.

>   chasing its shadow
>   along the saddle
>   a bluebird

The Visitation

The deep red linen cloth is torn at spine and heel. Inside the cover, in fading ink, I read: London, 1935. Above the name, the last vestiges of a paper clip. I fan the pages, inhaling the musty odour, and slow down at the *Wyves Tale of Bathe*. Vertical pencil lines mark particular verses. An odd word or sentence is heavily underscored. Glancing aside, a 1970s clock slides onto the wall, the minute hand barely nudging. I turn to the back of the book and linger over the explanatory notes. In the proper names index, by Apollo, scribbled marginalia: "God of intellectual illumination." I close the book. Chaucer looms out of the leaf medallion.

> silent classroom
> a warm ha'penny
> in my pocket

> pale windowsill
> and withered stem
> of an early bloom

> chalk motes
> in sunlight
> aslant

Sýko

After we left the island for the big city, Mother and Father refused to talk about the past. Yet, there was a sense, Mother, you longed for the homeland. On market days, you often came home with a bag of figs. When done with housework, you'd sit on the porch peeling the violet-tinged fruit, then gaze into the melting shadows as if countless trees were bearing plump little globes. Cradling the bowl you'd whisper, *sýko, sýko*.

        stolen fig
      memory's shape
       in my hand

Learning English

shifting clouds
the changing colours
of a bougainvillea

Opening grandmother's handmade notebook at C, I find a carob pod and recall her story about John the Baptist subsisting on its fruit. At M, her favourite culinary herb, a sacred myrtle leaf. Certain of an olive leaf, I turn to O and imagine those maroon orbs bobbing in brine. At J, a sweet fragrance rises from the page; I see her gathering fresh sprigs, pockets stashed with jasmine.

notebook
vine tendrils link
the faded script

The Spinning Top

As a child cherishes a spiral shell or blue-eyed china doll for solace, I keep a wooden top and pump the handle until the circus comes to life: hoops and umbrellas twirl, a trapeze artist flies through the air. To hear the different tones, I vary the speed, glimpse the fortuneteller's turning card, and fill in visions of magicians pulling rabbits out of hats. Pumping the top faster and faster, the colours blur into a glare of white light until it loses momentum and wobbles in ever-widening circles, eventually tipping back into the silence.

    the Milky Way arms winding toward brightness

Richard S. Straw

Richard S. Straw copyedits technical documents on health and substance use, prepares bibliographic databases on the same topics, and has lived in or near Raleigh, North Carolina, since 1984. Before then, he lived and worked in central Ohio, where he taught freshman English composition at Ohio State University, edited technical papers for a trade journal, proofread for a digest of news from the former Soviet Union, and graduated from Ohio State University (BA in English, 1977; MA in English, 1980).

He has been interested in haiku, senryu, haiga, and haibun since 1966. In the late 1980s, he served as an editor of *Pine Needles*, a quarterly newsletter for the North Carolina Haiku Society (NCHS). In 1988, he compiled *late afternoon bum*, a trifold Haiku Canada Sheet. During most of the 1990s, he took a hiatus from haiku activities, but tried writing again in late 2000. He self-published in 2001 *A Hiker Sees His Shadow*, an eight-page chapbook dedicated to the memory of his dad. In 2005, he put together another trifold, mostly of his published haiku, and titled it *Opening a Window*. In 2006, he began sending work again to various haiku and haibun journal editors. In 2009, 35 of his published haibun were arranged in a 44-page, self-published chapbook, *The Longest Time*.

First Impressions

The two-storied brick building's still in use, facing west on the village's main street, about a block from an Indian-named river that every few years floods cornfields and the road going north. Little else is the same, however, in my childhood neighborhood and home, which was in a walk-up apartment above a soda shop. The meat locker, barbershop, and restaurant in the building's ground floor have all changed hands or closed altogether, their former owners gone elsewhere, some to the cemetery on the river's other shore.

The photographs at least haven't faded. In one snapshot taken half a century ago, cars are still angle-parked in tree shade in front of the restaurant's doorway where dad in his factory clothes carries my sister, wrapped in a blanket, in his arms. Another shows mom on the same sidewalk with my preschool sister and me as a toddler, all in our Sunday best. Indoor shots reveal a high-ceilinged living room with flower-patterned wallpaper, a playroom with Jack and Jill painted on a wall, and a kitchen with a wooden shelf shaped like a crescent moon with stairs.

Our parents often talked at meals about the past. One of their stories was about an elderly baby-sitter who roused the firemen across the street to run their hose up our apartment's stairwell to douse the curtains that caught fire above the gas stove. Another time, acting on a tip from the barber, our mom in her waitress uniform ran to find us on the nearby bridge, where my sister was urging me to jump into the greenish-brown river. One night in my bedroom alcove off the living room, where the soft light of the neon sign from the restaurant below filled the air with an undersea glow, I dreamed of fish swimming out of water, the first dream mom and dad ever remembered me telling them.

> faraway stars
> over a distant hometown
> autumn chill

Stone by Stone

After a late afternoon visit to dad's grave, I start heading south on Route 23, but exit at Norton and detour east a mile past a gun and tackle shop, a rifle range, and a country graveyard. Dad once said on our way to one of his fishing spots that the 19th-century occupants of that cemetery had been moved stone by stone to higher ground from their original resting places so that Delaware Dam could be built by the Army Corps of Engineers.

Just past a long bridge that crosses the Olentangy, which feeds the reservoir north of the dam, a dirt road that looks familiar slopes to the water. Dust rises as my van descends toward a mud-rutted boat ramp. On a day too hot for fishing, I park in a tree's shade by a clearing, the only vehicle in sight.

Using one of dad's 35-mm cameras and a new roll of black-and-white film, I take a dozen photos of the still water, the rocky outcrops in the bridge's shadow, the weeds and cattails, and a stone slab by the ramp. And I know as I frame it that it's the same slab where dad sat grinning with a just-lit cigarette dangling from his mouth more than 40 years ago. He was in a folding lawn chair, had caught a catfish, a tiny one, and was holding it up with his right hand for me to photograph with his Kodak Baby Brownie. Beneath the shadow of his fishing cap, his young eyes smile into the lens.

Before getting back in the van for the long drive home, I try to remember where the bait shop was that we'd stop to buy bread, Moon Pies, and small three or four gulp bottles of Nehi. For bait, we'd bury small hooks in Wonder Bread spitballs. Sometimes, though, dad bought a cup of slimy night crawlers that would squiggle and bleed when pierced. The savvy catfish and brim nibbled on the worms' wiggling exposed parts as our red-and-white bobbers occasionally slipped below the water's surface and floated eventually, weightlessly, toward us through the low sun's glare.

                dark shoreline
                one last cast
                with the wind

Perennials

I used to call the nursing center so my kids could get on the line to say, "Hi, Grandma!!! We love you!!!" They'd only met her once or twice. I showed them family photos of her when she was young. They'd tell her what they'd been doing in school and with their friends. They'd talk briefly so she wouldn't become wearied. "Sounds like fun!" she'd reply or would parrot their words in a tired voice. Sometimes, before I hung up, she'd tell me that she and dad were doing fine. But he had died in hospice care less than a week after they'd moved into the center.

After 50 years with multiple sclerosis, every nerve she has is scarred. And since dad's death, premature senility has taken her mind.

Mom belonged to a mystery of the month book club when I was a boy, so I sent her some used detective novels to read. They're still in their shipping box in her armoire though. I don't send her anything to read now, not even letters, unless I have school photos of the kids to share. And those I mail in a greeting card to a cousin who drives to the nursing center, opens the envelope, reads the message aloud for her, and shows her the photos before putting them in an album in her night table.

My kids and I don't call her anymore either, not even on her birthday, Mother's Day, or Christmas. She no longer can hold the receiver of a phone to her ear or carry on the simplest of conversations. The nursing staff spoon feed her and tell me that she's very quiet: "Just sleeps, eats, and stares ahead."

During her first winter there, mom told me she'd been studying "a large menacing goldfish" in the front lobby's aquarium. She said that most of the other fish in the tank had disappeared, except for one or two hiding in corners. She whispered, "I've always been a small fish watching and staying out of the way of larger fish."

long winter
in an untended flowerbed
tulip bulbs

Desert Places

In omnibus requiem quaesivi et nusquam inveni nisi in een Hoecken met een Böcken.

Thomas à Kempis

"Everywhere I have sought rest and found it nowhere, save in little nooks with little books." His monastery cell and lancet window reappear now on a second-hand bookstore's shelf, where I find him again remaindered, but translated afresh.

I trust and collect such personal jottings, especially those published anonymously or collected posthumously by friends. Steady correspondents; meditative diarists and fiction writers; reclusive poets, aphorists, and parable tellers; and especially this speaker of homilies to common brethren—all capture the small moments. The words are not short-sighted, despite their authors often being short-winded. Without them, there's no antidote to the daily bluster.

At home, going at a labyrinth walk's pace, I begin this updated version of the *Imitation*, penciling in light marginal notes and comparisons with its prior translations. My eyes close to visualize the words. My wristwatch ticks as I breathe air from the past.

mountaintop
I reach out to feel
clouds

Note: The Thomas à Kempis quotation is from an article by Vincent Scully that appeared in The Catholic Encyclopedia (New York: Robert Appleton Company, 1912, Volume XIV; http://www.newadvent.org/cathen/14661a.htm).

Whether Together or Apart

A bumblebee sits motionless for at least 10 minutes on our deck near the kitchen door. Ants go up to it tentatively. It moves slightly, turns around finally, with an adjustment of its left hind leg and a stretch of its wings, which had been folded back. Its furry yellow patch is square and contoured to the shape behind the head. One ant tugs a leg, stirring the bee to fly over thin brown grass.

> no one else home
> African violets
> strain for the light

People say they dream of me, but I don't remember dreaming much at all, let alone of them. Their dreams are very vivid and personal. Mine are usually flat and sketchy, hardly ever retold to myself or to others. What should I think and say when they share their detailed dreams of me? How can I hide my embarrassment and sense of failure?

> fishermen
> standing knee deep in waves
> a surfer paddles out

In the spot I use, a weed and a seedling grow in two cracks. I park between them and avoid stepping on them. Eventually, the landscaping crew will whack them, or the sun will dry them up. Nonetheless, today's rain should keep them green for a while.

> silent prayer
> the church's furnace
> kicks on

What was it I told myself last night before going to sleep? Just before the headlights dimmed against the wall, after the last neighbor pulled into the parking lot outside my window, I'd promised myself something that I can't remember now, even though with three cups of coffee drunk and a fourth one brewing on the hotplate. I haven't been able to remember anything lately unless I wrote it down.

> winter night
> losing track of my breath
> at a kitchen table

I remember November days as a teenager in Ohio. Slow-moving clouds shaded the leaf-covered courtyard during an afternoon study period, 11th grade. I had plans to do something after graduation, if I could wait that long. Now, having done something, I wish the anticipatory feeling would return. Sometimes, it almost does.

> monks loading hay
> a few bales snow-topped
> under a cross

Note: The title "Whether Together or Apart" alludes to Robert Frost's "The Tuft of Flowers" in Collected Poems, Prose, & Plays (New York: Library of America, 1995, pp. 30-31).

Bill Wyatt

Bill Kembō Wyatt was the first ordained British Zen monk.

Ordained in 1972 he has studied with various Japanese teachers, traveled to Shasta Abbey in California and spent time with Robert Aitken Roshi in Hawaii.

This book, *Gleanings from the Throssel's Nest* is a record of events in Bill's life, takes us from rescuing small animals from the terrors of the cottage cat, to close encounters with nuclear reactors and the haunting sounds of Northumberland pipes. Through the poems we are offered a microcosm of the everyday world. Bill is a prolific and widely respected writer of haiku. Written through the winter and autumn months the book takes impermanence as its main theme and explores this through Bill's experiences of monastic life, retreats, celebrations and love in haiku, tanka and renku form. The book is both a physical and metaphysical journey filled with vibrancy, humor and reality. With his latest collection, Bill Wyatt gives us a glimpse of a life lived with zen.

It is one of those rare books where the whole is greater than the sum of the parts.

His previous poetry was published by both Penguin and Fontana, and he remained an active and passionate man till his death in late May, 2016.

Homeless in the Universe

>Carrying this useless baggage
>eternity merges in an endless flow
>Clouds scatter at their leisure
>seagulls call out in earnest
>In a dream I return
>to the temple where I first
>heard wind bells chiming
>in the summer breeze

I'm three days into the retreat. Returning from the hall, walking up the stairs, gurgling sound in my throat. I cough up a mouthful of blood! Don't panic, keep calm. I feel OK and settle down. Same thing happens next morning after meditation.

>Blown by karmic winds
>here and there–I stand alone
>gazing at infinity

One of the monks, concerned, whisks me off to Hexham A&E. Lots of tests, full m.o.t. The doctor and nurses very thorough. Finally an X-ray. In the next cubicle, an old fellow has been brought in from a nearby nursing home. We cannot see each other because of the curtain dividing us. I try chatting to him. Further down the corridor, an old lady is crying out, Help me, help me. I want to help them, but I'm wired up to machines.

>Mind a silent flower
>something wanting to cry out–
>a road beyond the sky

The old lady sails past me on a trolley for an X-ray. She had been found, collapsed, in the High Street. She's crying and moaning. I feel helpless. The nurses check up on me every half hour or so, blood tests, blood pressure, E.C.G.s etc. After a couple of hours, I hear the doctor discussing my case with the nurses: Looks from the X-ray like he's got a spot on the upper left lung, looks like cancer.

-After Ikkyū-

> In a dream breaking all the precepts—I won't die and I won't
> go away—so don't ask me—
> poetry's bullshit!

Eventually the doctor turns up. He mentions the spot on my lung and says that I should return home and get it checked. As they didn't have facilities for doing the scan, he suggested that I contact my own doctor as soon as possible. I recollect a poem written earlier in the year, thinking it would make a fine "death" haiku—

> Wandering down the years
> arriving at now—sheep bones
> bleached by the wind

The monk drives me back to the monastery. We are both starving, no food since breakfast. Everyone else had eaten earlier, so we heat up some left-overs in the micro-wave oven, which goes down a treat. Suddenly it's time for late afternoon meditation. Never sit on a full stomach! My tummy rumbles, sounding like an earthquake. I apologise to the girl sitting next to me, saying sorry about the noise, it's not as nice as the birds singing outside. She laughs.

> Flying to the edge
> of space—swifts sing out
> their homecoming song
>
> Trying to part the grass
> and see the wind—I stop
> and laugh at the passing clouds

Next day goes OK and I attend the Festival for Achalanatha Bodhisattva. Most of the work periods I spend in the kitchen, preparing vegetables for the monks and lay people. After a talk by one of the monks, I feel that gurgling sensation again.

> Coughing up blood
> and out of touch with the world
> I bow to Buddha

I make the decision to cut short the retreat. The monks agree and I book up a train and return home, not looking forward to the 8 hour journey. But all goes well, with no further incidents. Next day, check out with my local doctor, which is followed up over a period of 3 weeks with visits to Hastings and Brighton hospitals with further X-rays, tests and cat scans.

> With nowhere to dwell
> all dharmas are created—
> growing old and weary
> I watch the birdless flight
> of departing swifts

After seeing the surgeon at Guy's Hospital, it's decided that an operation is needed. I'm admitted and on the next day the op is performed. Out for the count for 4 hours. Waking up to find a chest drain going through the tube, leading into a bottle, stuck in my side. It monitors air leaks and fluid from the lungs. I have to walk around with it. A friend has loaned me a "Walkman", so I listen to CDs of Jack Kerouac, Gary Snyder, Charlie Mingus—

> Goodbye Pork Pie Hat
> on the thoracic ward—the swish
> of draining bottles

> After his lung op
> the old monk feels like he's been
> kicked by a mule

The pain is intense. During the night I self-administer morphine from a bottle attached to a needle in my arm. It brings relief, but I have barely slept for 3 nights. So I keep hitting the button.

> Not getting any wiser
> the old monk on a morphine high
> chatting to the clouds

At one stage I slip into a series of dreams and drift through alternative universes. A night of déjà vu. The nurse gives me an oxygen nebulizer, as I might have difficulty breathing. The shoes under my bed turn into a dog, the night nurse becomes a black angel, comforting me. Meanwhile, during all this, moans and cries coming from other beds as the pain relief nurses make their rounds.

> Listening to Charlie Parker–
> Bird looked like Buddha
> on his death bed–gazing out
> at the setting sun

After a couple of days, the surgeon visits me and says that after the vats wedge resection op there was no evidence of malignancy on the frozen section and that I was making a good post op recovery. So I can go home in a couple of days' time.

> Moon a distant flame
> crossing the sea–don't blame clouds
> for laughing at me

The Early Days of Throssel Hole Priory

Back in 1972, having become fed up with the world (or so I thought at that time), a unique opportunity arose. The previous year I had attended a sesshin at Purley, Croydon, Surrey. I had gotten wind of an English Zen Teacher, who had studied and practised Soto Zen in Japan. She had gone to America where she established a Zen training monastery. As England was her native land, the Rev. Master Jiyu Kennett came back over here in 1971, to conduct a couple of retreats. I was fortunate enough to catch the tail end of the retreat. I became so impressed with her that I undertook lay ordination, receiving the name of Zengetsu Kembō (which translated into English came across as *the moon of zen shining over the cliffs*). Rev. Master Jiyu returned to America, vowing to come back the following year. She was soon followed by an Enqlishman, whom she ordained as a monk. He came back to England as Rev. Daiji Strathern in 1972.

I met up with him and he told me that he had come into an inheritance, and was about to purchase an old farm in Northumberland, with the view of turning it into a monastery. I was working as a gardener at the time, and jumped at the chance of going up to Northumberland with him.

> Northumberland pipes
> welcome me–memories return
> with the fading light

Throssel Hole Farm (its name being taken from the throstle, or song thrush, which nested in the eaves, now an endangered species), had been taken over by a bunch of hippies and was run as a commune. When we arrived, the farm and surroundings were in a bad state of repair. We spent a couple of months doing the place up, painting and decorating the property in anticipation of the Rev. Master Jiyu's arrival. A lot of hard work went into preparing the old farmhouse. Though it was still very basic, it became liveable.

> Walking up the hill—
> but no longer a burden
> the clouds on my back

Rev. Master Jiyu arrived with monks from Shasta Abbey, California. Four sesshins were conducted during that summer, and on the first one, I undertook ordination as a junior monk. During the summer period I was given the opportunity to become Tenzo (Chief Cook), a responsibility from which I shuddered. I had never cooked before, apart from the occasional vegetable curry. The cooking was basic, as we only had an aga and limited budget for food. During this period I acquired a reputation for steamed puddings and custard! Ideal for the Northumberland climate. Another speciality being 'toad in the hole' and scotch eggs, made from peanuts, flour and herbs. We survived.

> Remembering that
> full moon haiku—nearly
> burnt the porridge!

Throssel Hole Priory, as it was then called, became the first and still is the only Zen monastery in England. Looking back, I can only say that this was a wonderful opportunity to engage with a long line of Zen ancestors, and a rare chance to encounter the Buddha's teachings.

> A face appears
> through the zendo window—
> full moon of autumn

At the end of the summer period, I undertook the ceremony of Nyudo-no-hai, whereby I became Chief Junior, whose task it was to lead all the other trainees. As well as being Tenzo, I was now responsible for everyone else. I was also given the job of Ino, Chief Disciplinarian, and further duties were added. But I survived and learnt that I had so much more to learn. Rev. Master Jiyu returned to Shasta, leaving the Rev. Mokurai (Silent Thunder), as prior, and me as his Chief Junior for the next year. Autumn drifted into winter.

> Snoring so loudly
> not even in harmony—
> monks in the zendo

I remember snow bound weeks, frozen toilets and wash bowls. One morning, awakening everyone for morning service and zazen, only to find that our zafus were covered by a couple of inches of snow that had drifted in through the eaves. I remember paraffin stoves to keep us warm at night, camp beds to sleep on.

> Morning service—
> the snow on my zafu
> was it a dream?

Winter drifted into spring, with the arrival of the Rev. Master Jiyu and three monks from Shasta Abbey. Four retreats were held during this period, and 35 people received lay ordination, whereby they affirmed their commitment to do good, cease from evil, and help others. On the first retreat, Rev. Mokurai completed his duties as prior with the ceremony of Jōdō, and I as Chief Junior, was examined in the ceremony of Hossen, 'Dharma Battle", whereby I had to answer (mondo) questions put to me from the other monks. I remember a great feeling of peace descending upon me as I answered their questions, yet feeling at the end of it, that there was still so much more to learn.

> After all those years
> plunging into the void—
> no moon, no finger

The summer retreats intensified. For the most part, my duties as Tenzo would occupy me for a good part of the day, and left me out of the talks and lectures given by Rev. Master Jiyu, there were however occasions when she would let me sit in on talks given to the senior monks, and I no longer felt left out It was very intense during this period, and I remember one of the lay people coming up to me saying that my eyes were like spinning tops and how could I keep up with the pressure?

By now, training no longer seemed like a chore, and I would not become disconcerted as the work load increased. The more difficult it seemed, the more I would respond positively. It was a time when I thrived on what would normally be described as stress. I learnt that ultimately there is nothing that could harm me, save my own delusive thinking.

>What's it all about?
>samsara and nirvana
>nothing but snowflakes

I was taken aback, when the Rev. Master Jiyu said that I was ready for transmission. Of course, I had read about it, but only vague hints, shelved in mystery. This would put me in direct line with all our ancestors, going right back to Shakyamuni Buddha. I felt that I was not ready for it, but as Rev. Master Jiyu explained, transmission only occurs when the teacher has acknowledged that the trainee has changed and wants to do something about his or herself. Transmission was not the end, but rather the true beginning of training.

>Early autumn frost–
>a woodpecker, pecking holes
>in eternity

I will be forever indebted to Rev. Master Jiyu for having that faith in me, a faith that I always lacked. Rev. Master Jiyu invited me out to America, and I took up a year's further study and practise at Shasta Abbey. But, after a while, ultimately, on my own decision, I decided to return to lay life as a gardener back in England.

>Afternoon zazen–
>late autumn snow turns to rain–
>this dream within a dream

I moved to Bexhill on the Sussex coast, working as a hospital gardener for a couple of years. All the while remembering the advice that Rev, Master Jiyu had given me, that if nothing else, meditation would give you peace of mind, but only if you kept it up.

I attended a couple of retreats in the early 1980s at Throssel, but due to misunderstandings and karmic circumstances I was not to return again for another 18 years.

By 1996, Rev. Master Jiyu had passed away, unbeknown to me. I was not to find out until a couple of years later. Throssel Hole had now become an Abbey, with priories scattered throughout the country. The monastery has increased in size, with new buildings and 50 or so monks, both male and female.

> Morning zazen–
> rain on rooftops, in one ear
> and out the other

Having attended 2 week-long retreats in 1998, I made the decision to return as a lay person for a period of 6 months in the following year. Out of respect, and in memory of my teacher, I offered my services to help out in the Rains Retreat of January and February 2000. I worked in the kitchen, preparing and cooking food for the monks and community. When not doing this, the time would be spent in meditation. I made lots of new friends, and no longer felt homeless, as I had for the previous few years.

> Night of endless rain–
> how refreshing the sound
> of the zazen bell

Ancestral Voices on Kos

Arrived at appartments in the early hours of morning. A meteor flew across the balcony and gone in the blink of an eye. Sky glittering with stars, Orion my neighbour. Distant hoot of an owl—

> Waiting for the moon—
> clouds drift by like orphans
> banishing my sorrows

Up early for breakfast. Then a short walk across the main street of Tigaki, once a small fishing-village. Flamingoes winter here in small numbers. Sometimes white storks and pelicans drop by, on their way to Northern Turkey and Eastern Europe. October, the month when the festival of Thesmophorica is celebrated. Held in honour of Demeter and only attended by women, to assure the fertility of the fields.

Back at Tigaki for the evening meal . . .

> Impromptu dance
> to Zorba the Greek—waiters
> spring into autumn

> October's full moon—
> from the taverna, 'doo-wop'
> mingles with cicadas

Mosquitos a problem. After an evening of wining and dining, I'm in no fit state to combat them. Defenceless, when I retire to bed, straight into the arms of sleep and Demeter. In the morning wake up to many lovebites—

> As an offering
> to this floating world—my blood
> accepts the mosquito

Just outside the hotel found several plants new to me. On looking them up, turned out to be Bladder Hibiscus. Pale, large, solitary flowers, yellow with dark purple centres, opening only in early morning. Native of Asia.

Bill Wyatt

> Just like an autumn leaf that has lived its day—
> soft breeze whirls me away
> after Theocritus

Theocritus, the Sicilian and bucolic poet lived on Kos for a while. He wrote one of his most ambitious poems here, the idyll knows as The Harvest Home, in which he describes the Koan countryside, with its singing linnets and larks, bees that loitered above fresh flowing streams. When "elms and black poplars make a shady place/ its green freshness roofed in by unkempt leaves"

> Cicadas welcome
> in the evening twilight—
> ancestral voices

Cicada Immortals part 2

I arose earlier than the others and made my way up to the old Genoese Castle in the morning light. Two Rock Nuthatches obliged after some waiting, with a dancing display. The Little Owl put in an appearance, looking more than bleary.

> 'Bringing news of spring
> the nightingales love song'
> Sappho

After breakfast we drove out to Scala Kalonis. Walked along a dried out salt pan area, managed to see two much wanted birds—Whiskered Tern and Olivaceous Warbler. Plants were few and far between. We later found that the winter had been one of the driest on record.

> A barefoot girl
> the wind lifting her skirt
> made me forget about myself

Just outside of Molivos, we stopped and found growing by the roadside a clump of Syrian Thistle (Notobasis syriaca). The purple-flushed Syrian Thistle, despite its wonderful colouring, comes from a Greek derogatory word meaning "donkey thistle".

> It must have been
> your lips that sent
> your friends away

Plenty of Isabelline Wheatears, their Latin name, Oenanthe, meaning a bird that appears at the same time as the first shoot of the vine.

> Down by the sea shore
> all the world was shining—
> just for you and me

It was getting late, so we headed for our "breakfast bar", no time for a wash and clean up. They were laying on the satellite Cup Final for us. Exciting match, especially as we had a "stuffed" eagle staring at us from the television set. The match 3-3 after extra time. Crystal Palace leading Manchester United 3-2 with 8 minutes of normal time left. Replay next Thursday, the day we get back home.

We finished up back at our digs with wine and listened to some blues and jazz tapes. One of those nights when dreams become immortal. Remembering Plato's words, just as I fell asleep, "Some say nine muses—but I count again, behold the tenth, Sappho of Lesbos."

> In the meadow
> horses graze on
> the flowers of spring
> *Lesbos, May 1990*

Dragon's Breath and Mountain Madness

We eventually arrived at the Pyrenees to be greeted by Red and Black Kites and Griffon Vultures. Elated we found a nearby campsite and brewed up. It started to rain, not heavy, so we set off for a local restaurant and had an evening meal. Weather beginning to break up, dragon's breath rolling down mountains.

After breakfast we walked round some of the Cirque de Gavarnie. Very dramatic treading along wood edges, finding endemic plants including Dragonmouth, Pyrenian, Columbine, P. Squill, P. Cranesbill, P. Valerian and P. Saxifrage. Also a snowfinch, not more than ten feet away, happily eating seeds. Maybe a Golden Eagle too, high up in the sky. After a wet evening, we broke camp and pushed on through the French and then the Spanish Pyrenees, rain following us as we climbed up and then down the mountains. Dragon's breath not far behind us.

Once we reached the plains, clouds disappeared, opening up into vast clear blue sky. We stopped off for Spanish bread. I'm sure that by then we were all suffering from mountain madness. Too many late nights of endless rain and that French Old Lady Gin, leading to big bluesy Jack Kerouac hangovers.

> Mountain madness—
> soaking wet, like tattered rags
> laughing at ourselves

Steve spoke to the shop owner, in English, "Hello mate, a loaf of bread please." This had brother Tony in stitches, and I had to help him out of the shop, before he finally flipped. It turned out that Steve had thought the shop owner was speaking to him in English.

We drove off and stopped again for cheese and bread, Tony in fits whenever we mentioned the bread shop. As we ate, relaxing in the heat, a quail walked indifferently past us.

> Sweltering sun
> "wet my lips"—the quail seems to
> have the right take on things

After further adventures in Spain, only to be rained off, we made our way back to Gavarnie and found an ideal campsite on a farm. Rain holding back as we put up our tents. We explored the countryside, finding in the meadow above us five different orchids, Tunic Flower, and Carthusian Pink. We had a cook up, tin of beans, lentils and sausages, onions, garlic and carrots. Just as we finished the meal, the sky opened up and off to bed. Woke up around 4 a. m. to find that the tent was awash with water. Tony soaked right through in his sleeping bag. I wasn't too badly off, as I had a camp bed, which kept me off the wet floor. But rain coming in through the sides of the tent. Tony disappeared into Steve's car until daylight.

So, enough was enough and we broke camp in the morning. In dismal rain we headed back for the coast and England. Followed by dragon's breath, always on our tail.

> Dragon's breath
> covering the morning sun—
> muffling birdsongs

Section III:
Excerpts from Japanese Books

Travel Diaries and the Development of
Modern Haibun

Awesome Nightfall:
The Life and Times of Saigyō

The Journal of Sōchō

Traces Of Dreams: Landscape, Cultural Memory,
and the Poetry of Bashō

Dew On The Grass:
The Life and Poetry of Kobayashi Issa

A Translation of Kurita Chodō's
Sketches of Moonlit Nights

Masaoka Shiki: His Life and Works

Literary Creations on the Road–Women's
Travel Diaries in Early Modern Japan

Slocan Diary

Travel Diaries and the Development of Modern Haibun
By Rich Youmans

> "Among diaries of the road, those of Ki, Chomei, and the Nun Abutsu are consummate works, bringing to fulfillment the feelings of the journey . . . [T]he scenes of so many places linger in the heart, and the aching sorrow of a mountain shelter or a hut in a moor become seeds for words and a way to become intimate with wind and clouds."[1]

This passage from Bashō's *Oi no Kobumi* (*Knapsack Notes*) provides entry into one of Japan's earliest literary genres, diary literature (*nikki*), which reaches back over a thousand years. As the renowned scholar and translator Donald Keene has noted, "only in Japan did the diary acquire the status of a literary genre comparable in importance to novels, essays, and other branches of literature." In many of these works, the prose was punctuated by poems–typically by classical waka, the forebear to the modern tanka (5 lines of 31 sounds total), adding new dimensions to the narrative. In total, the diaries offered portals into the lives of the Japanese over centuries, from aristocrats and courtesans to religious pilgrims.

An important segment of this genre is the *kikobun*–the "diaries of the road," as Bashō referred to them. Rooted in the travel poems of the *Man'yoshu* (*Collection of Ten Thousand Leaves*, the classic eighth century Japanese poetry anthology), these diaries depicted both the pleasures and the hardships of the road, and also commemorated the country's culturally and poetically significant landmarks. They became especially popular following the rise of the shogunate in the 12th century, and in the hands of the 17th century poet Matsuo Bashō they became works of literary art. To read and study them today, and to understand their place in the history of diary literature, is to become acquainted with the seeds of the modern haibun.

A Starting Point: *Tosa Nikki* and Court Diaries

Poetic diaries date back at least to the Heian era (794 to 1185 AD), and the majority were actually written by court ladies about their day-to-day lives. Among the earliest of these diaries is *Kagero Nikki* (typically translated as The Gossamer Years), a three-volume work by a woman known only as the mother of Michitsuna, her son by a highborn statesman. A self-portrait of the author's life over the course of 20 years (approximately 954 to 974), the diary describes with often brutal honesty the bitterness she felt over her husband's many paramours, as well as her despair at being trapped in a lonely life. It is widely considered to have begun a "golden age" of court diaries that continued for several hundred years.

However, not all diaries concentrated on daily court activities. Some focused on travels beyond the court, as exemplified by the oldest surviving diary in the Japanese language: the famed *Tosa Nikki* (*The Tosa Diary*) by Ki no Tsurayuki, the same "Ki" referenced by Bashō. *Tosa Nikki* records the author's return journey in the years 934 to 935 to Japan's then capital, Heian-kyo (now modern-day Kyoto), after he spent several years as governor of the province of Tosa on the island of Shikoku. It is written from the vantage point of a young woman in the entourage, a persona that Tsurayuki might have adopted in order to explain his use of Japanese script (*kana*), which was known as "women's writing" (as opposed to the language of men, Chinese). As a travel journal, the *Tosa Diary* is not perfect: the narrator often ignores passing scenery and even gets some place names incorrect. Such lapses can be forgiven, though, since Tsurayuki's main reason for writing the diary was seemingly not to record the details of a journey, but to honor the memory of his daughter, whose death is referenced throughout the diary—most poignantly in the work's final poem:

> though born here,
> she has not returned with us;
> how sad now, to see
> the little pine trees
> that have grown in my garden

Another Heian-era diary worthy of note—and one of the earliest examples of *both* court and travel literature—is *Sarashina Nikki* (*The Sarashina Diary*). As with *Kagero Nikki*, the birth name of the author has been lost to history. Generally known as "Sugaware Takasue's daughter" or "Lady Sarashina," she wrote the book later in life, and at times it reads more like a memoir than a diary. It begins when she is around 12 or 13 (circa 1021) and covers a wide span: the young girl's trip from her native province of Kazusa to the capital city, Heian-kyo; her time as a court attendant; her marriage; and various religious pilgrimages. It ends when the author is in her fifties (1059). By then, her husband has passed away and she lives alone and lonely, her days "wasted in weeping." Many scholars have commented that her life was one of shyness, isolation, and dreaminess, with her youthful days spent obsessively reading and thinking about the fictions of the day (especially *The Tale of Genji*). As the author herself notes, "I . . . dwelt in the romances from morning to night, and as long as I was awake."[2]

Sarashina Nikki is also renowned for its vivid descriptions of the author's travels, beginning with her trip to Heian-kyo. She presents small portraits of the landscape she and her family cross (she memorably refers to snow-capped Mount Fuji as someone wearing "a white veil over a violet-blue gown") and the villagers they encounter along the way, some of whom recount local tales. She periodically notes how frightening it could all seem—an unsurprising sentiment, given her young age—and especially so in the mountains, where she and her family seem to be traveling on clouds. Later in the diary, after she has left behind the "fancies" of her youth and spends more time in religious devotions, she recounts various pilgrimages—including one to Ishiyama Temple, where, ironically, Murasaki Shikibu allegedly began writing *The Tale of Genji*. These travel accounts have greatly contributed to the diary's status as one of the major works of nikki literature.

The Growth of Kikobun

As legislative and judicial power transferred to the Kamakura shogunate in the late 12th century, travel became increasingly frequent between Kamakura and the Emperor's court in Heian-kyo. As Haruo

Shirane points out in his book *Traditional Japanese Literature: An Anthology, Beginnings to 1600*, this set the stage for an "unprecedented" rise in kikobun that lasted through the the end of the Kamakura period in 1333 and into the Muromachi era (1336 to 1573)[3]:

> Travel [appeared] as a literary topic in every major genre of the time, from military chronicles to anecdotes, diaries, classical poetry, linked verse, and [noh] drama . . . authors who recorded their journeys viewed themselves within a history of travel poetry, which included *The Tales of Ise*, *The Tale of Genji*, and the poetry of Saigyō, which served as an inspiration for their journeys. [4]

The notable travel diaries that recorded this Heian-kyo/Kamakura trek include *Izayoi Nikki* (commonly translated as *Diary of the Sixteenth Night* or *Diary of the Waning Moon*) by the nun Abutsu (1221? to 1283), one of the trio of diarists referenced by Bashō in *Knapsack Notes*. A rather strong-willed woman, Abutsu led an eventful life: she served in the Imperial court as a teenager; suffered a disastrous love affair that led her to run away and take vows as a nun when she was 17; left the convent shortly afterward and had a son and daughter while in her twenties; married a renowned poet, Fujiwara no Tameie, in her thirties; had two more sons, Jogaku and Tamesuke; and upon her husband's death took the name Abutsu-ni (nun Abutsu) along with the Buddhist tonsure. She also initiated an ultimately successful lawsuit against Tameie's son by an earlier wife to protect what she felt was Tamesuke's rightful inheritance. In so doing, she ignited fierce rivalries within the Mikohidari house—a major poetic family of that time, of which her husband had been a member—and started, as the scholar Steven Carter put it, "one of the longest and most all-encompassing literary disputes in world history."[5]

Abutsu's journey to Kamakura to argue that lawsuit lies at the heart of *Izayoi Nikki*, even though the travel account itself takes up only a portion of the book (which also includes family correspondence and a final long poem of 151 verses). Still, the work has become a minor classic among travel diaries and is among the most widely read works of the Kamakura era, even though scholars rate her earlier diary about her teenage years, *Utatane (Fitful Slumbers)* as more inviting and direct. *Izayoi Nikki* conveys Abutsu's dynamic personality and also serves as a historical exhibit of its time, especially in its emphasis on wordplay and puns. Its poems also reflect how imitative Japanese verse overall had become by then, dominated by literary allusions and the strictures of families with long poetic traditions (like the Mikohidari house). Similar to feudal overlords, these families portrayed themselves as the country's only true literary heirs[6]—a belief that was as much at the heart of Abutsu's lawsuit as her son's inheritance.

Another tradition exemplified in *Izayoi Nikki* is the reverence toward sacred shines and to landmarks of poetic or cultural significance; of the 55 poems in the travel section of the diary, 49 are about sites that had been memorialized previously in poems. [7] These sites—*utamakura*—served to connect travelers with the past, to honor that cultural memory, and to pass along that memory as part of a continuous narrative. For instance, upon arriving at the Fuwa barrier, Abutsu composed this poem:

> The cracked eaves of
> the Fuwa barrier house . . .
> how the drizzle
> and the moonlight
> must leak through

Located near Sekigahara in what is now Gifu Prefecture, the Fuwa barrier had once been one of three central checkpoints in Japan before being abandoned in the late eighth century. Abutsu's poem recalls a similar one written by Fujiwara Yoshitsune (1169 to 1206) and published in the *Shinkokinshu*, the eighth anthology of waka poetry compiled by the Imperial court: "The eaves of /the abandoned guardhouse/ at Fuwa barrier/have gone to ruin–/ only autumn wind." By alluding to Fujiwara's poem and recognizing a landmark of significance, Abutsu's waka served as a "link in a chain of poetic and literary transmission," as Haruo Shirane writes in *Early Modern Japanese Literature: An Anthology, 1600-1900*:

The interest of travel literature, at least in the Anglo-European tradition, generally lies in the unknown—new worlds, new knowledge, new perspectives, new experiences. But for medieval waka and renga poets, the object of travel was to confirm what already existed, to reinforce the roots of cultural memory. By visiting utamakura, the poet-traveler hoped to relive the experience of his or her literary predecessors, to be moved to compose poetry on the same landscape, thereby joining his or her cultural forebears. [8]

This reverence toward utamakura can also be seen in the travel diaries of Sōgi (1421 to 1502), a Zen monk and renowned renga master. His two diaries—one about a trip in 1468 from Mount Tsukuba to the Shirakawa Barrier, the other a journey in 1480 to the island of Kyushu (which Sōgi referred to by its old name, Tsukushi)—contain many visits to famous poetic sites. Even though a majority of these sites were unexceptional and, in some cases, had fallen into disrepair and ruin, the past associations still held sway. In his book *Travelers of a Hundred Ages: The Japanese as Revealed Through 1,000 Years of Diaries*, Donald Keene notes that Sōgi "never questioned the importance of visiting the various utamakura":

> Any landscape, no matter how ordinary or even unattractive, was redeemed in his eyes, providing someone had composed a poem about it . . . Sometimes there was uncertainty concerning the exact location of a particular place that was known from the old poems. Several different places, none of them impressive, had been identified as the site of the vanished Barrier of Shirakawa, but this did not bother Sōgi when he set out. He was not an archaeologist but a poet . . . as long as he supposed that he was at an original site, that was quite sufficient. [9]

Upon arriving at the Barrier's neglected ruins, Sōgi wrote the following:

"Moss served for its eaves, and maples made its fence, and in place of sacred streamers, ivy hung before the altar. At the thought that now only cold winds came to make offerings here, I could not check the tears of emotion. I imagined how deeply Kanemori and Nōin must have been moved and, although I hesitated to compose a poem that would be so much rubble when compared with their masterpieces, my thoughts were too many to keep to myself.

> There was mist and wind
> When I left the capital
> But today I looked:
> They had vanished from the sky,
> Dreamlike, and wintry rain fell.
>
> I do not expect
> The future to bring me fame,
> But I hope to keep
> Future poets from forgetting
> Shirakawa Barrier. [10]

Keene goes on to say that the whole point of that journey may have well been for Sōgi to write those two waka. Of course, Shirakawa Barrier was not forgotten; it continued to be visited by poets through the years, including Matsuo Bashō (1644 to 1694). By the early 17th century, classical linked verse (which had primarily been an aristocratic pursuit) had been surpassed in popularity by haikai no renga with its more playful (and often vulgar) approach. A master with his own school, Bashō often traveled throughout Japan as much for business as enlightenment, conducting renga sessions and gaining new disciples. From these wanderings emerged five travel journals that Keene has called "the summit of Japanese diary literature."[11] Just as Bashō is credited with transforming renga (as well as the hokku, a renga's opening verse) from something initially deemed as inelegant to a true poetic form, so did he transform diary prose, marking a new path that led to the modern haibun.

Bashō, Kikobun, and the Development of Modern Haibun

Unlike those written by others before him, Bashō's five travel journals–from *Nozarashi Kiko*, an account of his return to his native Ueno after his mother's death in 1683, to his masterpiece, *Oku no Hosomichi* (often translated as *Narrow Road to the Deep North*)–have the honed character of a man writing for posterity. That is especially true of *Oku no Hosomichi*, where Bashō's lapidary language–poetic prose, really–signaled a departure from the past. The trip to the northern country took place in 1689, and for the next five years Bashō sought to recount that trip with a new mode of expression. As Haruo Shirane points out,

> Bashō wrote haikai prose throughout his literary career, but it was not until around 1690, shortly after his noted journey to Mutsu, the Deep North (Tohoku), that he [Bashō] consciously strove to develop prose with a haikai spirit as a new literary genre and that he began to use the word *haibun*. Haibun in the broad sense existed before Bashō in the form of prefaces, headnotes to hokku, and short essays written by haiku masters ... Bashō's new notion of haibun, by contrast, is characterized by the prominent inclusion of "haikai words" (*haigon*), particularly vernacular Japanese (*zokugo*) and Chinese words (*kango*). [12]

Shirane goes on to note that Bashō's haikai-style kikobun "may best be understood as an attempt to reveal the different possibilities of haibun in the form of travel literature. The resulting fusion of vernacular Japanese, classical Japanese, and classical Chinese, with its parallel and contrastive couplet-like phrases, had a profound impact on the development of Japanese prose. Of particular interest is the close fusion between the prose and the poetry, a salient characteristic of haibun, in which the prose creates a dramatic context for many of the best hokku that Bashō wrote."[13]

Keene, too, remarked upon this fusion and its importance in Bashō's diaries even prior to *Oku no Hosomichi*. Keene points to the famous passage in *Nozarashi Kiko* where Bashō meets his brothers and sisters for the first time after their mother's death, a passage that ends with the haiku, "if taken in my hand/they would melt with my hot tears–/autumn frost." Various commentators have noted how the haiku no doubt compares autumn frost to the whiteness of the mother's hair (indeed, to the "frost" evident on all their heads), and how it vividly conveys the ephemerality of life. But Keene uses the passage as an example of just how prose and poetry relied on each other in Bashō's art, so that neither could be removed without damaging the other:

> It is not merely that the prose explains the circumstances of the poem, in the manner of the prefaces found in collections of waka. The haiku expresses Bashō's grief more compellingly than the prose, but the prose sets the scene, describing the sorrow of the brothers over their mother's death, their aging, and the difficulty they experience in trying to speak to each other. [14]

In addition to creating a new haikai-infused writing style, Bashō also sought to breathe life into the utamakura tradition. Bashō valued that tradition, as shown in *Oku no Hosomichi* when he reacts to the ancient Tsubo stone monument marking the site of Taga Castle: "Now, before this monument from a thousand years ago, I can see into the minds of the ancient people. This is the blessing of pilgrimage, the joy, the journey's aches forgotten, my eyes shimmering with tears." However, that heritage could also pose limitations: Confirming what already existed left little room for exploration. Peipei Qiu, the director of Asian studies at Vassar College in New York State, points out that in classical Japanese poetry,

> each poetic toponym or seasonal word (*kigo*) has its established essence (*hon'i*), which determines not only what but also how landscape should be portrayed. In addition, the canonical literary travel journals bear a predominately melancholy tone inherited from classical poetry . . . When Bashō aspired to develop a new type of travel journal in *haikai* style, he confronted the same

challenge *haikai* had faced when it reflourished in the early seventeenth century: in the shadows of tradition, Bashō had to re-present a classically defined landscape through a popular *haikai* vision and by using *haikai* language. [15]

As Qiu notes, Bashō accomplished this by re-casting himself as "reckless" (the term the poet applied to himself in *Oi no Kobumi*) and a "carefree wanderer," employing a lightness that was characteristic more of haikai than the conventional travel narratives of old. While mindful of the kikobun's traditions, Bashō strove to imbue new poetic associations and emotions to the locales he visited, and to capture not just historical significance but beauty—his celebrated description of the Matsushima islands, with their twisted pines and their interweaving, almost embracing topographical features, remains a classic. He also sought out not just time-honored utamakura locales, such as the Shirakawa Barrier or Matsushima, but also lesser sites, such as Sado Island, a home of political exiles; the latter, in fact, inspired one of his more famous haiku: "above the rough sea/surrounding Sado Island/the River of Heaven." Bashō once advised a disciple, "Do not seek to follow in the footsteps of the men of old; seek what they sought,"[16] and that dictum captures perfectly what Bashō hoped to accomplish through his own travels.

When Bashō traveled to the northern country, it was not simply to commemorate the memory of past poets or recount history, but to enrich and revitalize his own art. And in doing so, he developed a model for haibun and travel writing that others were invited to follow.

Diaries of the Road: Haikai Travel Writing Today

More than 300 years later, the haibun tradition has dwindled in Japan but ignited elsewhere throughout the world, particularly in the United States and Great Britain. However, while many haibun still revolve around travel (including those in the first English-language haibun chapbook, Robert Spiess's *Five Caribbean Haibun*, published in 1972), they tend to be short pieces, from a few hundred to a thousand words.

They take their inspiration from specific people and places encountered on a trip–episodes in a journey.

However, true "travel diaries"–the kikobun of old, narratives that weave individual episodes into a rich tapestry, often with varying styles of prose–are rare. Only a few haibun writers have attempted such extended accounts. They include Tom Lynch, whose *Rain Drips from the Trees: Haibun Along the Trans-Canadian Highway* (1992, privately published[17]) recounts a hitch-hiking trip that begins at a Pennsylvania roadside fruit stand and ends on the deck of the Vancouver Island Ferry, as the distant lights of Port Angelis appear. Another volume, *Met on the Road: A Transcontinental Haiku Journal* by William J. Higginson with Penny Harter (1993, Press Here), includes a diary of the couple's move from Scotch Plains, New Jersey, to Santa Fe, New Mexico. Both works feature some nice observations: Lynch's depiction of a bull elk, its rack glimmering in "mercury light" and its breath misting the darkness, and Higginson's description of the passing Illinois landscape as "corn fields, corn fields, and occasional fields of the deep green leafiness of soy."

But probably the earliest and best example of a true modern kikobun is *The Spring Journey to the Saxon Shore* by David Cobb (1997, Equinox Press[18]). As Cobb acknowledged in a 2013 essay, *The Spring Journey* "is a frank attempt to adapt the model of Bashō's *Narrow Road to the Deep North* and contextualise it into a contemporary British setting."[19] As such, it followed the traditional tenets, with many references to British utamakura that separate it from the previous English-language travel haibun. *Spring Journey* details a several-day bicycle trip that Cobb took across East Anglia, "from the 'lower part' of Essex (that is its north) for a cottage on the Norfolk coast." It doesn't just relate the brief encounters he has along the way, including those with a tea shop waitress, a half cousin recently widowed, and a child who asks him if he believes in heaven and hell. The book also plumbs local history, from historic sites (castles, churches, shrines, etc.) to poets, writers, witches, painters, kings, and revolutionaries. (In the village of Ixworth, not only does he remember a local poet, Robert Bloomfield, who "wrote in these parts an ode about smallpox," but he even has an imaginary conversation with him.)

Another exemplary work is *Stallion's Crag: Haiku and Haibun* by Ken Jones (2003, Iron Press). The title piece of this book (which also contains shorter haibun and individual haiku) is described by its publisher as a "6, 000 word haiku-studded prose poem (haibun) set in the wilds of Plynlimon in mid-Wales." Plynlimon (or, or in the original Welsh, Pumlumon) is the highest point of the Cambrian Mountains– the "sacred mountain of Wales," as Jones refers to it. (It is also the site of a cave where Jones, a Zen and Ch'an practitioner/teacher, spent years as a part-time hermit.) *Stallion's Crag* chronicles the author's wanderings in the Pumlumon range during his retreats there. "This bare landscape was once alive with *names*," he writes, "many signalling myths and stories–even histories and biography. They mapped a landscape of collective memory." Jones delves into this "collective memory" with a keen eye and a deep appreciation of the region's history, lore, and beauty, all mixed with the poet's own reflections. Take the following passage, which references Owain Glyndwr, the last native Welshman to hold the Prince of Wales title, who led the last Welsh independence movement in the early 1400s.

> The stallion of Stallion's Crag is Grey Fetlocks (Llwyd y Bacsiau), Glyndwr's great war horse. Galloping across the crag in one death-defying leap he delivered the hero from his pursuers.
>
> *In the falling light*
> *soft rain*
> *in rock hoof prints*
>
> I grope my way down back to the cave, the flickering candle lantern a small delight. My sleeping bag is already stretched out peacefully.
>
> What kind of night will it be? Sometimes the clouds clear from the mountain and I am moon-struck. Wide awake, I listen to my most-constant companions:

In floods of moonlight
enchanted stonechats
sing the night away[20]

Two other works worthy of note are *Water Shining Beyond the Fields: Haibun Travels Southeast Asia* by John Brandi (Tres Chicas Books, 2006) and *Border Lands: Travels in the Old Country* by Jim Kacian (Red Moon Press, 2006). *Water Shining Beyond the Fields* recounts three trips the author and his wife, Renée, took to southeastern Asia in successive autumns. The countries they visited–Cambodia (October into November, 2002), China (November, 2003), and Thailand (November into December, 2004)–come alive through Brandi's engaging details: He takes us to Cambodian wats (i.e., temple compounds) where families lay out picnics as pilgrims pass by; to backstreets in old Chinese villages, far from the region's more urban zones (where even a Wal-Mart now sits); to temples and shops of small Thai towns, where outdoor markets arise as the sun sets, and the streets fill with the tastes and aromas of local cuisine (lime leaf, jasmine rice, roasted taro, curries). Haiku punctuate the prose periodically, revealing (as Brandi describes in his introduction) "an unexpected flash, core, essence, of what the prose didn't quite capture or describe."[21]

In *Border Lands*, Kacian is asked by a friend (referred to as "Z") to bear witness at his father's funeral in the "old country," which is situated in the war-torn Balkans. The author begins by acknowledging his nervousness–"Only a fool or a saint or a media correspondent travels in a foreign land on the brink of war not his own"–then adds that "there are things which at times we must honor, beyond consideration of risk . . ." What follows is a captivating account of Kacian's trek, from the sublime (hikes into the mountains, the camaraderie of Z's friends and family) to the historical (remains of a Roman outpost, cenotaphs of an ascetic cult) to the sad and mournful:

> The crossing is even slower going back. We are told an airstrike took place just over the border last night, and the area remains unsafe. From up here on the ridge we can see the cratered valley. A few vehicles are left behind,

smoking, but all else is quiet. The driver asks around, and we agree to go on.

> after the bombing
> random flights
> of swallows[22]

As shown by the above examples, travel journals do surface from time to time. However, they generally compose a fraction of the haibun now being written. Which is a shame, since for those willing to invest the time in a true account of a journey–perhaps even to map out a destination that includes some modern-day utamakura–the rewards can be immense.

As Bashō and his forebears knew, such travels can serve as catalysts toward new forms of expression, new perceptions, even a revitalization of one's art. A long work such as the kikobun also enables writers to "flex" their writing muscles–to flesh out the characters they encounter, to introduce prose styles that modulate in tone and help the reader experience the rhythm of the journey. And since so much of travel contains moments of new perception, the inclusion of haiku offers a perfect way to record and honor them. To quote Brandi again from *Water Shining Beyond the Fields*, a haiku can serve as "a kind of imagistic, miniature, sixth-sense portrait of something not described in the prose; something unexpectedly essential that eye-ear-nose-taste-touch did not reveal."[23] Haiku help to crystallize those moments in a journey that stay with us, even if we sometimes don't know why.

In his essay "Potentials of Two Different Haibun Forms: Nikki and Kikobun," David Cobb noted how most haibun being written today were close to the Japanese nikki, or diary entries. "In musical terms," he wrote, "a *kikobun* may be rather like a *suite*, *nikki* like a *moment musicale*."[24] It's an apt comparison, and perhaps it can also be viewed as a call to action: to get beyond just "moments," no matter how beautiful, and create something larger, grander.

There are so many places that can "linger in the heart"; through haikai travel journals–the kikobun–they perhaps can linger a bit longer.

1. Translation from *Bashō's Journey: The Literary Prose of Matsuo Bashō*, translated and with an introduction by David Landis Barnhill; State University of New York Press, Albany, 2005. Page 30.

2. From *Diaries of Court Ladies of Old Japan*, translated by Annie Shepley Omori and Kochi Doi; Houghton Mifflin Company, Boston and New York, 1920. Page 21.

3. The three-year gap between the two eras was named the Kenmu (or Kemmu) Restoration, an ultimately unsuccessful effort by the emperor of that time, Go-Daigo, to end military rule and restore a civilian government.

4. From *Traditional Japanese Literature: An Anthology, Beginnings to 1600*, edited by Haruo Shirane; Columbia University Press, New York, 2007. Page 777.

5. From *Dictionary of Literary Biography, Volume 203: Medieval Japanese Writers*, edited by Steven D. Carter; The Gale Group, 1999. Page 6. "Abutsu-ni" biographical entry written by John R. Wallace, University of California, Berkeley.

6. Edwin O. Reischauer, "The *Izayoi Nikki* (1277-1280)," *Harvard Journal of Asiatic Studies*, Vol. 10, No. 3/4, December 1947. Page 261.

7. Ibid, page 271.

8. From *Early Modern Japanese Literature: An Anthology 1600-1900*, edited by Haruo Shirane; Columbia University Press, New York, 2008. Pages 99-100.

9. From *Travelers of a Hundred Ages: The Japanese as Revealed Through 1, 000 Years of Diaries* by Donald Keene; Henry Holt and Company Inc., New York, 1989. Pages 218, 220.

10. Ibid, page 221. Taira no Kenemori and Nōin were poets of the middle to late Heian era (Kenemori died around 990, Nōin around 1050). They were both on the list of "Thirty-six Immortals of Poetry" (*Sanjurokkasen*) compiled by poet/scholar Fujiwara Kinto (996-1075).

11. Ibid, page 11.

12. From *Early Modern Japanese Literature: An Anthology 1600-1900*, edited by Haruo Shirane; Columbia University Press, New York, 2008. Pages 98-99.

13. Ibid, page 101.

14. From *Travelers of a Hundred Ages: The Japanese as Revealed Through 1, 000 Years of Diaries* by Donald Keene; Henry Holt and Company Inc., New York, 1989. Pages 294-295.

15. From *Bashō and the Dao: The Zhuangzi and the Transformation of Haikai*, by Peipei Qiu; University of Hawai'I Press, Honolulu, 2005. Page 76

16. From *Travelers of a Hundred Ages: The Japanese as Revealed Through 1,000 Years of Diaries* by Donald Keene; Henry Holt and Company Inc., New York, 1989. Page 220.

17. The book was later reprinted in its entirety in *Journey to the Interior: American Versions of Haibun* (1998, Charles E. Tuttle Co., ed. Bruce Ross).

18. From *"Transmissions of Haibun"* by David Cobb, *Haibun Today*, Vol. 7, No. 3.

19. A revised *Spring Journey* can be found in David Cobb's book *Business in Eden* (Equinox Press, 2006).

20. From *Stallion's Crag: Haiku and Haibun* by Ken Jones; Iron Press, Northumberland, England, 2003. Pages 36-37.

21. From *Water Shining Beyond the Fields: Haibun Travels in Southeast Asia* by John Brandi; Tres Chicas Book, El Rito, New Mexico, 2006. Page 12.

22. From *Border Lands: Travels in the Old Country* by Jim Kacian; Red Moon Press, Winchester, Virginia, 2006. Page 54.

23. From *Water Shining Beyond the Fields: Haibun Travels in Southeast Asia* by John Brandi; Tres Chicas Book, El Rito, New Mexico, 2006. Page 12.

24. *"Potentials of Two Different Haibun Forms: Nikki and Kikobun"* by David Cobb, *Kyso Flash*, Issue 3, Spring 2015.

Awesome Nightfall:
The Life, Times, and Poetry of Saigyō
By William R. LaFleur

William R. LaFleur writes in his preface from *Awesome Nightfall: The Life, Times, and Poetry of Saigyō*:

"Free and easy wandering" designates an appealing way of life according to Chuang tzu, but it is, in fact, a path that few have entered either freely or easily. Saigyō's life was too difficult to be so designated, even though it included several extended journeys."

***

"Bashō, Japan's best-known poet, explicitly named Saigyō, who lived four centuries earlier, as the poet of the past to whom he was most indebted. And that debt is implicit in his writings, both prose and poetry. Yet there are real differences. There is something detectably modern in Bashō, whereas Saigyō's view of reality is clearly medieval." Saigyō himself prefaced many of his verses with prose introductions that located his writing in time, space, and occasion.

***

During the tenth lunar month of 1140, the twenty-three-year-old Norikiyo left the palace and became a monk. The dharma-name given him then was En'i (Level of Perfection), and some documents thereafter refer to him by this name. Although it appeared at a later point in his monastic life, the name Saigyō, meaning "Going West," came to be the popularly accepted appellation for this person, and it remains so today.

***

The following poem, written likely just before Norikiyo became a monk, oscillates interestingly between the future and the past.

> When facing crises,
> what will be gone completely are
> thoughts of their perfect beauty—
> that of blossoms known intimately
> in the sage emperor's palace.

The term *hakōya*, derived from the Chuang tzu, was a term for a hermit sage's refuge in mountains. In Norikiyo's day it had rather recently come to refer to the palace of the retired emperor.

***

During the first couple of years after being tonsured, Saigyō lived either on the periphery of the capital or within walking distance of it. We have poems from this period expressing worry that living on the Eastern Hills was not giving him the necessary distance from "the world." Then he went further—for instance, to Kurama, on mountains within two or three day's journey by foot from Heian. Since he left the court during the fall, it was probably during his first winter alone that he records the misery he had been feeling within the capital. He felt the impact of his decision physically.

> Having made my escape from a worldly way of life, I was in the interior of Kurama at a bamboo conduit, the water of which was frozen and not flowing. Hearing from someone that this would be the state of affairs until the arrival of spring, I wrote this poem:

> > It was bound to be:
> > my vow to be unattached
> > to seasons and such—
> > I, who by a frozen bamboo pipe
> > now wait for water, long for spring.

***

From the perspective of the capital, Kōya was very remote, and Saigyō employed this theme of remoteness as the opening line in a series of ten poems. He notes that he wrote them at Kōya and sent them to

Jakunen, a monk living at that time in Ohara. Jakunen sent ten of his own poems in response. Saigyō records that what he sees in this place differs greatly from what would be seen back in the city. Two of this set are:

> Deep in the mountains—
> sitting upright on moss
> used as a mat for himself,
> with not a care in the world—
> is a gibbering, chattering ape.

> Deep in the mountains—
> no song of birds close
> to what we knew at home,
> just the spine-tingling
> hoots of owls in the night.

In verses such as these, the poet accents the physical and social distance placed between himself and urban society.

A more rigorous practice of Buddhist regimens for both body and mind shows up in the multiple poems he wrote about being on Mount Omine, a site in that period for undergoing severe, often painful, disciplines. Saigyō hints at the rigors of Omine's routes in the following:

At a place called Ants' Crossing:

> Crack-of-morning
> climb from caves in thick
> bamboo grass beyond
> the mists: body now bending along
> stark rock forms at Ants' Crossing.

Some of Saigyō's splendid poems about the moon and the increasing clarity of his own mind seem to flow directly from the austerities undertaken at this point in his life.

On seeing the moon at the place called Shinsen on Mount Omine:

> Passage into dark
> mountains over which the moon
> presides so brilliantly . . .
> Not seeing it, I'd have missed
> this passage into my own past.

> So brilliant a moon
> up there that the clouds
> have sunk down
> into the valley, urged along
> by winds sweeping the peaks

A far more extensive kind of pilgrimage came next. At some point before he turned thirty Saigyō journeyed to Mutsu Province in the far northeast, no small undertaking at that time. It is estimated that if a person left the capital in the spring, he or she would reach that destination some time in autumn. This route, at least by the time Bashō retraced the footsteps of Saigyō, gradually became famous—in part because it was arduous. In winter it was cold.

***

> Boulder-encircled
> space, so far from everything
> that here I'm all alone:
> a place where none can view me
> but I can review all things.

The impulse to put distance between himself and the capital resulted in another journey, this time westward and on to the island of Shikoku. At age fifty-one he departed with a sense that he might never return. It had been exactly twenty-eight years since his tonsure. Before leaving the capital he wrote:

> Just as had always been so, I continued to go to the
> Kamo Shrine even after becoming a monk. Now at an
> advancing age, I was about to pilgrimage to Shikoku,

thinking that I may never return. So I made a night visit to this shrine on the tenth day of the tenth month of 1168. I wanted to present a votive request. But since I was wearing the clothes of a Buddhist monk and could not go inside the shrine, I requested someone to present it on my behalf. Through the trees the light of the moon was filtering softly, so that the atmosphere of the place was even more sacred than usual, and I was deeply moved. I wrote this:

> Awe is what fills me
> as my tears fall onto the sacred
> branch I here present:
> my feelings are of someone
> wondering if he'll ever return.

This journey was to result in very important poetry. Part of its purpose was to pay homage to two persons who, although now dead, had been important to Saigyō. The first was Retired Emperor Sutoku, the second person whose memory he wished to honor there was Kōkai, the early Japanese transmitter of esoteric or tantric Buddhism and the founder of Japan's Shingon School.

***

In two poems Saigyō makes reference to being at Ise, not Mount Kōya, when writing a poem for someone in the capital. He moved in 1180 when he was sixty-three years old. Saigyō had written:

> I grew tired of living on Mount Kōya and went to a mountain temple at a place called Futami in the vicinity of Ise. The sacred mountain of the great Shinto shrine there is referred to as the mountain traversed by sacred beings. Reflecting on the fact that the great goddess Amaterasu, who is worshiped at the imperial shrine in Ise, is a manifest expression of Dainichi Buddha, I composed the following:

> Following the paths
> the gods passed over, I seek
> their innermost place;
> up and up to the highest of all:
> peak where wind soughs through pines.

***

Saigyō rather brilliantly turns doctrine into a concretized image in his verse. He does so by noting how the branches or, perhaps, even the dangling stalks of early summer flowers of the sakaki tree, the variety of tree most sacred in Shinto, are literally pendant. They hang down from a base at the top of the tree. Saigyō wrote:

> Having gone to Ise, I worshipped at the great shrine.
>
> Adoration for
> the sacred sakaki tree—
> pendant branches
> with both gods and buddhas
> depending on each other.

***

The imagery of the following poem shows Saigyō's belief in Ise's capacity for both strength and clarity.

> Shrine pillar
> rooted firmly in the rocks;
> sun in the sky
> casting down a shaft of light
> never overcome by clouds.

It is, one may hope, not an intrusive interpretation to see in such a verse, an implicit contrast between what the poet saw as Ise's peaceful ambience and the strife, both secular and religious, in most places elsewhere in his day. Saigyō's poems composed about the astonishing beauty of the blossoms observed there are abundant in Saigyō's work.

While undertaking religious disciplines, I was in a place that had attractive blossoms:

> If my rapt gaze
> would not give rise to rumor
> and disgrace, I'd
> want to spend all spring fixed here,
> feasting my eyes on these flowers.

It is, I think, not wrong to view Saigyō's efforts to make sense of his passion for the beautiful phenomena of the natural world, no doubt epitomized for him by the blossoms at Yoshino, as one of the major intellectual and religious concerns of his life.

The Journal of Sōchō
By H. Mack Horton

Introduction to the Translation

The Journal of Sōchō (Sōchō shuki) was compiled from 1522 to 1527 by Saiokuken Sōchō (1448 to1532), the preeminent linked verse (renga) poet in Japan at the time. It depicts four major journeys between the Kyoto area and Suruga (now part of Shizuoka Prefecture), where Sōchō served as the poet laureate of the Imagawa daimyo house, as well as several shorter excursions and long stays at various hermitages. Much of Sōchō's time in and around the capital was spent at Daitokuji or other temples related to his spiritual master, the Zen prelate Ikkyū; in the east, he generally divided his time between lodgings in the Suruga capital and in his Brushwood Cottage (Saioku) in Mariko not far away. Sōchō's journal, which includes more than 600 verses in predominantly the 17-syllable hokku and 31-syllable waka genres, is one of the longest and most variegated and evocative literary works of Japan's late medieval period.

The journal was written during the Age of the Country at War (Sengoku jidai, 1467 to 1568), a century of unprecedented collision between warrior houses, social groups, and artistic genres. Renga masters, like Sōchō and his own teacher Sōgi, traveled between the capital, still Japan's cultural center, and the periphery, facilitating interaction and cultural borrowing as they linked verses into long renga sequences. In this, as in his travel writing, Sōchō was one of Bashō's vital antecedents.

Second Year of Daiei (1522)

Departure

In the fifth month of the second year of Daiei, I set out on a journey to the northland with an acquaintance from Echizen. Though Kaeruyama, the Mountain of Returning, reminded me that I could not expect to return home again, I pressed on past Utsunoyama mountain, and when I reached Sayo no nakayama, I composed this:

> Even though I hope
> I will pass this way again
> on my journey home,
> this is the hill of old age.
> Sayo no nakayama.

Kakegawa

Stayed at the residence of Yasuyoshi. A construction project is just now under way. The outer castle is about thirteen or fourteen hundred yards in circumference. Around it they have dug a moat and built earthworks, after the manner of the main compound. The ground here is hard as rock; they might as well have built of iron. There is also a moat between the main and outer compounds. The ramparts are so steep it is frightening to look over.

I composed this hokku at the castle:

> Summer rain—
> on cloud-covered cliffs,
> willow trees!

There is a lake to the south. With its tall cliffs and expanse of water, it is like the sea itself. One might call it "Dragon Pond." Another hokku here:

> The surface of the pond—
> clear cliffs like Suminoe
> by the springtime sea.

***

Hamamatsu

Spent two days with the commissioner of the Hamamatsu Estate, now Iio Zenshirō Noritsura. Then went by boat from Yamazaki in that estate past Inasa Inlet to the manor of Hamana Bitchūnokami, where we had a day of renga:

> Clear now over the water–
> the sky has dressed
> for the fifth-month rain.

Kachiyama

We crossed Honsaka and were guided to lodgings with the Saigō, then spent a day at Kachiyama, castle of Kumagai Echigonokami. We composed renga:

> Bead trees blossom
> in the clouds, though dust
> covers the slope below!

Lodgings with the Makino

Near Yawata, at lodgings at the residence of Makino Shirōzaemonnojō, in a field called Honnogahara, we had a day of renga:

> Grasses tall enough
> to touch a traveler's sleeve–
> a summer field!

Kariya

Fighting has been breaking out from time to time with no warning in this province, so we could not cross Yahagigawa river and the Eight Bridges. We went by boat to the castle of Mizuno Izuminokami in this province and lodged in Kariya one night.

Tokoname

Stayed a day at Mizuno Kisaburō's in Tokoname in Chita District, Owari Province. Minamoto Yoshitomo's tomb is located at a place called Noma.

Ise Senku at Yamada in Ise Province

We crossed to Ōminato harbor in Ise and proceeded to Yamada, where we visited Ise Shrine . . . Sōseki then left for Owari. Knowing it was likely to snow before long, I decided to set out for the north on the sixteenth. There has been fighting in this province beyond

Kumozugawa river and Anonotsu, making it difficult to get from place to place . . . We left Hirao when it was still dark. It began to rain in earnest at about nine o'clock in the morning . . . We were accompanied to the town by many people and palanquins from Moritaka. Anonotsu has been desolate for more than ten years, and nothing but ruins remains of its four or five thousand homes and temples. Stands of reeds and mugwort, no chickens or dogs, rare even to hear the cawing of a crow. The wind and rain at the time were terrifying.

Our escorts all returned home and no others arrived to meet us. We lost our way, and after wandering in the wrong direction we hired a local foot soldier on the advice of an acquaintance. The soldier took us two leagues to a place called Kubota. That night the party sent by Kajisai, equipped with palanquins and such, found us. I am amazed we saw the day through safely.

Stayed there one night and had a bath. On waking in the night:

> How bitter
> to set out at my age
> across the Suzuka Mountains—
> what is to become of me
> as I travel on my way?

Kameyama

As I feared, the road to Ōmi has been impassable since yesterday. Kajisai's castle at Kameyama is three leagues into the mountains. We stayed at the Jōjuin subtemple of the ritsuin Shinpukuji, three chō away. I was surprised by how clean and neat it was. Rested there more than ten days. Each day's pleasant company moved me deeply. There was a renga session:

> High, the headwaters
> of the eighty rapids.
> The sound of autumn.

This simply refers to the lines "the eighty rapids / of Suzuka River" . . .

***

Anonotsu

We were taken from Kajisai's to a thatched dwelling like a salting hut in a village outside Anonotsu. Stayed there the next day waiting for our escort from Miyahara Moritaka. At the urging of some people from Anonotsu, we composed some linked verse:

> When will they return?
> The pines know not, nor the white waves
> of the autumn sea.

These villagers are no doubt waiting for the time they can move back to Anonotsu.

I went out to the beach when evening fell. I could see into the far distance, and "the shore at the border of Ise and Owari" stood out bright and clear. As I lingered there, some young men gathered, bringing things on hand to eat and drink, as well as flutes and drums, and we made merry. I recalled the poem "neither cherry blossoms / nor colored foliage" and composed this in response to it:

> Here this evening
> cherry blossoms and colored foliage
> abound
> in the heart of one
> by the thatched-roof huts beside the bay!

Later that night they left. There I was, feeling "pillowed on the waves," when one of the youths returned from somewhere to ease my travel loneliness. After he left the next morning, I sent this poem:

> Of that unexpected,
> brief rest upon the reeds,
> touched then abandoned
> by the ceaseless waves,
> can no trace still linger?

Kumozugawa

On the first of the ninth month we left and went back to Anonotsu harbor, taking sake with us. Later we departed with regret and reached Kumozugawa river, where we were met by a mountain ascetic sent by Asakura Tarōzaemon Norikage. I read the letters he brought, and we then accompanied him to lodgings in Hirao. The next morning, I wrote a reply:

> What is the point
> of its being in Koshi,
>   one wonders, vexed.
> Today the name Returning Mountain
> means those of Suzuka instead!

Moritaka too got word of our stopping here, and he once more sent the day's escorts. On the second of the month we reached Yamada, and I recorded my old and bent wanderings of the last few days.

Saigyō Valley

After the twentieth of the same month, I visited Kenkokuji temple of the Inner Shrine at Ise. There it was decided that we should all go to Saigyō Valley, site of that great priest's ancient dwelling. We crossed Isuzu Mimosusogawa river downstream and walked along the narrow paths between the rice paddies of Yamada, pressing through the bush clover and pampas grass withered under a thin frost.

When we reached the grounds all was quite desolate. Mountain water brought in by a bamboo pipe, pine posts from the days of old, a fence of woven bamboo, a dozen or so nuns in tumbledown quarters, paper coverlets, stitched hempen garments, the smell of anise incense—I felt the past before my eyes and put into verse what arose in my breast:

> More poignant the sight
> than anything I had heard—
>   how moving, this dwelling,
> so redolent of the past,
> in which he renounced the world!

I wrote it on a pine fence post and went back to Kenkokuji.

***

Take

In the tenth month we left Yamada and stayed two or three days at Take. There was a renga session

> The tenth month—
> roof eaves thatched
> with colored foliage!

Hasedera

I made a pilgrimage to Hatsuse and stayed a day or two. An old acquaintance came to visit from the capital, and we spent the day chatting. After he left, I sent this after him:

> At Mount Hatsuse
> we talked until we heard
> the temple's vesper bell,
> bringing the past to life
> on a day never to be forgotten.

Tōnomine

I had an invitation from Tōnomine to observe a festival and so climbed the mountain. It was even more impressive than I had heard. Stayed at An'yōin. We composed renga. The hokku:

> A frost of damask,
> with leaves at branch tips
> woven into rich brocade!

Konparu Shichirō came late at night, and we invited temple boys and drank sake. Continued until dawn.

Nara and Takigi

The next day I visited Tachibanadera temple and lodged a night in Yagi, capital of Yamato Province . . . My hokku for a renga sequence:

> When is winter?
> At Wakakusa Mountain,
> springtime sun!

Then to Jison'in. Lodged there more than ten days. This renga hokku:

> They fall this morning—
> snow-blossoms in the garden,
> blown by a brisk wind.

At Rengein:

> Mingle and scatter!
> tempest-tossed snow-blossoms
> and colored foliage.

A pilgrimage to the Great Buddha, then up to Takigi in Yamashiro . . . A few cups of sake at a temple building at Hannyaji before setting out. On the slope I went to get out of my palanquin and landed flat on my backside. Whereupon:

> Breaking the cane
> on which he so long relied,
> the old warrior
> with no lookout to the rear
> carelessly took a tumble.

We finally made our way to Shūon'an in Takigi.

***

Year's End

I hope to end my days at Shūon'an. Even so, I composed the following in private celebration at the end of another year:

> This is my request—
> that I might vanish
> before the snow on the peaks
> where they cut firewood
> in the last days of the year

***

Third Year of Daiei (1523)

Shirakawa

On my way from Takigi to the capital in the third month, I composed this at the Tsujinobō retreat in Shirakawa in Uji:

> Spring! and the blossom
> that continues to remember—
> the first cherry.

This is related to the "Sawarabi" chapter of *The Tale of Genji*, in which "the temple across the way" appears.

To the Capital

At lodgings in the capital:

> Fleeting as the cicada,
> pale cherry blossoms
> are now in bloom!

***

Journey to Echizen

The abbot of Shinjuan at Daitokuji then did me the honor of calling on me at my travel lodging and told me that the temple wished me to go to Echizen again and revive the matter of a donation.

***

Hokku I composed while in Echizen:

> Coming and going,
> they meet in bead-tree branches—
> the clouds on the peak.

> The rain is redolent
> of orange blossoms
> in the fifth month!

At Sakuuken, the garden of which boasts unparalleled rocks and trees:

> An evening shower—
> rivulets of rain run off
> onto rock pent sedge.

***

At Shiga:

> The autumn sea—
> on its billows blossom
> a thousand flowers!

Composed for a linked-verse session in the capital with a merchant from Bōnotsu in Satsuma:

> A rocky strand
> tinted and retinted by myriad waves
> on an autumn evening!

At Shijo, Bōmonchō:

> Chilling rain at night,
> then frost outside the door at morning—
> a plank-roofed cottage!

Arima

While taking the waters in Arima, at Kōyadera temple, I composed these:

> Passing through Inano,
> a name recalling grebes side by side,
> in the morning snow!

> The moon before dawn—
> frost-withered against the sky,
> ears of pampas grass.

For a thousand-verse sequence at Nose Gengorō's, at Shiroyama:

> Sunset, and yet
> gentle still—the light
> of the passing year.

***

Fourth Year of Daiei (1524)

The Water Wheels of Ujigawa River

As we went upriver from Fushimi toward Uji Bridge, we could see Mizu no mimaki pasture and Yawata Mountain. Kotsugawa and Ujigawa rivers flow together there to form an expanse as broad as a lake. The people we invited from Kyoto enjoyed themselves, "beating in time on the boat sides," playing shakuhachi and pipes, and singing popular songs like "Water wheels revolving in Uji's rapids—are they turning over thoughts of this woeful world?" The deutzia on the banks and the irises at the water's edge looked lovely, blooming together. There were innumerable stretches of rapids, and the boatman sang old songs like "struggling against the current at a tow rope's end." We finally put into shore and alighted, sorry the trip was over.

***

Sightseeing at Washinosuyama

Two or three days later, we breakfasted at Shōhōji temple. Slept there the night before. A bath was provided for all in my company.

The next day we decided to see Washinosuyama mountain by palanquin at Kajisai's invitation. The narrow, mossy path was slippery, and the water cascaded down through the valley like the sea itself. The bearers reached out for what holds they could on the rock wall but could not stop their legs.

They say there was a mountain temple here in the past. Might the site be used in battle? A natural shield of cliffs. Pillars of rock to support a gatehouse. It appears to cover fifty square chō around the valley. Here one could confront tens of thousands of soldiers with impunity.

That day we visited Shōhōji and also Kōzenji, a branch temple of Tōfukuji. The abbot arranged a session of linked Japanese and Chinese verse:

> Is it because this is
> the mountain where eagles dwell
> that the cuckoo is so distant?
>
> In the fifth month
> one feels cool.

When we reached the back of the single sheet, sake was brought out, and we shared several cups with the acolytes. Did not leave till evening.

Again on the twenty-fifth of this month, at a monthly dedicatory linked-verse session for a temple called Jionji:

> In the summer rains,
> water builds on the outer leaves
> of the sedge grass!

***

Fifth Year of Daiei (1525)

Return to Brushwood Cottage

I have maintained a place of retirement by Utsunoyama mountain for some time, and I decided to take up residence there on the twenty-sixth of the twelfth month, after having been away five or six years in the capital:

> Though I only just left
> for Takigi, where I planned
> to cut firewood at year's end,
> I have taken shelter instead
> by Reality Mountain.

By "though I only just left," I meant that I had set out for Takigi in Yamashiro only a short time ago.

> From this day onward
> I must cut my firewood
> for the ages here,
> placing my trust in the pines
> of Reality Mountain.

I repaired the thatched fence, coarse rush blinds, and bamboo flooring of this mountain dwelling and straightaway took up residence. Then on the morning of the twenty-seventh a heavy snow fell, and everything took on a new, fresh look:

> Here at my cottage
> the thatched roof and rice-straw fence
> and blinds made of reeds
> all seem somehow to set off
> the snow to its advantage!

***

> Now beneath the snow,
> I understand his advice
> about stacking it up.
> I do not have brushwood left
> to make a single bundle.

I was recalling the satisfaction with which that great priest [Saigyō] wrote, "While I stack brushwood / in the yard of my cottage, / how little is this year's end / like others I have seen!" He seems to be saying that people's desires can be satisfied with little.

Already New Year's Eve:

> The eve of the day
> the New Year begins—
> soon I too will know
> if the things they say are true
> about spirits coming back.

Thus ends the entry for 1525 in *The Journal of Sōchō*.

Book Two of the journal describes a second trip west to the Kyoto area in 1526 and back to Suruga the following year. He chronicled the years 1530 to 1531 in his last journal, *Sōchō nikki* (The diary of Sōchō), then passed away at his Brushwood Cottage in 1532, lionized as one of the greatest renga poets and most prolific diarists of the medieval era.

Traces Of Dreams: Landscape, Cultural Memory, and the Poetry of Bashō
By Haruo Shirane

In the winter of 1680, Bashō moved to Fukagawa, where he began composing haikai that drew on his own life as a recluse, creating, probably for the first time in haikai history, what appeared to be a personal, confessional mode–a movement no doubt influenced by his readings of Chinese recluse poets such as Li Po and Tu Fu. At Fukagawa, Bashō wrote poems and *haibun* (haikai prose) such as "The Brushwod Door" ("Shiba no to," 1680).

> After nine years, growing weary of living in the city, I moved my home to the bank of the Fukagawa River. "Ch'ang-an was, from long ago, a place of profit and fame, making it difficult for those who were empty-handed and penniless to survive." Is it because I found the person who said this to be so wise that I am now so poor?
>
> > against the brushwood door
> > gathering tree leaves for my tea–
> > a storm

Bashō here emerges as a "poet of life" who implicitly asks us to read his poetry against his personal life. One consequence has been that generations of readers have imagined Bashō eking out a lonely and humble existence in a small grass hut, an image sustained and fostered by Edo artists and later poets such as Chōmu. At the same time, Bashō's Chinese-style poetry, opened a window on to another world, on to the "past," as in the following *haibun*, which Bashō composed in the winter of 1681.

> In the window, the snow of a thousand autumns
>   on the Western Peak
> Stopping at the gate, the ships traveling
>   a thousand leagues to the Eastern Sea
>   —Owner of the Hall of Stopping Ships
>   Flower Tōsei

I know this poem, but I do not know his feelings. I can imagine his poverty, but I cannot know his pleasure. I am superior to the elder Tu Fu only in the sense that I have more ills. Hidden in the leaves of the plantain at the side of my simple thatched hut, I call myself "beggar old man."

> oar sounds hitting the waves
> guts freezing at night–
> tears

> a kettle at Poor Temple
> whistling in the frost–
> a cold voice

> Buying water

> quenching its thirst
> with bitter ice–
> a sewer rat

> Year's End

> as the year ends
> echo of rice-cake pounding–
> a lonely bed

This haibun opens with the last two lines of a *chüeh-chü* or quatrain, by Tu Fu, in which the Chinese poet looks out from his hermitage. The result is a double vision (*mitate*).

***

In the following haibun called "Crafting a Hat" ("Kasa hari") Bashō parodies Sōgi's verse.

> When I grow weary of living alone in my grass hut and the autumn wind sounds lonely, I borrow Myōkan's sword and, imitating the Bamboo Cutter, cut pieces of bamboo, bend them, and call myself the Old Maker of Hats. Having little skill, I am unable to finish a hat even if I devote an entire day to it. Short on patience, I grow tired as the days pass. In the morning, I stretch paper over the bamboo; and in the evening I dry it and stretch on more paper. I dye the hat with persimmon dye, apply lacquer, and wait for it to harden. After twenty days, it is finally finished. The hat slopes down and turns inward and outward at the edges so that it resembles a half-opened lotus leaf. Its form is more interesting than a perfectly balanced hat. Is it the shabby hat that Saigyō wore? Or the hat that Su Tung-p'o put on his head? Shall I travel to see the dew on Miyagi field? Or shall I take my walking cane to see the snows of distant Wu? As my heart quickens at the thought of falling snow pellets and I wait impatiently for the winter showers, I find myself admiring the hat and finding special pleasure in it. In my excitement, I suddenly have a thought. Drenching myself once more in Sōgi's winter shower, I take up my brush and write on the inside of the hat.
>
> > life in this world:
> > just like a temporary shelter
> > of Sōgi's!

The poetic madness emerges not only in the poet's childlike purity of spirit but also in the manner in which the poet treats material objects as poetic signs. The misshapen hat (*kasa*), which reminds Bashō of the hats worn by such poets as Su Tung-p'o, Saigyō, and Sōgi, becomes a medium—much like the grass hut and the Japanese plantain—through which the poet communes playfully with the "ancients."

The following passage comes at the end of *Record of an Unreal Dwelling* (*Genjuan no ki*; 1690), considered to be Bashō's model haibun.

> This is not to say that I sought to escape into the mountains and fields out of a love for quiet and loneliness. I am simply like someone who, growing ill, finds it tiresome to be with people and turns his back on the world. When I look back over the years, I am painfully reminded of my shortcomings. I once coveted public office with property. At another time, I decided that I should enter the priesthood. But desiring to capture the beauty of the birds and beasts, I was swept away by the floating clouds and drifting winds. For a while that alone was my life. Now at the end, I cling, without talent or ability, to this one thread: the art of poetry. Po Chü-i, it is said, exhausted his five organs composing poetry, and Tu Fu grew lean doing the same. Needless to say, I have none of their wisdom or poetic talent. But is there anyone who does not live in an illusory dwelling? With those thoughts, I lie down.
>
> > for now I will turn
> > to the large pasania tree–
> > a summer grove

This haibun is also a greeting to Kyokusui represented by the large tree, thanking him for lending Bashō a relaxing dwelling that has allowed him to recover from his long journey through the Interior.

***

A typical haibun was written in gratitude to a host on a journey with the praise often expressed in Chinese allusions and forms, which were often the prototypes for Bashō's haikai prose. The well-known "Tower of Eighteen" ("Jūhachirō no ki"; 1688), for example, was written when Bashō was invited to the house of Kashima in Mino (Gifu), on his way back from the *Backpack Notes* journey.

A stately tower stands on the banks of the Nagara River in Mino Province. Mr. Kashima is the owner's name. Inaba Mountain rises in the rear, and mountains, which are high and low, neither too near nor too far, stand to the west. A cedar grove hides a temple in the middle of the rice fields, and the dwellings along the shore are wrapped in the deep green of bamboo. Water bleached cloth has been stretched out to dry here and there, and to the right a ferryboat floats on the water. The villagers walk back and forth ceaselessly; the houses of the fisherfolk stand side by side; fishermen pull in their nets and cast out their lines, each one working as if to enhance the setting of the stately mansion. The vista is enough to make one forget the heat of the lingering summer sun. The moon at last replaces the rays of the setting sun, and the light of the flares reflected in the waves gradually comes closer as the residents begin cormorant fishing at the base of the mansion—a startling sight! In the cool breeze I find the famous Eight Views of Hsiao-hsiang and the Ten Sights of West Lake. If one were to give this tower a name, Eighteen Sights would be appropriate.

> from this spot
> all that meets the eye
> is coolness

The haibun, which is written in prose couplets with contrastive and parallel images, is an elegant homage to Bashō's host, climaxing with a comparison of the dwelling to the famous sights of China—the views of Hsiao-hsiang and West Lake—and the image of "coolness" in the hokku. The compact parallel structure, the terse Chinese style, and the gentle poetic overtones quickly turned it into an exemplary haibun that was widely admired and repeatedly anthologized.

Bashō gathered a number of these haibun, prose in haikai spirit, and wove them into commemorative travel accounts, which he sometimes sent to the primary host of the journey. *Skeleton in the Fields*, Bashō's first travel account, is based on at least five such appreciatory haibun. Almost all the haibun Bashō composed during his visit to the northern region—at least thirteen notable works survive—were later incorporated into *Narrow Road to the Interior*. The same applies to *Backpack Notes*. After passing the Shirakawa Barrier, the symbolic entrance to Michinoku, Bashō gave Tōkyū, the station master at Sukagawa, the following haibun, which contains the hokku examined earlier.

> Looking forward to the various famous places in the Interior, I traveled north, where I was drawn, first of all, to the ruins of the Shirakawa Barrier. I followed the ancient road to that former checkpoint, crossing along the way the present barrier at Shirakawa. I soon arrived at Iwase County and knocked on the fragrant gate of the gentleman Satansai Tōkyū. Fortunately, I was able, in the words of Wang Wei, "to cross the Yang Barrier and meet an old friend."

> > beginnings of poetry
> > the rice-planting songs
> > of the Interior

Compared with the corresponding passage in *Narrow Road to the Interior*, this haibun is far more flattering, comparing the host to a figure in a Chinese poem by Wang Wei and making no mention, as *Narrow Road to the Interior* does, of the visitor's laborious trek across the Shirakawa Barrier. After accumulating a sufficient number of such haibun, Bashō rewrote and recontextualized them to fit into a larger travel narrative.

***

> When I stopped for the night at Ōgaki, I became a guest at Bokuin's residence. Since I had begun this journey from Musashi Plain with thoughts of a weather-beaten skeleton, I wrote:

> > end of the journey
> > and still alive!
> > the last of autumn

Bashō's poem, which echoes the opening poem on the "skeleton in the field" (*nozarashi*), is an expression of gratitude to Bokuin, thanking him for his warm hospitality, which has saved Bashō's frail body from the vicissitudes of the road.

***

The interest of travel literature, at least in the Anglo-European tradition, generally lies in the unknown, in new worlds, new knowledge, new perspectives, new experiences. But for medieval waka and renga poets, the object of travel was to confirm what already existed, to reinforce the roots of cultural memory.

***

Pilgrimages to scared places, to temples and shrines, were popular as early as the Heian period and formed an integral part of the travel account tradition, particularly those written by hermit priests. A typical passage begins with a description of the landscape, the history of the shrine or temple, usually giving some detail about the founder or the name. The climactic hokku, which may be a greeting to the divine spirit or to the head of the temple/shrine usually conveys a sense of the sacred quality or efficacy of the place. In the passage on the Ryūshaku temple, or Mountain Temple (Yamadera), in Dewa (Yamagata), that quality is embodied in the word "stillness" (*shizukasa*), which later became the poetic essence (*hon'i*) of this new poetic place.

> In the Yamagata domain there is a mountain temple called Ryūshakuji. It was founded by the High Priest Jikaku and is an especially pure and tranquil place. Since we had been urged to see this place at least once, we backtracked from Obanazawa and traveled for about seven leagues. When we arrived, there was still light outside. We borrowed a room at a temple at the foot of the mountain and then climbed to the Buddha Hall at the top. Boulders were piled on boulders, creating a mountain; the pines and cypress trees had grown old; the soil and rocks were aged, covered with smooth moss. The

doors to the temple buildings atop the boulders were closed and not a sound could be heard. We followed the edge of the cliff, crawled over boulders, and then prayed at the Buddha hall. As the beautiful surroundings settled into silence, I felt my heart growing pure.

> stillness—
> sinking deep into the rocks
> cries of the cicada

***

For Heian court poets, who had no need to visit the physical *utamakura*, there was only the *utamakura* of the poetic tradition: composing on *utamakura* meant travel without traveling. Bashō, by contrast, followed in the shoes of poet travelers such as Saigyō and Sōgi, who had visited the physical *utamakura*. A poem on an *utamakura* was implicitly a greeting to the spirit of the ancient entombed in the *utamakura*, enabling the poet to join the company of those who had written memorable poems on the same toponym. At the same time, the poet, hearing the voices of the past, could be overwhelmed and silenced by his poetic predecessors. In the following scene in *Backpack Notes*, Bashō visits the cherry blossoms at Yoshino, perhaps the most famous *utamakura* in Japan.

> We stayed for three days at Yoshino, while the cherry trees were in full bloom, and saw Yoshino both at dawn and at dusk. The beauty of the early morning moon sent my heart racing, filling me with emotion. I was swept away by thoughts of that famous poem on Yoshino by Fujiwara Yoshitsune, was left directionless at Saigyō's signpost, and recalled the poem that Teishitsu had tossed off–"What a scene! What a scene!" Unable to compose even a single poem, I regretfully closed my mouth. I had come charged with enthusiasm, only to see it all disappear.

***

Whenever Bashō felt that his haikai was stagnating, he embarked on a journey and sought out new poets who could stimulate him. Like other traditional Japanese arts, haikai demanded years of training, but Bashō welcomed young or new disciples, who brought a fresh and flexible perspective.

***

Bashō's haikai, like his travel, moved fundamentally in two directions, linking participants together and linking them with the past, with a sense of tradition.

***

Ultimately, travel in Bashō's work becomes a metaphor for the haikai imagination. As Bashō's poetics of the "unchanging and everchanging" (*fueki ryūkō*) suggest, the pursuit of what he called the "truth of poetic art" (*fūga no makoto*) required unceasing forward movement. Travel meant a constant effort to explore new territory and new languages as well as the perpetual search for new perspectives on nature, the seasons, and the landscape, the carriers of poetic and cultural memory. The same can be said of reclusion, the other central topos of Bashō's literature. In the Chinese and Japanese poetic traditions, the recluse distances himself from the established in order to gain a critical distance on it. At the same time, however, travel for Bashō, as for his medieval poet-priest predecessors, was a movement through time, a retracing of the steps of the ancients (*kojin*), who became the source not only of spiritual and poetic inspiration but of cultural authority. Travel was a means of both expanding and acquiring cultural identity.

***

Dew On The Grass:
The Life and Poetry of Kobayashi Issa
By Makoto Ueda

In his preface, Makoto Ueda writes:

> "The received opinion is that, while Bashō with his mystic ascetiscism and Buson with his romantic aestheticism immeasurably enriched the haiku tradition, it was Issa who, with his bold individualism and all-embracing humanism, helped to modernize the form to a degree matched by no other poet."

It also reveals his awareness of the travel journal as a literary genre in which factual truth may sometimes take second place to poetry. *The Journal of Travel in the Third Year of Kansei* ends with Issa's arrival at his old home on the evening of May 20. As the author tells us,

> I entered my native village at around the time when lamps begin to be lit in the houses. Then there came the moment I had been looking forward to all those days: at long last I saw my father and mother, both in good health. My joy, happiness, and gratitude at that moment were like those of the blind tortoise encountering a piece of driftwood in the ocean, or those of the man who found a shining star in the blackest sky. Overwhelmed with happiness, I was lost for words for a while.

>> the tree by the gate
>> is here as it always was
>> evening coolness

In describing the climactic moment of the journey, Issa again resorts to classical allusions. The blind tortoise refers to a parable in Nirvana Sutra that compares the difficulty of meeting Buddha to the chance of a blind tortoise bumping into some driftwood in the middle of an ocean. The image of a man delighted to find a star on a dark night had often been used in various books before Issa's time. The ending hokku, which expresses the relief of finally finding a place of rest, echoes Bashō's verse that concludes "The Record of My Life at the Genju Hut".

The *Verse Notebook* ends with poems written in or around 1794, but it is succeeded by The Journal of Travel in the Western Provinces, which records Issa's life in some detail from February 19 to June 17, 1795. His purpose was to pay a visit to a certain Sarai, the chief priest of a local temple, who had been a close friend of Chikua's.

***

> At Nanba Village in Kazahaya Country I inquired about Sarai and was told he had passed away fifteen years before. Thereupon I asked the new head priest if I could stay overnight at the temple, but he declined my request. I felt totally helpless, since I had come all this way depending solely on Sarai's goodwill. Now I had to grope my way through the field and gardens.

> dark, dark–
> I step into a puddle
> on an unknown path

Issa arrived at Matsuyama on March 5 and spent the next twenty days enjoying the cherry blossoms. His host was Kurita Chodo (1748-1814), the owner of a brewery whose fame as a haikai poet was known all through the western provinces.

***

Through a hole in the shoji screen: 1812-1816

Determined to settle down in his native village, Issa left Edo on December 20, 1812, and arrived in Kashiwabara one week later.

> As I reflect upon myself, I have to think I was born to be part of the undergrowth. A bellflower, a karukaya grass, or a lady flower that sprouts in the shade of miscanthus

and other bushes does not grow to its full height no matter how much time passes. If by the rarest of chances the bush hanging over it should die, the plant underneath will look happy and revitalized because of the precious sunlight it has begun to receive. Still, it will be lacking in its natural color and stand feebly like a lamp that flickers. It gathers its strength and tries to live its own life in the gusty wind of the world, it will end up being scratched by the sharp prongs of a rake.

I have lived as a dreamer for fifty years, but now the dream is gone without a trace. I am only waiting for my time to expire. All this must be in retribution for my previous birth.

> for me, no share
> of New Year's happiness—
> this wretched plight!

> In the outside world
> plum blossoms, cherry blossoms
> other people's spring

Issa spent many days on the road in the spring of 1822. During the months of March and April, the days he stayed home totaled only fifteen. Since he still had a problem with his feet, he often hired a palanquin to go from one student's house to another. The physical handicap did not interfere with his poetic activities or dampen his spirits. A haibun he wrote at around this describes the kind of life he was leading:

> Today the sky was clear for a change. The scenery around us finally began to show something of vernal warmth. It was pleasant to see trees and grass sprouting buds in the spring breeze. Because several old friends of mine came for a visit, we decided to have a little drinking party out in the field. As we went out to a field by the gate, we saw many bog rhubarbs budding out at sunny spots and

waiting to be picked. The sight assured us that we would have plenty of food for the party.

My companions for the occasion were close friends whom I had known for over twenty years and with whom I had often exchanged jokes while eating from the same pots and pans. Together we spent the entire day drinking. Even when the clear moonlight began to fall on the gate, we were so absorbed in the pleasure of the party that we did not come to our senses. At last, having consumed nearly two gallons of sake, we got utterly drunk and writhed like big serpents till we fell asleep. We slept well into the night.

>   lying on my back, I gaze:
>   like a child's rag ball
>   a spring hill

The haibun is one of the happiest prose pieces Issa ever wrote. The type of life described in it is perhaps what is meant by becoming a "fool." He pursued his pleasures to his heart's content, with no qualms over the question of religious salvation.

A Translation of Kurita Chodō's Sketches of Moonlit Nights
By Patricia Lyons

Kurita Chodō (21st August 1749 to 21st August 1814), was a Japanese poet of the Edo period (1600 to 1867), regarded as a leading figure in the poetry world in Matsuyama, the former Iyo Province. Gotō Masanori, commonly called Teizō, was born in 1749 in Iyo, now Matsuyama, and married into the Kurita family at the age of 17. The Kurita and Gotō families both owned prosperous sake breweries, and they served Katō Kiyomasa, who built Matsuyama Castle. Chodō became the 7th owner of the brewery when he was 23. Around this time, under the encouragement of his wife and his father-in-law, who were haiku poets, he began to compose haiku. He built Kōshin-an in 1800 to devote himself to haiku activities, and retired from governmental service.

Kobayashi Issa, one of the greatest haiku poets of their period, was an important friend of Kurita Chodō. Issa was younger than Chodō by fourteen years, and Chodō gave him guidance about haiku. Issa visited his house in 1795 and 1796 and they enjoyed composing haiku together. Their friendship lasted until Chodō's death. In 1807, Chodō moved to Mitarai-jima, a small island of the former Aki Province, now Hiroshima Prefecture, where he spent the rest of his days. He died at sixty-five in 1814. Masaoka Shiki praised Chodō as the best poet in Iyo of his age. Chodō was widely known as a disciple of the famous haiku poet Kato Kyodai, having a connection with poets in Edo, Kamigata, and Owari provinces.

His first travel writing, *Tsumajirushi*, a journal kept during his trip to Setouchi, Kii, Yamato, and Kyoto, was completed in 1787. In 1805, five years after his building of Kōshin-an, he wrote about his reclusive life there in the journal Kōshin-an-ki. Kōshin-an is a retreat including a Japanese garden and a house in Matsuyama, Ehime. Today, part of the house has been restored to preserve its original form as one of the special historic sites in Ehime, and the NPO corporation GCM Kōshin-an Club is involved in voluntary activities to promote it.

The Third and Fourth Day Moons

In autumn one is moved more deeply by things, and gazing at the moon is especially delightful. When thinking of the moon, we feel as if we have just met someone who lived long ago. Around the hour the moon comes into view, close friends come to call uninvited. At such a time, their familiar faces stir up fresh, new feelings. How amusing it is that, for some reason, we rush to begin talking of this and that. In the season when the miscanthus begins to rustle and the leaves of the willow by the eaves to fall, the crescent of the third and fourth day moons sinks softly in the west.

> on a rough straw mat–
> eating my meal and above,
> the River of Heaven

Note: "Amanogawa" is the Japanese name for the Milky Way.

The Waxing Moon

By the seventh and eighth days, the moon takes on a lovely shape. As people come and go along a broad street, they may look familiar, but it is difficult to know for sure. How delightful it is to exchange glances for no reason at all. At this time, the moon hidden behind pine needles is especially wonderful.

> going out in autumn
> it always seems to be
> a moonlit night

The Tenth Day Moon

The tenth day moon is also such a delight. As it glides across the sky, we talk of things at length. After a passing shower, the moonlight that seeps between the clouds makes an even deeper impression. To sleep would be a shame, we say, as we rush to delay one who would go home. How enjoyable it is to press upon him one more cup of wine. Katydids gathered among thick clumps of grass, crickets on the wall, each one chirps out its own sad song. That all should gather this way lends to the beauty of autumn nights.

> a bell cricket's call
> tells of night's deepening chill
> from within the hedge

The Midpoint of Autumn

At the midpoint of autumn, when the fifteenth day moon comes round to a darker part of the sky, it shines more brilliantly than ever. Both now and in days gone by, people of nobility took great delight in gazing upon it. Even more so was this true in the palace of the emperor, but we cannot know the pleasures of life in grand palaces. People of high rank and great wealth lack composure, and of what use are their riches for looking at the moon? There are those who play about, wandering among the hills and fields or punting on rivers and lakes, but as amusing oneself elegantly must be done with a true heart, they are only acting foolishly. Some turn blank faces to the moon and lament the passing of time. Others bemoan the troubles of the world and think of dwelling deep within the mountains. Most of what they do brings no gain and is utterly pointless. If there is somewhere a convenient place and one has obtained even a bundle of straw, one can spread it out and, without cares or worries, sit alone simply gazing at the fifteenth day moon. In the purity of the moon's light, of what is there to be ashamed? How truly wonderful this is.

> coming into sight
> quickly brightening the dark
> tonight's moon

The Sixteenth Night

The uncertain moon of the sixteenth night is matchless in beauty. Even as we wonder when the tide rising to the reed-lined shore will reach its crest, already bands of small waves are retreating over the tidal flats. What is there that can remain the same for any length of time? Saying that the memory of the night before is unforgettable, wandering farther than we could have thought to the edge of the plain of pampas grass, on a path where dew drops fall, carried away, walking aimlessly, all this comes from the greediness of the human heart.

> higher than other nights
> taking its place in the sky
> the autumn moon

The Last Quarter of the Moon

The twentieth day moon is even more moving. Especially when its half-circle appears near the ridge of a mountain, with impudent clouds coming and going, it is even more touching. And the mood is deepened when we hear the sound of a distant bell, the call of a stag for its mate, or the wind rushing through pine trees.

>   a mountain village–
> fleas, mosquitoes forgotten
>   the autumn moon

The Moon That Rises in Early Morning

The twenty-sixth and twenty-seventh day moons, which rise around two or three in the morning, shine down like a dusting of frost, and we are fortunate indeed to hear, from a roughly-built wooden house with a loosely barred gate, the notes of koto and bamboo flute. How delightful! You wish that someone would come out and wonder what they are like. The depth of night is made so moving by the lovely sound from a rude house of reeds of someone beating cloth to soften it or by the cries of wild ducks on the edge of a marsh calling their companions.

>   uneven clip-clop
> of a mallet beating cloth
>   as the night deepens

Daybreak

The moon at daybreak is truly moving. On a journey with no destination, with grass for a pillow, when passing through some border crossing, the mountains of home growing ever smaller, how sad and alone one must feel. How much more so is parting from one's beloved. Indeed, autumn moves the heart most of all.

> leaving them behind
> a lingering sadness comes
> autumn mountains

Note: Written and assembled in the eighth month of the tenth year of Kansei (September 1789) by the aged Sokuin, as he sat by his window through the long nights.

Masaoka Shiki: His Life and Works
By Janine Beichman

In *Descriptive Prose*, Shiki emphasized the need for selection in prose as he had in poetry:

> If one makes central the most beautiful and moving, the scene comes alive of itself. And the most beautiful and moving part is not always large, conspicuous or essential. Often it is obscure, as though half-hidden in shadows. A single red camellia discovered amidst the obscure and frightening darkness of a forest is extremely beautiful and creates a feeling of joy. One can make the camellia the center of the composition then, but this does not necessarily mean describing it in detail. If you describe the dim, fearful aspect of the forest in rather complete detail and then merely indicate the red camellia, a strong feeling can be conveyed to the reader by a single word.

In *A Drop of Ink*, Shiki had written, "I feel the pain and see the beauty." This ability to hold two opposites in suspension, preserving both yet yielding to neither, has already been described in the poetry and it characterized Shiki himself as well, for he tended both to perceive and to describe in dualities.

Excerpt from *A Drop of Ink*

In the entry for March 7, Shiki relates at length how the birds outside his window bathe, then notes at the end that *he* has not been able to bathe for five years. The sudden shift of viewpoint here, as in the entry for February 11, gives a flourish and vivacity to all that comes before:

> After I became sick, someone borrowed a large wire birdcage for me to take my mind off being confined to bed. I had it placed in front of the window with ten birds inside. I enjoy watching them from my sickbed, for they have a funny way of rushing down to bathe when the

water in their basin is changed. Before one can even take one's hand off the water basin and out of the cage, the finches fly down, ahead of any of the others. They are the best bathers, too, splashing away so energetically that half the water is gone in a minute. Then the other birds have to take turns bathing in what little water is left. I doubt whether the two black-headed manikins consciously decided to change matters, but lately they fly down just as the finches are about to hop in, then chase them away and bathe themselves side by side. After them come the Jakarta sparrows and then the zebra finches and the canaries. Finally the basin's edge is thronged with birds arranged in order of arrival. Each flies up to the perch as it finishes bathing and flaps its wings furiously. They look so happy. Now that I think of it, it must be about five years since I could take a bath. (XI, 130-131)

The mood of the two public diaries, even when Shiki is describing emotions that were truly pitiful, is always informed by this quality of playfulness.

Literary Creations on the Road–Women's Travel Diaries in Early Modern Japan
By Keiko Shiba and Motoko Ezaki

In her *Translator's Introduction*, Motoko Ezaki states–

The author *Shiba Keiko* in her *afterword* says, "This is not a thesis, nor did I attempt a new theory or anything so ambitious as to make contributions to academia with this book." For years she has searched for materials written by the women of early modern Japan, her quest being to "simply read what they actually wrote" and possibly "learn something universal from them."

Shiba majored in Japan's early modern history at college in the 1960s. While learning, she felt strong doubts about the then predominant view that the era under the Tokugawa bakufu was the darkest time for women, when "the oppression of women marked a nadir in our history."

Shiba's achievement in *Literary Creations on the Road–Women's Travel Diaries in Early Modern Japan* stands unique by virtue of the sheer number of authors and their journeys that it introduces; her collection of travel diaries had reached nearly two hundred when the book was written, and is a manifestation of her efforts to describe as many works as possible while minimizing her own analytical comments on each text.

The Reasons Women Traveled Volitional Travel: Pilgrimage and sightseeing

The well over one hundred women's travel diaries from early modern Japan that I have so far collected may be grouped into two broad categories in terms of the purposes and motives for the travel: volitional or compulsory.

Among voluntary journeys, sightseeing trips together with visits to temples and shrines are predominant, accounting for nearly half of all these diaries. The popularity of sightseeing and pilgrimage is apparent from the "Decree of the Keian Era" (*Keian no ofuregaki*) that the Tokugawa government issued in 1649; it dictates in detail daily routines for peasants to observe. Interestingly, the officials felt compelled to add the following provision: "A wife who drinks tea excessively, has a penchant for visiting temples and shrines, and likes to go on outings should be divorced." Nevertheless it did not stop women from taking to the road for excursions and visits to temples and shrines.

Yamanashi Shigako, the housewife and mother of a sake brewing family of Iharamura in Suruga province, departed for a pilgrimage to Ise Shrine with her fourth son Tōhei and an attendant in 1792, when she was fifty-five years old. They headed west along the Tōkaidō (a highway), stopped at Mt. Akiha and Hōrai-ji temple, visited both the Inner and Outer Shrines of Ise, and arrived in Kyoto via the Ōmi road. There they watched with amazement the procession of a court aristocrat accompanied by a number of ladies-in-waiting. Passing through Uji, Nara, Yoshino, Mt. Kōya, and Osaka, they viewed the sea of Hyōgo from Mt. Maya. In the Grove of Ikuta, they recalled the historic Genji-Heike battle, then visited the ruins of the Heike clan at Suma and Akashi.

Passing the castle towns of Himeji and Okayama, they reached Marugame in Shikoku by boat. After visiting Konpira Shrine, the party again boarded a boat for Miyajima. During a tour of islands on the Seto Inland Sea, they watched with interest children grazing cows on the grass near the shore of Momoshima. Landing at Hiroshima for the return trip, they visited temples, shrines, and various sights on their way, later resting in Osaka. The party stayed for nearly one month in Kyoto. They apparently saw the famous Kamo Festival and enjoyed other noted events in Kyoto, but their activities are not recorded in her diary, except for the author's simple note that says, "The capital was too splendid for words, and my brush is inadequate for its description." Leaving the city on the thirteenth day of the fifth month, her party passed Fuwa-no-seki and Nagoya, then finally reached Mitsuke (in present day Shizuoka prefecture) in their home province. From

Mitsuke one beheld gorgeous Mt. Fuji (the word *mitsuke* can mean *to view*, hence the town's name). Having thoroughly enjoyed their journey during prime flower season, the second month through the fifth month, Shigako titled her diary "*Haru no michikusa*" (Dawdling along Spring Roads) and concluded it with a *waka*:

> Traveling clothes—
> putting on layers of those for many days
> have I returned home
> and beheld beautiful Fuji,
> What joy, just to hear the name *mitsuke*!

Like Shigako, many women enthusiastically visited famous scenic locations on their way to and from their pilgrimages to Ise Shrine.

Abe Mineko, the matron of the medicine-trading Abe family of Uekimura in Chikuzen province, traveled to Ise Shrine at the age of forty-eight in 1840 and authored a diary entitled "*Ise mōde nikki*" (*Diary of a Pilgrimage to Ise*). With her friends she left Uekimura on the twenty-third day of the second month and sailed across the Seto Inland Sea to Kyoto. On their way they stopped at Iwakuni, Miyajima, Onomichi, and Okayama to offer prayers at local religious sites. From Marugame they proceeded to visit Konpira Shrine. At Kagaku-ji, a temple remembered for its association with the forty-seven rōnin of *Chūshingura* fame, Mineko and her friends were moved to tears by the unveiling of a sacred Buddha. The party then visited Sumadera temple and the gravesite of Taira no Kiyomori, enjoyed sightseeing in Osaka, and arrived in Kyoto via Uji. They roamed the imperial capital for about ten days and made a tour of the eight famous picturesque spots of Ōmi (known as the *Ōmi hakkei*). At Kusatsu they bought rice cakes called *ubagamochi*, a local specialty of the area, then crossed the mountains of Suzuka heading for Ise Shrine.

On their return trip after staying for about three days in Ise, Mineko and her friends crossed the mountains of Iga, toured Nara and Yoshino, then set out to the Seto Inland Sea from Osaka on the second day of the fifth month. They arrived home on the ninth day of the month. It was approximately a forty-day journey.

There were those of strong faith who, often in spite of illness, would embark upon a pilgrimage circuit of holy temples. Iwashita Isoko was the proprietress of a brothel at the Shinagawa post station in Edo. She started her journey to the Chichibu circuit of thirty-three temples accompanied by two attendants in 1860. Isoko, who was of weak constitution, had long been a faithful follower of Kannon Bodhisattva. She departed in a palanquin on the twenty-sixth day of the eighth month and on her way offered prayers at *kishimojin* (the goddess of childbirth and children) in Zōshigaya. In a station at Warabi she saw prostitutes soliciting patrons. The scene must have particularly moved her, being intimately knowledgeable of the lives of such women. Stopping along the way at Ōmiya and Kumagaya, they reached the hot springs of Ikaho. By then, however, Isoko was in poor health, and the party ended up resting there for several days. Afraid of possibly meeting her end in Ikaho, she prayed for the favor of deities and Buddhas. Fortunately she gradually regained her appetite, and they hurried for Chichibu while offering prayers on their way at various temples and shrines. Completing the circuit of Chichibu Kannon temples, the party came home after a seventeen-day journey. The following day Isoko began to write an account of her travel, which was to be completed and entitled *"Chichibu zumrai no ki"* (Pilgrimage to the Chichibu Circuit of Kannon Temples).

Kutsukake Nakako, the mistress of a *sake* brewing house at Sakaki in Shinano province, visited the thirty-four Kannon temples at Chichibu with her third son Engyo and an attendant in 1803, when she was fifty-five years old. They left Sakaki on the fifth day of the third month, taking the reverse route of the circuit, which would normally start from Edo. Stopping at their relatives' homes and family temples on their way, they arrived at the thirty-fourth temple Suisen-ji on the ninth of the month, where they offered prayers to *Senju*-Kannon (Kannon with one-thousand arms). Nakako wrote,

"This was the pilgrimage that I had long wished to accomplish, therefore I was determined to go wherever others went and do whatever others could," and indeed she never hesitated to clamber up the hills no matter how steep they were. She obviously embraced the challenges of her life, having shouldered both the family business and the raising of four sons and two daughters after being widowed at the age of forty. Completing her long cherished pilgrimage, Nakako stopped over at Edo, Enoshima, Kamakura, and Nikkō on her way home. She recorded her accounts of the journey in "*Azumaji no nikki*" (Diary of Traveling East).

Ōkuma Tsugi-jo, the mother of the village headman of Matsudo in Shimōsa province, went on a pilgrimage accompanied by attendants to Chichibu.

***

A Bride's Journey

Fujiki Ichi, the daughter of a chief retainer of Aizu domain, was separated from her father in childhood and grew up with her mother's natal family, the Fujikis, in Kyoto. Her father, Hoshina Masaoki, had fallen from power and been banished to Mizusawa in Ogawashō (in present day Niigata prefecture), across the Agano River. Her maternal grandfather was the chief priest of Kamigamo Shrine.

When she was fourteen, Ichi's marriage was arranged to the eldest son of the Kishi clan, a chief retainer of Kurume domain in Chikugo province (Kyūshū). Ichi recorded an account of her journey as a bride:

> It wasn't that I attempted to follow the example of famous writings of olden times, but I simply wanted to keep a journal to console my melancholy mind during the journey.

Thus begins the diary of a girl who left the house of her mother and grandfather to travel to a strange and faraway land. It vividly depicts her longing for the capital, where she had grown up, and anxiety for the future.

At the end of the year 1700, the bride's procession made a torchlit journey to Fushimi, and then headed for Naniwa (old name of Osaka) by boat. At the mouth of the river, Ichi parted with her maids, who had come that far to see her off. The boat sailed further and further from the capital, passing famous scenic spots in the Seto Inland Sea, such as Naruo, Nishinomiya, Wada-no-misaki, Suma, and Akashi. Ichi's homesickness intensified.

> Sea breeze of Onoura—
> you blow far, away from me
> as our procession moves forward,
> Pray, tell my people there
> of my longing for home

Various landscapes impressed her, however. She found Akashi Bay too splendid for words, and Awaji Island was "one thousand times" more beautiful than she had imagined while living in Kyoto.

On 12. 29, the ship anchored at Murozumi, deviating from the original itinerary, which had them stopping at Kaminoseki. Ichi took a great liking to the place, describing it as "a charming beach, indeed." The sea was dotted by Kasadoshima and other small islands, and on land, luxuriant with evergreen trees, the *fugen-bosatsu* (Samantabhadra) was enshrined at a local temple. The party could not depart on New Year's Eve due to lack of wind and therefore ended up welcoming the New Year there. The boatmen ceremoniously dedicated young sake to the spirit of the ship, erected auspicious pine branches at bow and stern, and enshrined a guardian deity in the boat. Ichi observed, fascinated.

***

Nearing Yonezawa, they found a number of *sekisho* erected here and there, making their passage extremely difficult, and eventually they were told to turn back and go home. At one checkpoint the party was made to wait. While eating the rice balls offered to them, "talking about refugees of ancient times, and lamenting over our own fate with tears," one of the retainers patiently negotiated with the officials and finally obtained permission to pass in the evening.

Rejected by Yonezawa domain, they headed for Sendai. They staggered along the sawyer's road and fearfully crossed many suspension bridges covered with wisteria vines across the horrifyingly deep ravines, rough waters swirling at the bottom. On 8th September, after a dangerous, frightening journey of some fifteen days, they arrived in Sendai and finally settled into a temple assigned to be their lodging. They remained there for about two months. After the war ended, they departed for Nagaoka on 9th November. The return trip was free of the terror of war, and though challenged by the snowy, mountainous roads, the party could occasionally appreciate beautiful views along the way.

On 28th November, they ended their six-month journey as refugees and came home to Nagaoka. Tsune wrote, "It is still hard to believe that we really traveled as far as Ōshū. It feels as if I was just having a long dream." She added three verses of waka at the end of her diary and a one line foreword:

I composed the following poems at the departure of a certain lord for the east.

>Gathering clouds—
>cloud the heaven as you wish,
>Someday will we see
>the moment when all the clouds are
>cleared from our clouded minds

>Those who punish
>and those who are punished,
>Could there be any
>difference between their loyalties
>towards their beloved countries

>Melancholy or joyousness,
>whichever the heaven may bring to us,
>have we not to
>lament over our destiny
>should we still be alive together

"A certain lord" in her foreword implicitly refers to her husband Tadakuni, who had originally come from Miyazu domain of Tango province to marry into the Makino family. After the war, Tadakuni subjected himself to voluntary confinement at the Shōei-ji temple in Tokyo to express his fealty to the new government.

***

Illness and Death away from Home

Onoike Matsuko of Hayashima in Bizen province vistied the Western circuit of thirty-three Kannon temples and extended her journey to Ezo (present-day Hokkaidō), where she sojourned for about one year before returning home. When she reached Ōdate in Dewa province, Matsuko fell ill. In spite of the inn master's warm nursing, she died in November, 1809, in her fifties. Although travelers who died during their journeys were normally buried where they passed, with no particular notice sent home, Matsuko's death was reported to her family through the good will of the Satakes, the local daimyo family. Matsuko's son Ihei made the long journey to Ōdate, expressed the family's profound gratitude to the inn master and other people, and returned home with his mother's remains, a lock of hair, her travel diary and *waka* poems she had composed. Unfortunately neither the travel diary nor poems have been preserved, nor is it known why Matsuko travelled to Ezo. Only one of the *waka* she wrote is found in *Ruidai kibikoku kashū* (A collection of *waka* from Kibi province classified according to themes) edited by Matsuda Yamadakyū in 1848:

I composed this poem at Ezo in autumn, 1807.

> Like the blue of the ocean—
> is my mind, so clear, unclouded with
> any shade of worry,
> so, too, is the moon of the autumn night
> shining above the Chishima islands in Ezo

Having raised her children, with the son inheriting his father's name and her daughter married into another family, Matsuko must have been deeply content when she looked up at the moon in the clear autumn sky. Nothing else of her own writing is available now, leaving us no clue as to what she had to say about her life. But with this waka we know that Matsuko had accomplished an ambitious, extensive journey before departing this world, a journey on a scale that many women at the time might have found inconceivable.

Joys of Travel
Experiencing the Wider World

Travel was full of challenges and difficulties for women of the early modern era, but it provided great joy, as well. Once on the road they could actually experience that which they had heard and read about. It was more than just visiting temples and shrines or places of scenic beauty and historic interest. They would climb mountains, cross the ridges and plains, ride horses, travel in palanquins, stroll through the fields, collect sea shells on the beach, get on boats, sail across the inland sea by steamship, lodge at an inn, drink tea at a tea stall or go shopping. Each was a valuable, fresh experience, rarely a part of people's daily lives at home.

The seasonal flora and fauna must have appeared much more vivid than in books. Appreciating nature deeply through all their five senses, women travelers composed deeply felt poems.

> Evening cicadas
> with your loud chorus–
> Are you trying to make me forget
> the loneliness of traveling through fields of
> grass wet with dew?

> Whose robe is this
> left on a tree branch, I asked,
> to which replied
> the cicadas in their vigorous chorus
> "it's mine," "it's mine," "it's mine."

The above poems are both from "*Ikaho-ki*" (Ikaho Diary) by Nakagawa

Man, the wife of the Oka daimyo in Bungo province. In 1639, when the rulers were in turmoil due to the Shimabara Rebellion, Man set out on a journey to see the beautiful mountain villages in Ikaho and the various flowers found in the Musashino grove. Passing through Musashino on her way, she was greatly comforted by the singing of the evening cicadas and was inspired to compose those verses; both sound as if she was conversing directly with the insects, a theme she might not have conceived had she been sitting in her living room.

Chiyo-jo, the *haikai* poetess of Mattō in Kaga province, who traveled to various places in the Kantō and Kansai regions, did not leave much of a diary, but her works of *haikai* reveal to us her footsteps. When she was sixty years old in 1762, she attended the memorial service for Rennyo at Yoshizaki-gobō.

> I went to visit Yoshizaki. Deeply grateful and moved by its ambience, I offered prayers and composed this:
>
> > With my head bowed
> > did I see the gentle petals of violets,
> > the seat of Buddha

Surrounded by the beauty of nature, Chiyo-jo was obviously jubilant and able to experience Buddha's great mercy.

Escaping from Daily Routine

Travel in those times absolutely required physical fitness and vitality. It made women face various situations that often forced them to make their own judgments and decisions. Once on the road, they could not afford to merely remain obedient wives or daughters, as moral texts for women instructed. In fact, normal precepts for women would be of no particular help in managing the dynamic relationships with their travel companions throughout their long journeys. They also had to weather winds, rains, and thunderstorms, endure the hardships of climbing mountains, crossing rivers and ridges, and many more. Travel required a new resourcefulness of them.

Slocan Diary
By Kaoru Ikeda

Introduction

This book *Stone Voices Wartime Writings of Japanese Canadian Issei*, Edited by Keibo Oiwa is about the Issei, their presence and wartime experiences. It is a selection of some of the finest written accounts by Issei themselves, translated for the first time from Japanese into English. *Stone Voices* focuses on the period of the Pacific war as it was experienced by the Issei. The entire Nikkei history in Canada continued to revolve around the wartime experiences of uprooting, incarceration and dispersal.

***

Kaoru Ikeda (1875–1946) kept her diary, selections of which are included here during her stay from 1942–1945 at Slocan "relocation camp" in the interior of British Columbia. Her Slocan diary has been retained for more than seventy years by her daughter who has been its sole reader.

***

With the bombing of Pearl Harbour in December 1941, all persons of Japanese descent were declared "enemy aliens." Their assets were seized and most of the Japanese Canadian population was relocated or sent to internment camps. Stone Voices is a selection of memoirs, diaries, and letters written by four Issei, the first generation of Japanese to settle in Canada.

***

Departure

On Wednesday, June 3rd, one hundred and forty people, including us, were assembled and sent to Slocan, British Columbia. Two trains had gone at the end of May and this was the third one. The day before departure I cut as many flowers from the garden as I could and went to visit the family graves. I offered the flowers to my dead husband, my son Ken, and my older brother, and bid farewell to them all. Not knowing when I would be able to come back to visit their graves, I could not help but weep. When my husband passed away, although I knew he had a full life, my sadness was profound. However, now that we faced these recent disturbances, I began to feel that his death was timely. With his various connections to Japan, if he had been alive, he would have been put in jail. Even so it was much better to have died before being exiled to a godforsaken "ghost town" and forced into a miserable life in his old age. He was a happy man to die surrounded by his family and friends. We took rice to the Ts house, cooked it and made many rice balls to stuff in our lunch boxes. We also packed our bags with bread, butter, roast chicken, canned goods, and fruits to take with us on the long trip. This was enough food for about three or four days.

***

Exiled at Slocan

Surrounded by dark green hills and a mirror-like lake, Slocan presents some fine scenery. It's just like a summer resort and the water is so clean that it runs through pipes which go directly into the kitchens. we must think it lucky to move to a place like this, since there are said to be camps where water is not in such abundant supply.

The greater part of the Slocan Valley spreads out widely around the clear stream which flows from Lake Sloca. This area was to be the home of the Japanese evacuees. When I arrived there were about five hundred of us, but I heard that there were plans to bring in four to five thousand people. There were about three hundred or so *hakujin* settlers already living in the area.

***

Tokunaga acquired some scrap lumber from the nearby mill and made shelves. The rest of us were also busy putting plates, food and other small things in order. We began to clear the land around the house and made a garden. We planted lettuce, radishes and beans although it was a bit late in the season. We also transplanted chrysanthemums, trefoil, and coltsfoot that we had uprooted in such a hurry the morning we left Vancouver. There were so many tough thickets, dead trees and a network of bracken roots that a spade wouldn't even break through, so that even with Chisato and the kids helping, it was dreadful back breaking labour for Tokunaga.

The 21st was the anniversary of Ikeda's death, but we could not visit him at his grave. His photograph, enlarged and framed, was hung on the kitchen wall. Since there were plenty of little lilies blooming behind our house, I picked some, put them in a small empty bottle and left them as an offering on the makeshift altar that Tokunaga had nailed together from a piece of board. I consulted with Chisato about some favourite dish of her father's we could offer him, but what could we get our hands on in such a remote place? With some leftover flour and red bean paste we made dumplings and boiled some fiddleheads we picked on the mountain. We put these dishes in front of a framed photograph of Ikeda as an offering and we humbly shared a meal with him. I am sure my deceased husband must have been surprised to have this service in such unfamiliar, poor surroundings. It made me think of how he loved fiddleheads. Every year we went to the woods near Burnaby to pick them. In order not to create unemployment problems the Commission tried to supply work to as many Japanese as possible. Carpenters and skilled craftsmen, people to collect firewood from the forests, others to transport and chop it, warehouse hands, truck drivers, janitors, bath house workers, stovepipe cleaners, sales people in shops, hospital attendants, busboys and waitresses in restaurants.

There were over a thousand people in all. Tokunaga became very busy, pressured by his responsibilities which made me worry for his health. Wages were as small as they were in the road camps but since we did not have to pay for housing we made enough to buy food. The old and the sick who could not work or did not receive any money from family members working in road camps were given government assistance. There were many people with complaints, but considering that we were regarded as enemy aliens I thought we should be rather thankful for the generous way the authorities in Slocan were treating us.

Since I never much liked the hustle and bustle of the city, I would just as gladly be living on the slopes of a mountain where we could hike out back daily. We found huckleberry bushes everywhere in the woods. In August when the berries became dark red and ripe, we picked and ate them with sugar and milk–they were so delicious. After having heard that the local people gathered bushels of them to make jam, we too went to pick and make jam two or three times. Both the colour and the taste were first class. Every day, however warm it was, I put on a sweater and two pairs of socks as protection against the mosquitoes, and wandered off into the mountains. Chisato would see me off, making fun of my outfit and wishing me luck on my quest. Sometimes I was frightened to find big paw prints and bear droppings in the mountains, but my forays were too much fun for me to stop. I could only hope that they wouldn't come out during the day. I had also heard that noise would scare them off, so I loudly sang made-up songs as I walked. If somebody had seen me they would have thought I was crazy. At this thought I burst into laughter.

> Picking berries
> I happened on a bear print
> In the Slocan mountains

The fall scenery of Slocan was especially fine. From the mountain tops we could see the clear water of the lakes down below. The mixed yellows of the willows and deciduous trees against the deep green of the mountains and the red maples composed a beautiful canvas. When the berry season had passed we began to gather pine cones and dead twigs. Some of the cones were extraordinarily large, ranging from five to eight sun. And they were filled with so much sap, they burned extremely well in our morning fire.

> Mountain life
> Gathering fallen wood
> The right job for an old one

Searching for mushrooms was also fun. The mountains being so full of pine, one would expect matsutake mushrooms to appear. So on

Sundays there were many people who went hiking in search of matsutake mushrooms but could not find any. Anyway, whatever place one lives in offers unique pleasures.

Waking on the morning of October 31st, we were all amazed to discover a blanket of pure white snow. Although previous mornings had been cold and frosty, no one could have imagined that we would have snow so soon. Looking at each other, somebody said what we were all thinking: "We should have known better, Slocan is not Vancouver!" That night was Halloween but how could it mean anything in this place. Mariko discovered a few fireworks that were left over from the year before. After dark we divided some apples and fireworks with the children across the way until they had two or three each.

Then to everyone's delight we set off a firework display.

***

Christmas in Slocan

Our neighbour Mrs. Urabe gave us two pretty boxes, one large and one small. They will serve as pickle casks. Several days ago when Chisato bought vegetables from the Doukhobors, (who come by in their old fashioned wagons to sell vegetables, chicken, eggs, etc.,) she said in passing to Mrs. Urabe, that she wished she had some barrels so that she could make pickles. Urabe-san kindly made her two casks for pickles. So we immediately bought cabbage. We are all happy to be able to make enough pickles to last us the whole winter. Chisato baked cookies and gave them to Urabe-san as thanks. It was also Urabe-san who was kind enough to bring the shovel he had made on the morning after another heavy snow fall. He is so kind.

The recent shortages of goods in this country are unbelievable. Last year aluminium products were disallowed, next it was rubber; gas rationing goes without saying. Similarly there are severe shortages of steel, and glass products are also restricted. So are shoes and other leather goods. Synthetics have replaced cotton and among foodstuffs, sugar was first rationed so there is hardly any candy available. We manage to buy a few sweets for Christmas, but jams and canned fruit are almost completely out of stock.

Time is passing so quickly, the year is almost over. There was a Christmas concert at the church and the children from Sunday school and kindergarten received some presents. Mariko was baptized on the Sunday of Christmas week. Despite a shortage of ingredients, Chisato managed to make a delicious Christmas cake and baked lots of cookies. We sent my son Arimoto cake and cookies as well as a leather half coat. He was so pleased with his gifts that he sent, special delivery, a letter of thanks which arrived on Christmas Eve. I was most relieved to know that he was celebrating Christmas in good health. Ayako and Mariko went into the mountains to find a small Christmas tree. Sadly their many Christmas ornaments were left in Vancouver, but they are imaginative enough to make their own. They waded through the snow and picked heaps of red berries they found thrusting up from the ground. Then they threaded them alternately with balls of cotton into 5 to 6-inch-long pieces and with these draped over the tree's (branches, with some store-bought silver "icicles" sprinkled on, we had first class-decorations—quite lovely. Here and there we placed three or four birds I made from rags.

We had a wonderful dinner of delicious roast chicken which Chisato cooked in place of turkey, which our stove was too small to accommodate. Then a whole crowd of kids from the other building descended upon us to admire our Christmas tree. Each of them was very happy to receive the cookies and apples wrapped in paper and the little cloth birds and pin cushions that we divided among them. Later in the evening the older kids played cards exuberantly and were pleased when we served them Christmas cake and cocoa. Thus our Christmas turned out to be an unexpectedly merry time.

Later I heard a funny story about Christmas. The women's committee, which I mentioned before, made a resolution to demand turkey and Christmas presents for each family. Anybody could see that such demands would be rejected, but the most aggressive actually dared to go to the Commission with their demands. They were immediately refused. How brazen they could be! To make demands for things like electricity and water, which are necessities, is understandable and we can all see that the Commission has been trying hard to accommodate our needs within their limits.

Now that we are given work and a wage, however small, I feel ashamed that people would demand to be given presents. Now we are at the end of the year. In this wandering life of ours, there isn't much we can do to prepare for the New Year. Knowing that the children long for kuri-kinton I substituted peas for chestnuts and managed to make mame-kinton. I chopped fruits into the leftover gelatin which made for a nice dessert. I cooked the few black beans that we had received from Mrs. M. and had been saving for this occasion. Chisato baked some cupcakes and made udon noodles which took her a long time. She cooked the chicken and made spaghetti, which was everyone's favourite. This was the whole list of our New Year's feast. The taste of our handmade udon was exceptional, thanks to Mrs. T., our neighbour, who had taught us how. Mariko helped her mother and has become quite adept. I hear that some people had planned ahead to store up their New Years foods and there were even those who had made mochi. Thus the year 1942 has come to a close, at last.

Banished
To a cabin in snow mountains
The year settles down

***

Diary
March 3, 1943

Clear and sunny. Today is the day of sekku, Girls' Day. But in this temporary world a celebration is hard to arrange. A while ago I decided to make dolls for my grandchildren, to celebrate sekku. I used rags and anything else I could find. Mrs. Kōyama's grandchild is supposed to have her hatsu-zekku so I gave as presents my handmade dolls and birds. She was so happy that she came over to say thanks. Here is my haiku that I attached to a doll.

> Hatsu-zekku
> A beaming newborn
> Peach blossom

In return Mrs. Kōyama gave me a strip of paper with two poems.

> Baby crawls
> Lovely
> Zekku dolls

> Remaining snow
> Lights up cabin
> Spring still young

March 6, 1943

Clear sky. Nothing happening. Temperature is five below. March in Slocan is as clear as crystal.

March 7, 1943

In the afternoon I went to a haiku group meeting with my family. I think we all did well. Chisato's poem with a theme of "spring mud" won the highest recognition.

> Spring mud
> Into the wheel tracks
> Cigarette thrown

***

September 27, 1943

Our chrysanthemums have small yellow flowers. These are the ones my grandchildren received in New Denver as Easter presents. Thanks to my son-in-law who took good care of them, they are doing well.

> Each morning
> More in blossom
> Garden mums

> Hand cut
> chrysanthemums
> Soaked in perfume

October 4, 1943

> Mountain lodge
> Leaves drift in
> Through morning windows

October 7, 1943

Clear and sunny. Beautiful autumn sky and a pleasant day. Today is the anniversary of my son Ken's death. Chisato cut some chrysanthemums and offered them along with various other things. Everybody seems thoughtful. It is hard to believe, eleven years have already passed.

October 10, 1943

Pouring rain. The rain hasn't stopped since yesterday. I have been sick the last few days. I have a terrible cough and therefore am staying in bed.

October 14, 1943

Clear and sunny. Feeling better I finally got up. The last few days suddenly became cold and this morning the ground was completely frozen and spoiled our garden. Everybody is busy salvaging whatever they can from their gardens. Our chrysanthemums withered. In the afternoon I walked into the mountains for a short walk. Probably because the summer was too dry or too many trees have been cut down the mushrooms are no good this year.

October 18, 1943

These days it has been raining and chilly, which doesn't make me feel very good. But today is nice. So in the afternoon I went to visit old Mrs. Sekine to give her white lily bulbs and the fuki roots.

> Morning frost
> Chrysanthemum flowers
> Drooping slightly
>
> Mountain gift
> For my hair
> Fallen red leaf

November 4, 1943

Today is my sixty-eighth birthday. I just keep on accumulating years without being very useful to others. But I'm grateful that I'm not sick and therefore a burden on everybody.

November 13, 1943

> Arranging chrysanthemums
> Silently
> I celebrate this day

***

December 7, 1943

Oh the unforgettable day has come around again! Snow was late this year but since yesterday it has been falling. The chill is now definitely in the air. For me it became impossible to go out for even a short time. I spent my day quietly reading and knitting.

December 24, 1943

In the afternoon on this Christmas Eve day we were surprised to see the Mounted Police go into the mountains and come back with a big radio receiver on a sled. We heard that somebody informed the Mounties that Mr. K., who lives above us, had a short wave radio. They raided his house and confiscated the radio. Deep in the mountains without much entertainment would it be so harmful for someone to listen to the radio? I'm shocked at the narrow-mindedness of the Mounties and the existence of a Japanese informant who will sell-out his own people. I cannot help feeling hateful. I feel sorry for Mr. K.

December 25, 1943

As we are already accustomed to this, we erected a small Christmas tree and when the neighbour's kids came over to play we gave them cookies. The roast chicken dinner was delicious. We received many beautiful Christmas cards. These days the children are enjoying opening their mail.

December 28, 1943

In the evening Mariko gave a Christmas party inviting her high school friends. Everybody cheerfully enjoyed themselves until around eleven o'clock.

December 31, 1943

Another humble New Year is upon us. The Inoue family from Popoff gave us precious white radish so I made everyone's favourite dish with it. I also made some sushi dishes for New Year's. For the last dinner of the year I made miso soup with my homemade miso that I opened for the first time. Mariko made a pun saying; "We eat miso on the night of omisoka [the last day of the year] So everybody laughed. I thought the miso was pretty well made. That made me happy. Well, so much for another year.

> I thought
> It would be just temporary
> In this mountain country
> Accumulating another year
> As snow deepens

January 25, 1944

For the last two or three days it has been severely cold. This morning the engine in the generator house stopped and there was a black-out. The water has also stopped flowing. Chisato went to a nearby water tank and came back with hot water and with that we prepared our breakfast. After breakfast Mr. Inoue kindly got some buckets and pots to fetch us some water.

January 30, 1944

Clear and sunny, very cold. Today there was distribution of the care packages from Japan at the Bay Farm school. I saw the people from across the street going with empty buckets to pick up their packages. My daughter and Tokunaga also went during the morning. One bottle of soya sauce per person, one pound of tea per family and half a pound of miso per family.

> Reaching out
> With compassion
> Precious gift
> From my native land.
>
> Old country memories
> Carried back
> With scent of tea

Sitting looking at this gift which has travelled across the world, sent by my compatriots I can barely restrain my tears, as the memories well up. At lunch we gathered to drink some of the tea, appreciating its beautiful scent, good quality and rich taste.

***

September, 1944

Last night our garden was trampled by calves. This morning I went out to inspect it and there were big hoof marks everywhere. I found carrots, radishes, and Chinese cabbage eaten. I hear that our neighbours' gardens also received a lot of damage. Although they were behind a log fence the cows either stepped over it, or if it was too high, pushed it over. Well what can we do?

***

November, 1944

This fall the mushrooms have been plentiful in the back mountains. So I have been enjoying my walks every day.

There are rumours that the mountain on the other side of the lake has many matsutake mushrooms and many people are hurrying over there to find them. From my neighbourhood there are people who came back with a big sack full of the mushrooms. They shared them with everybody and as a result we got two or three good mushrooms. To get to this mountain one has to row for three hours across the lake, then climb several miles towards the peak, so not just anybody can go mushroom gathering.

November 4, 1944

Today is my birthday. In the morning everybody wished me a happy birthday. Because I had been ill I was afraid that I would not be able to live until this birthday but I am grateful to have made it.

November 11, 1944

An exhibition of chrysanthemums was held at the Bay Farm school. Fortunately the weather was good, so I decided to go for a little exercise. The rest of my family had gone yesterday. There were many pots of various colours. A lot of energy and effort had been put into the flowers. On one wall there were fifteen or sixteen tanka poems with the theme being chrysanthemums. The calligraphy teacher, Mr. Miyake, copied the poems out.

The following poem of mine was among them.

> Desolate garden
> Of our temporary home
> Nobly
> Pointing to eternity
> The fragrance of white chrysanthemums.

***

November 20, 1944

At night the first snowfall of the year arrived. It came down for only about two hours. Since then it's been snowing and then melting, snowing and then melting. The road was washed out under mud and water, but thanks to the weather the air is good and clear.

November 30, 1944

Arimoto came to join us because his camp has closed. We heard that his camp was infested by bed bugs and we were afraid that he'd bring some of them with him. They put all his belongings into a small hut and the Commission's sanitation department disinfected everything. On top of that we had to boil sheets and other things just to be sure. The building across the way had been complaining that there were bedbugs but our house is isolated, and this has spared us from having the same problem.

December 7, 1944

This day is back again. It has been three long years since Pearl Harbour. What is happening in my native country? The Americans have been joyfully boasting of the bombing of Tokyo. But also I hear that Japan is doing very well on many battle fronts which the Americans haven't talked about.

I can only pray for good results.

Biographies of Other Contributors

Jim Kacian is founder and president of The Haiku Foundation; founder and owner of Red Moon Press; editor in chief of *Haiku in English: The First Hundred Years*, the definitive text in the field; and author of some score of books of and about haiku. When he isn't working on haiku he can be found paddling the east coast of North America in his hand-built kayak. He lives in the Shenandoah Valley of Virginia with his partner of 30 years, Maureen Gorman.

Keiko Shiba is a scholar of women's history of Japan's Edo period (1603-1867). Educated at Waseda University, she has traveled across the country over the last several decades, searching for various texts penned by women, including travel diaries, *waka* poems, and *haikai* verses, most of which had fallen into obscurity. Shiba is an eminent figure in the field; her books and articles are frequently quoted by scholars both in and outside of Japan. Among her publications are *Aizuhan no onnatachi* [Women of the Aizu clan] (Kōbunsha, 1994), *Edoki no onnatachi ga mita Tōkaidō* [The Tōkaidō Highway, observed by Edo women] (Katsura Bunko, 2002), and *Edo-ki onna hyōgensha jiten* [Encyclopedia of women writers and artists in Edo Japan] (Gendai Shokan, 2015). She delivered lectures on selected women writers on *Edoki ni ikita onna hyōgenshatachi*, an educational radio program of NHK, Japan's public station, from July through September, 2016.

Motoko Ezaki a Ph. D. in Japanese linguistics from UCLA, supervises the Japanese studies program at Occidental College. Her areas of interest cover a wide range including syntax, semantics, discourse analysis, as well as pre-modern to contemporary Japanese literature. She aspired to become a translator since childhood, and in 1990 won the second prize of *Hon'yaku shōreishō* (the annual literary translation competition) sponsored by Babel Press, a Tokyo publisher. Her current translation project is the entire text of a travel diary composed by Fujiki Ichi, a woman of the early 18th century, during her journey as a young bride, an excerpt of which has been printed in *Literary Creations on the Road*.

H. Mack Horton is Chair of the Department of East Asian Languages and Cultures at the University of California at Berkeley, from which he received his Ph. D. in 1989. He has written widely on Japanese poetry and self-reflective literature. *The Journal of Sōchō* was the topic of his Ph. D. dissertation.

He has taught premodern Japanese language and literature for nearly three decades. He is currently finishing a book under the auspices of the Guggenheim Foundation on linked verse (renga), a genre that flourished for five hundred years and eventually featured among its greatest practitioners Sōgi, his student Sōchō, and Bashō.

He spent a total of ten years in Japan, the first five as a language student, translator, and journalist, and the last five as a doctoral researcher and post-doc working with the renowned linked-verse scholar Kaneko Kinjirō.

In his off-duty hours, he plays jazz trumpet, and his partner runs her own music management business and so puts up with his evenings on the bandstand. She is also a translator (from French and Portuguese) and is thus his first and best reader.

Ray Rasmussen currently an editor of *Haibun Today*, lives in Edmonton, Alberta and Halton Hills, Ontario, Canada. His work has been published in a variety of journals and anthologies. He presently serves as technical editor for *Contemporary Haibun Online* and *Haibun Today*. When he's not busy writing and editing, he spends a good deal of his time hiking, canoeing, snowshoeing and photographing wilderness places including Alberta's Willmore Wilderness Park and Jasper National Park, Utah's Canyonlands and Ontario's Algonquin Provincial Park. http://raysweb.net/haiku

Imamura Takeshi Born in Matsuyama, Ehime Prefecture, in 1933. Currently Vice-president of the Matsuyama Shiki Society and Director of the Kōshin'an Club. Publications: Co-author of There Is Today: Kurita Chodō and His Writings

Patricia Lyons Born in the United States. Studied Japanese literature at the University of Washington and Stanford University. Has lived in

Matsuyama, Japan, for more than twenty years. Has worked as a translator after retiring from teaching English at Ehime University.

Minako Noma Born in 1937. Worked as an elementary school teacher. Has three children and nine grandchildren. Has composed haiku and studied English for more than 35 years. Has served as a Chairperson of the Shiki Memorial Museum English Volunteer Group.

Dr. Janine Beichman received her doctorate from Columbia University and is professor emerita, Daito Bunka University. She is the author of the literary biographies *Masaoka Shiki: His Life and Works* and *Embracing the Firebird: Yosano Akiko* and *The Birth of the Female Voice in Modern Japanese Poetry*, and also of *Drifting Fires*, an original Noh play which has been performed in Japan and the United States. Her translations include *Setouchi Jakuchō The End of Summer*, and two collections of the poet and critic Ōoka Makoto's work: *Beneath the Sleepless Tossing of the Planets: Selected Poems and Poems for All Seasons: An Anthology of Japanese Poetry from Earliest Times to the Present* (also published as A Poet's Anthology). She is currently at work on the second volume of her Yosano Akiko biography, as well as a revised edition of Poems for All Seasons and two books of translations. the poetry of Yosano Akiko and the poetry of Ishigaki Rin.

William R. LaFleur Born in Patterson, New Jersey in 1936, died of a massive heart attack in February 2010. He was 73 years old. Dr. LaFleur began his higher education at Calvin College in Grand Rapids, Michigan and continued with graduate training at the University of Michigan and the University of Chicago. Dr. LaFleur taught as an authority on Japanese intellectual history at Princeton University, the University of California at Los Angeles, and Sophia University in Tokyo. In 1989 he became the first non-Japanese scholar to receive the Watsuji Tetsurô Culture Prize.

Dr. LaFleur's published books covered topics from medieval literature in *Mirror of the Moon* (1978) and *Awesome Nightfall* (2003), both studies of the priest-poet Saigyô (1118-1180). Other works covered broader issues of religious thought, including *The Karma of Words* (1986) and *Buddhism in Cultural Perspective* (1988). He dealt with complicated issues of abortion in *Liquid Life* (1992). He edited *Zen and Western Thought: Essays by Masao Abe* (1985), recipient of a prize from the American Academy of Religion, and Dôgen Studies (1985). He also edited *Dark Medicine: Rationalizing Unethical Medical Research* (2008), a study on Japanese critics of American biotechnology and bioethics.

As a gifted poet and philosopher, Dr. LaFleur brought humanity and wisdom to the study of everything he encountered, from the taste of tea to the technology of medicine, from hungry ghosts to haiku poets.

https://www.sas.upenn.edu/news/death-william-r-lafleur-department-east-asian-languages-and-civilizations

Haruo Shirane Shincho Professor of Japanese Literature, Department of East Asian Languages and Cultures; Chair of East Asian Languages and Cultures teaches Japanese literature and cultural history, with particular focus on prose fiction, poetry, performative genres, and visual culture.

Professor Haruo Shirane received his BA (1974) and his PhD from Columbia University (1983). He is the recipient of Fulbright, Japan Foundation, SSRC, and NEH grants and has been awarded the Kadokawa Genyoshi Prize, Ishida Hakyō Prize, and, most recently, the Ueno Satsuki Memorial prize (2010) for outstanding research on Japanese culture.

He is currently interested in the relationship of classical and medieval cultures to early modern and contemporary cultures, looking at issues of gender, manuscript culture, print capitalism, performance and media. His most recent book, *Japan and the Culture of the Four Seasons* (Columbia University Press), explored the cultural construction of nature and the environment across a wide spectrum of literature, media, and visual arts from the ancient period to the modern.

Haruo Shirane has just been appointed as the 2016-2017 honorary curator of the American Haiku Archives at the California State Library in Sacramento. He is also affiliated with the Weatherhead East Asian Institute. Shirane also pursues his interests in the interaction between popular and elite cultures, issues of cultural memory and language, ecocriticism, and cultural constructions of nature. In 2010, he was awarded the Ueno Satsuki Memorial Prize on Japanese Culture for his contributions to the study of Japanese culture.

Makoto Ueda born 1931 is a professor emeritus of Japanese literature at Stanford University. He earned a Ph. D. in comparative literature in 1961.

In 2004-2005 he served as the honorary curator of the American Haiku Archives at the California State Library in Sacramento, California. He was given that honor "in recognition of Ueda's many decades of academic writing about haiku and related genres and his leading translations of Japanese haiku." The library added that "Ueda has been our most consistently useful source for information on Japanese haiku, as well as our finest source for the poems in translation, from Bashō to the present day." His work on female poets and 20th century poets "had an enormous impact".

He is an author of numerous books about Japanese literature and in particular Haiku, Senryū, Tanka, and Japanese poetics, some of which are *The Path of Flowering Thorn: The Life and Poetry of Yosa Buson* (1998), *Light Verse from the Floating World: An Anthology of Premodern Japanese Senryu* (2000), *Far Beyond the Field: Haiku by Japanese Women* (2003), *Dew on the Grass: The Life and Poetry of Kobayashi Issa* (2004), *Mother of Dreams: Portrayals of Women in Modern Japanese Fiction* (2004)

Jeffrey Woodward currently acts as General Editor of *Haibun Today*, a journal he founded in 2007. He formerly edited *Modern Haibun & Tanka Prose* and served, in 2010 and again in 2011, as adjudicator for the British Haiku Society's Haiku Awards. His selected poems, under the title *In Passing*, were published in 2007 and he edited The Tanka Prose Anthology in 2008. In 2013, collections of his haibun and tanka prose were issued under the respective titles *Evening in the Plaza* and *Another Garden*.

Keibo Oiwa (a.k.a. Tsuji Shin'ichi) is a cultural anthropologist, filmmaker, translator, environmental activist, and public speaker. Author of over 50 books, Keibo teaches in Meiji Gakuin University, is a founder-leader of the Sloth Club, an ecology and "Slow Living" NGO.

His books in Japanese, include *Slow is Beautiful: Culture as Slowness* and

It's Just Fine to be Slow. He has produced and directed five of the DVD documentary series "Asian Visions," featuring Satish Kumar, Kawaguchi Yoshikazu, Hwang Daegwon, Vandana Shiva, Sulak Sivaraksa, Pracha Hutanuwatra.

His books in English include *The Other Japan: Voices beyond the Mainstream* (co-authored by David Suzuki and originally published as *The Japan We Never Knew*), and *Rowing the Eternal Sea: The Story of a Minamata Fisherman*.

Rich Youmans's haiku, haibun, and related essays have appeared internationally in various journals and anthologies, including *Journeys 2015*. His collection of linked haibun with Maggie Chula, *Shadow Lines*, won a Merit Book Award from the Haiku Society of America, and his haibun collection *All the Windows Lit* was a 2015 Snapshot Press eChapbook Award winner. An editor and publisher by profession, he currently oversees the communications and publications of a U.S. trade association representing jewelry designers and manufacturers. He and his wife, Belle, live on Cape Cod in North Falmouth, MA, USA.

Publishing Credits

Section I: Early Adaptors

John Ashbery Six haibun from *A Wave*, Copyright 1981, 1982, 1983, 1984 by John Ashbery. Used by arrangement with Georges Borchardt, Inc. for the author. All rights reserved.

Jerry Kilbride All haibun have been taken with permission from Ms Adrienne Kilbride, from the book *Tracings / haibun* by Jerry Kilbride; edited by vincent tripi; drawings by Chukiat Jaroensuk. [Northfield, MA]: Lily Pool Press (2004)

Kenneth C. Leibman *Oleno* reprinted online from the chapbook *alachua* from The Haiku Foundation Website, *Hōryū-ji* reprinted from *American Haibun and Haiga Volume 1: up against the window*, Red Moon Press

Paul F. Schmidt *Kyoto Temples* reprinted from *American Haibun and Haiga Volume 1: up against the window*, Red Moon Press

Edith Shiffert *Yama-Biko: Mountain Echo* is reproduced with the kind permission of Dennis Maloney from *The Unswept Path, Contemporary American Haiku, Companions for the Journeys Series vol 8* Edited by John Brandi and Dennis Maloney, White Pine Press/Buffalo, New York.

Rod Willmot *The Ribs of Dragonfly*, 1984 Black Moss Press books are distributed in Canada and the United States by Firefly Books Ltd., 3520 Pharmacy Avenue, Unit 1C, Scarborough, Ontario M1W 2T8. ISBN 0-88753-121-0. Some of the haiku in this book first appeared in *Frogpond*, *Muse-Pie*, and *Wind Chimes*. Earlier versions of three chapters were published in *Cicada*.

Section II: Contemporary Writers of Haibun

Melissa Allen *Haibun Today, Chrysanthemum, Contemporary Haibun Online*

Cherie Hunter Day *Frogpond, The Unseen Wind: British Haiku Society*

Haibun Anthology 2009, Haibun Today, Modern Haiku.

Lynn Edge *Haibun Today, Contemporary Haibun Online, Modern Haiku.*

Judson Evans *American Haibun & Haiga 4, Contemporary Haibun, Modern Haiku, Frogpond, Trobar Clus: Mont Ventoux Journal, Japan Journal.*

Chris Faiers Initially self-published in 1990 as *Eel Pie Dharma*. In 2012 Hidden Brook Press published a professional reissue as *Eel Pie Island Dharma, Eel Pie Dharma: A Memoir/Haibun,* Toronto: Unfinished Monument Press, 1990.

Charles Hansmann *Modern Haiku, Frogpond, KYSO flash 3, Crack the Spine.*

Jeffrey Harpeng *Contemporary Haibun Online, Haibun Today.*

Ed Higgins *Haibun Today, Contemporary Haibun Online, Modern Haibun & Tanka Prose Volume 1.*

Ruth Holzer *Haibun Today, Contemporary Haibun Online, Frogpond.*

Roger Jones *Contemporary Haibun Online, Frogpond, Lynx.*

Gary LeBel *Modern Haiku and Abacus, Modern Haibun & Tanka Prose Volume 1.*

Tom Lynch *American Haibun & Haiga Volume 1, Contemporary Haibun Online,* http://digitalcommons.unl.edu/englishfacpubs/39, *Organization & Environment* 11:2 (June 1998), pp. 207–211. Copyright © 1998 Sage Publications. Used by permission.

George Marsh *Contemporary Haibun Online* and from his websites: http://www.haiku.org.uk/, http://darkislands.co.uk/category/haibun/

Michael McClintock *Modern Haiku, South by Southeast, Frogpond, Blithe Spirit, (Brushwood No. 1, Anthology of the Nobuyuki International English-language Haibun Competition,* British Haiku Society, August 2002).

Beverly Acuff Momoi *Lifting the Towhee's Song,* Snapshot Press 2011 eChapbook Award, *Contemporary Haibun Online, Frogpond.*

Lenard D. Moore *Frogpond, Valley Voices: A Literary Review, Pembroke Magazine.*

Peter Newton *Contemporary Haibun Online, Frogpond.*

Jim Norton Four haibun from *The Fragrance of Dust*, Published by Alba Press, 2012 collection, *Contemporary Haibun Online.*

Stanley Pelter Selected from the archives of *Haibun Today.*

Dru Philippou *Haibun Today, Jerry Kilbride Memorial English Language Haibun Contest 2009, Genjuan International Haibun Contest 2015.*

Richard S. Straw *Contemporary Haibun Online, Simply Haiku.*

Bill Wyatt *Presence 44, Haibun Today, Archive: American Haibun & Haiga Volume 3.*

Section III: Excerpts from Japanese books

William R. La Fleur *Awesome Nightfall The Life, Times, and Poetry of Saigyō,* © 2003 William R. LaFleur, Awesome Nightfall. Reprinted by arrangement with Wisdom Publications, Inc., wisdompubs. org. Wisdom Publications 199 Elm Street Somerville MA 02144 USA

Motoko Ezaki *Literary Creations on the Road: Women's Travel Diaries in Early Modern Japan,* by Shiba Keiko translated by Motoko Ezaki. University Press of America, A Division of The Rowman & Littlefield Publishing Group, 4501 Forbes Boulevard, Suite 200, Lanham, Maryland 20706 USA

Patricia Lyons's translation of *Sketches of Moonlit Nights* into English from *An Introduction to Haibun with A translation of Kurita Chodō's Tsukiyo sōshi,* Printed in Japan by Minako Noma in 2013

Minako Noma Excerpts from *An Introduction to Haibun with A translation of Kurita Chodō's Tsukiyo sōshi,* Printed in Japan by Minako Noma in 2013

Janine Beichman *Masaoka Shiki His Life and Works,* Cheng and Tsui Company, 25 West Street, Boston, MA 02111-1213 USA ISBN 0-88727-364-5

Kaoru Ikeda's Slocan Diary was taken from *Stone Voices Wartime Writings of Japanese Canadian Issei*, Edited by Keibo Oiwa Vehicule Press, POB. 125, Place Du Parc Station, Montreal, Quebec H2W 2M9, 1991 ISBN1-55065-014-9

H. Mack Horton These brief excerpts, slightly revised, have been adapted especially for *Journeys 2017* from *The Journal of Sōchō* (Stanford: Stanford University Press, 2002). For historical and literary context, see the companion volume, *Song in an Age of Discord:* The Journal of Sōchō and *Poetic Life in Late Medieval Japan*.

Keiko Shiba and Motoko Ezaki These brief excerpts, slightly revised, have been adapted especially for *Journeys 2017* from *Literary Creations on the Road–Women's Travel Diaries in Early Modern Japan* by permission from the Publisher-Rowman & Littlefield Publishing Group, Maryland, USA

Acknowledgements

I gratefully acknowledge the assistance given to me by Rich Youmans, for writing the *Introduction* and the essay *Travel Diaries and the Development of Modern Haibun* and by Jeffrey Woodward for his essay *Form in Haibun: An Outline*. I am indebted to all the haibuneers who laid the foundation of this fascinating genre from whom I have learnt so much namely–Bruce Ross, Jim Kacian, the late Ken Jones, David Cobb, Jeffrey Woodward, Ray Rasmussen, Bob Lucky, Glenn Coats and others too numerous to mention here.

I would also like to express my gratitude to the following people:

Prof. Haruo Shirane for allowing me to use excerpts from *Traces of Dreams: Landscape, Cultural Memory* and the *Poetry of Bashō*.

Laura Westbrook, Rights and Permissions Coordinator of Brill Publications, for allowing me to use excerpts from Prof. Makoto Ueda's *Dew on the Grass: The Life and Poetry of Kobayashi Issa*.

Will Vunderink, Agent for Georges Borchardt, Inc., who kindly gave me permission to reprint six haibun from John Ashbery's *A Wave*.

Prof. H. Mack Horton for allowing me to use excerpts from *The Journal of Sōchō*, Stanford University Press, Stanford California.

Minako Noma and Patricia Lyons for allowing me to use excerpts from *An Introduction to Haibun with A translation of Kurita Chodo's Tsukiyo soshi*, printed in Japan by Minako Noma 2013.

Joy Kogawa who helped me locate and contact Keibo Oiwa, who allowed me to use the diary excerpt of Kaoru Ikeda from *Stone Voices: Wartime Writings of Japanese Canadian Issei*, published by Véhicule Press.

Lydia Anderson for allowing me to use excerpts from William R. La Fleur's *Awesome Nightfall: The Life, Times, and Poetry of Saigyō*, published by Wisdom Publications, Inc.

Adrienne Kilbride for allowing me to use five haibun from *Tracings/haibun* by Jerry Kilbride.

Jim Kacian for allowing me to use Kenneth C. Liebman's *Oleno* Reprinted online from the chapbook *alachua* and *Hōryū-ji*. Reprinted from *American Haibun and Haiga Volume 1: up against the window*

Dr. Janine Beichman for allowing me to use excerpts from *Masaoka Shiki: His Life and Works*.

Dennis Maloney for allowing me to use Edith Schiffert's *Yama-Biko: Mountain Echo*, from *The Unswept Path*, White Pine Press.

Patricia Zline, Rights & Permissions Assistant, Rowman & Littlefield Publishing Group, for allowing me to use excerpts from *Literary Creations on the Road: Women's Travel Diaries in Early Modern Japan* by Shiba Keiko, translated by Motoko Ezaki.

A special thanks to Rich Youmans and Ray Rasmussen for their tireless guidance and to Ray who allowed me to use his own professional photo for the cover.

A big thank you to Raveesh Varma for providing me books and for many scanned documents.

I would also like to thank my son, Ananth Deodhar for his help in formatting this issue for publication and my daughter-in-law, Ishu Deodhar for her culinary support.

Last but not least, I am grateful to all the poets who cooperated with me and very generously honoured me by letting me have their work for this anthology, the third of my *Journeys*.

Angelee Deodhar

Made in the USA
Middletown, DE
12 March 2017